Bloodborne

TITAN®
COMICS

Bloodborne

TITAN COMICS

EDITOR: **TOM WILLIAMS**
DESIGNER: **WILFRIED TSHIKANA-EKUTSHU**

MANAGING & LAUNCH EDITOR: **Andrew James**
TITAN COMICS EDITORIAL: **Jonathan Stevenson, Dan Boultwood**
SENIOR PRODUCTION CONTROLLER: **Jackie Flook**
PRODUCTION SUPERVISOR: **Maria Pearson**
PRODUCTION CONTROLLER: **Peter James**
ART DIRECTOR: **Oz Browne**
SALES & CIRCULATIONS MANAGER: **Steve Tothill**
PRESS OFFICER: **Will O'Mullane**
MARKETING MANAGER: **Ricky Claydon**
COMMERCIAL MANAGER: **Michelle Fairlamb**
HEAD OF RIGHTS: **Jenny Boyce**
PUBLISHING MANAGER: **Darryl Tothill**
PUBLISHING DIRECTOR: **Chris Teather**
OPERATIONS DIRECTOR: **Leigh Baulch**
EXECUTIVE DIRECTOR: **Vivan Cheung**
PUBLISHER: **Nick Landau**

WWW.TITAN-COMICS.COM

Bloodborne

THE DEATH OF SLEEP

WRITTEN BY
ALEŠ KOT

ARTWORK BY
PIOTR KOWALSKI

COLORS BY
**BRAD SIMPSON
& KEVIN ENHART**

LETTERS BY
ADITYA BIDIKAR

ORIGINAL GAME
PUBLISHED BY
SONY COMPUTER
ENTERTAINMENT, LLC
DEVELOPED BY:
FROMSOFTWARE, INC.

#1 COVER A
BY
JEFF STOKELY

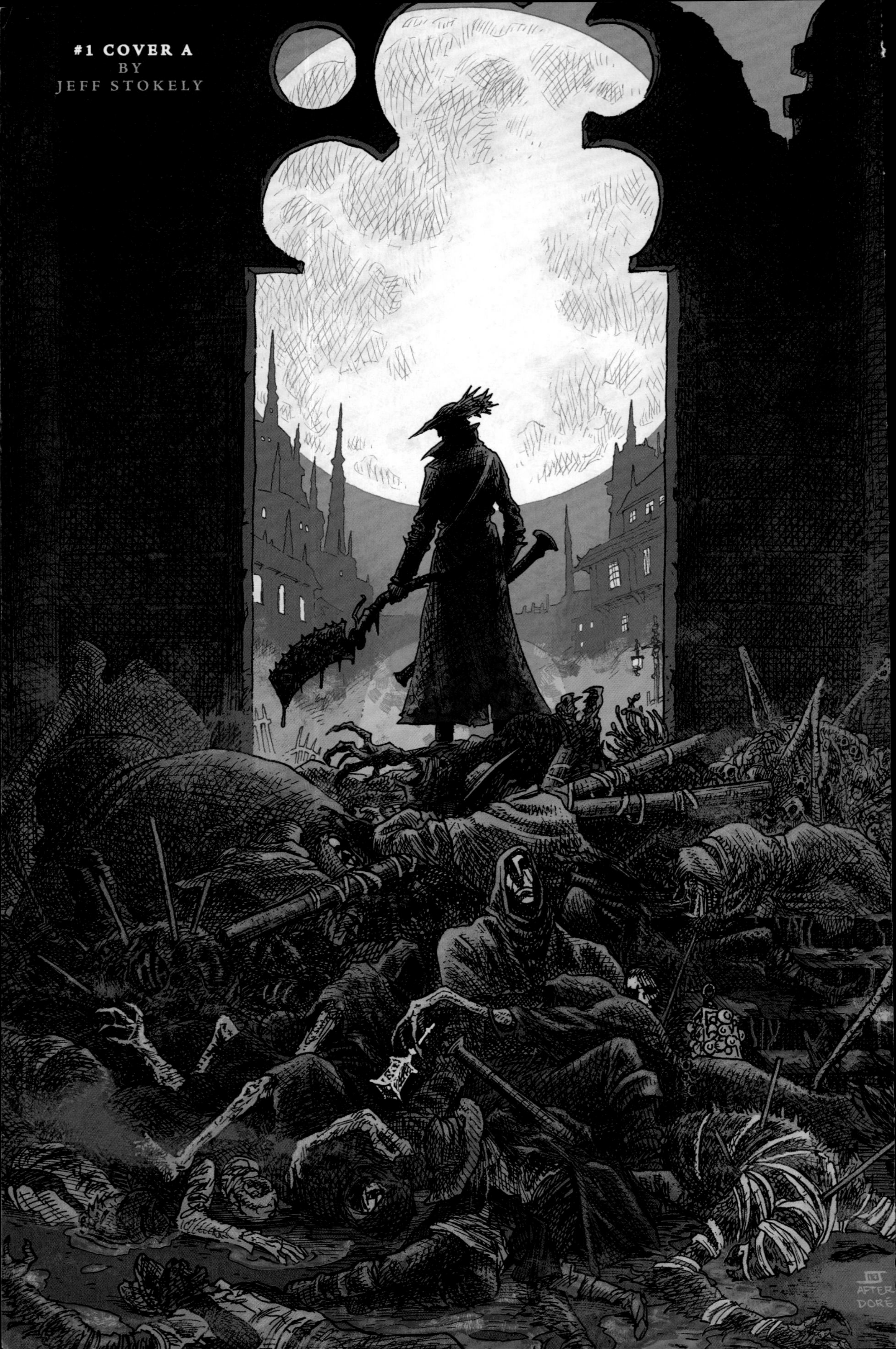
AFTER
DORÉ

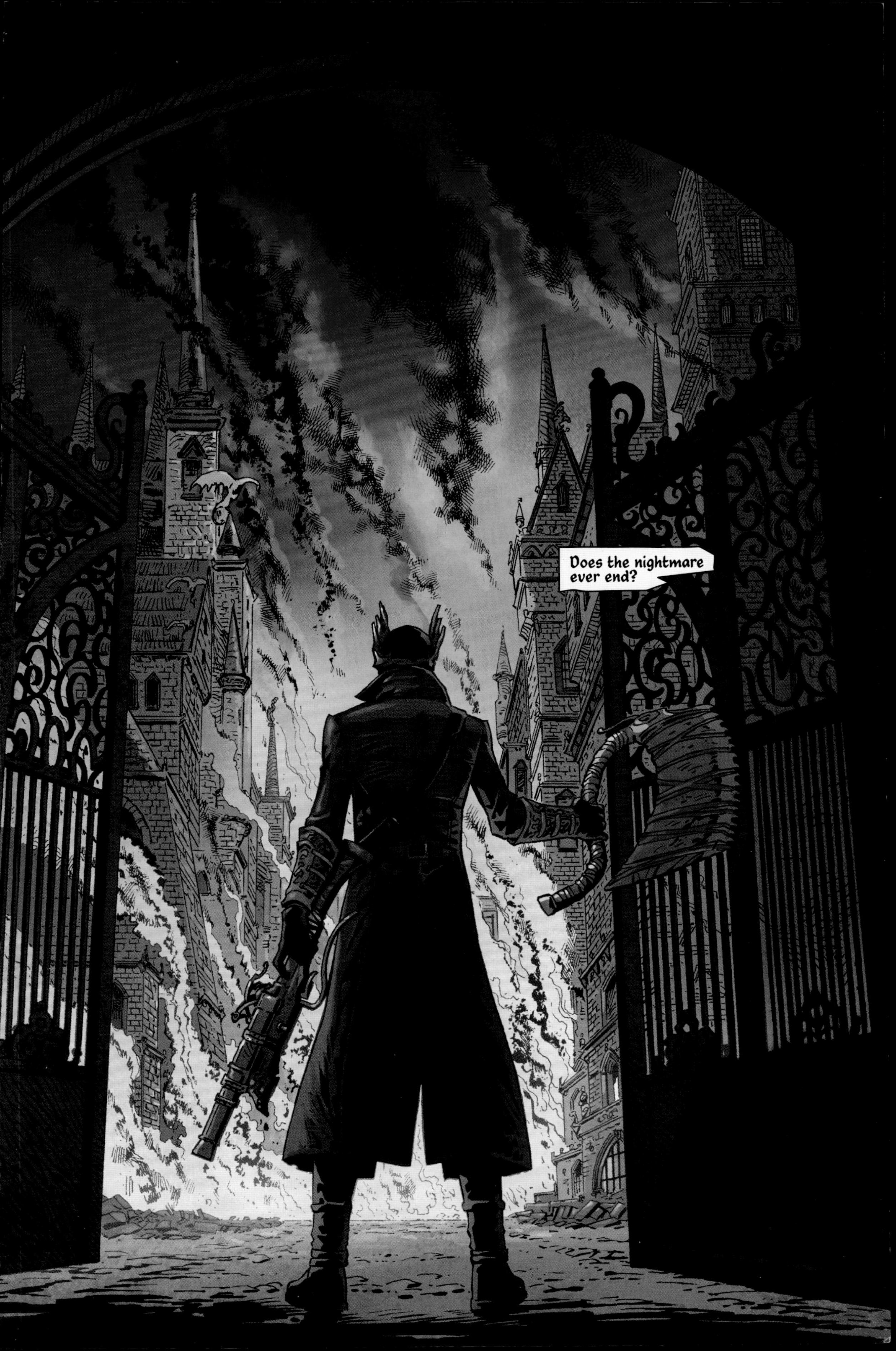
Does the nightmare ever end?

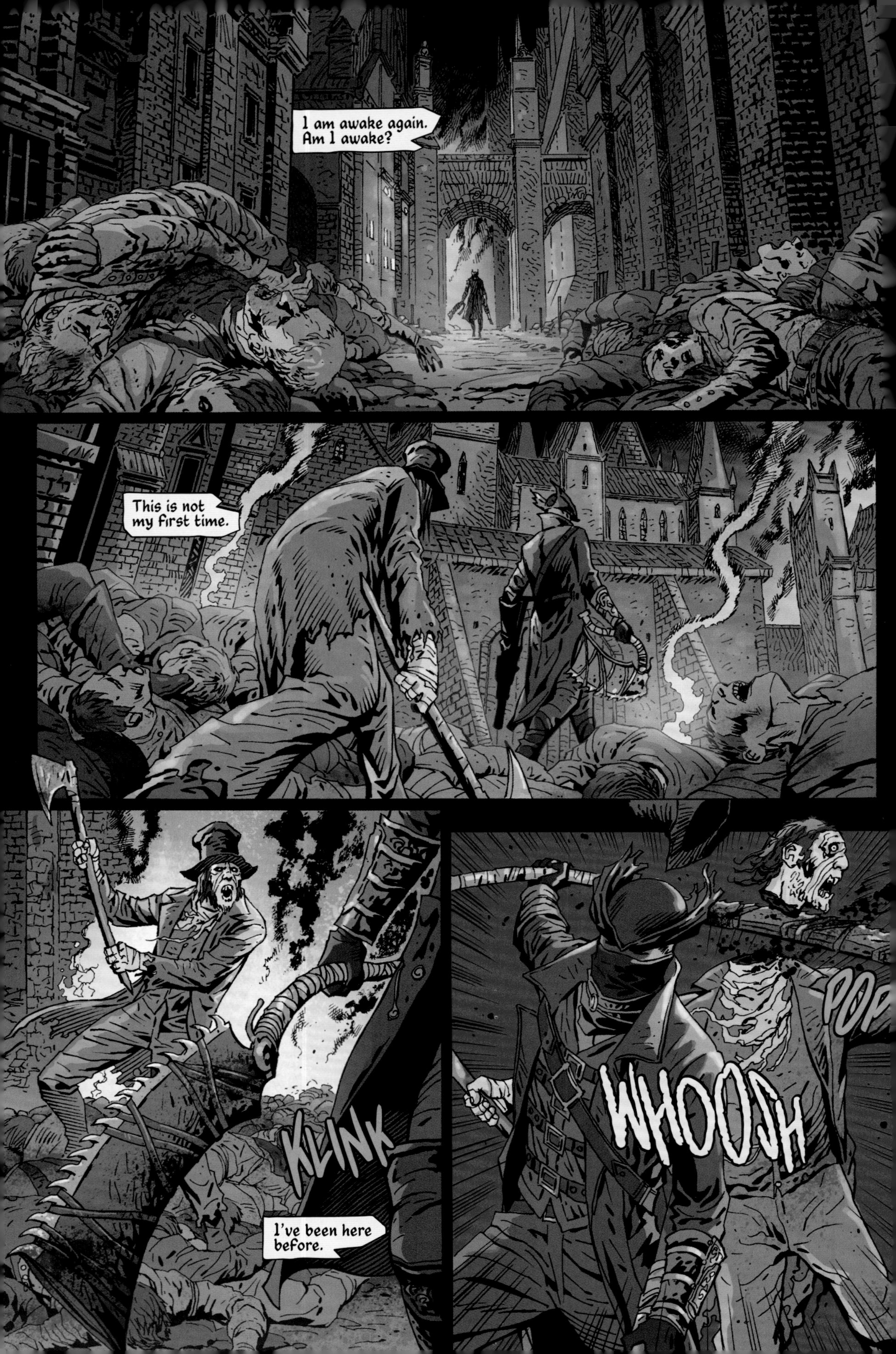
I am awake again.
Am I awake?
This is not my first time.
KLINK
I've been here before.
WHOOSH

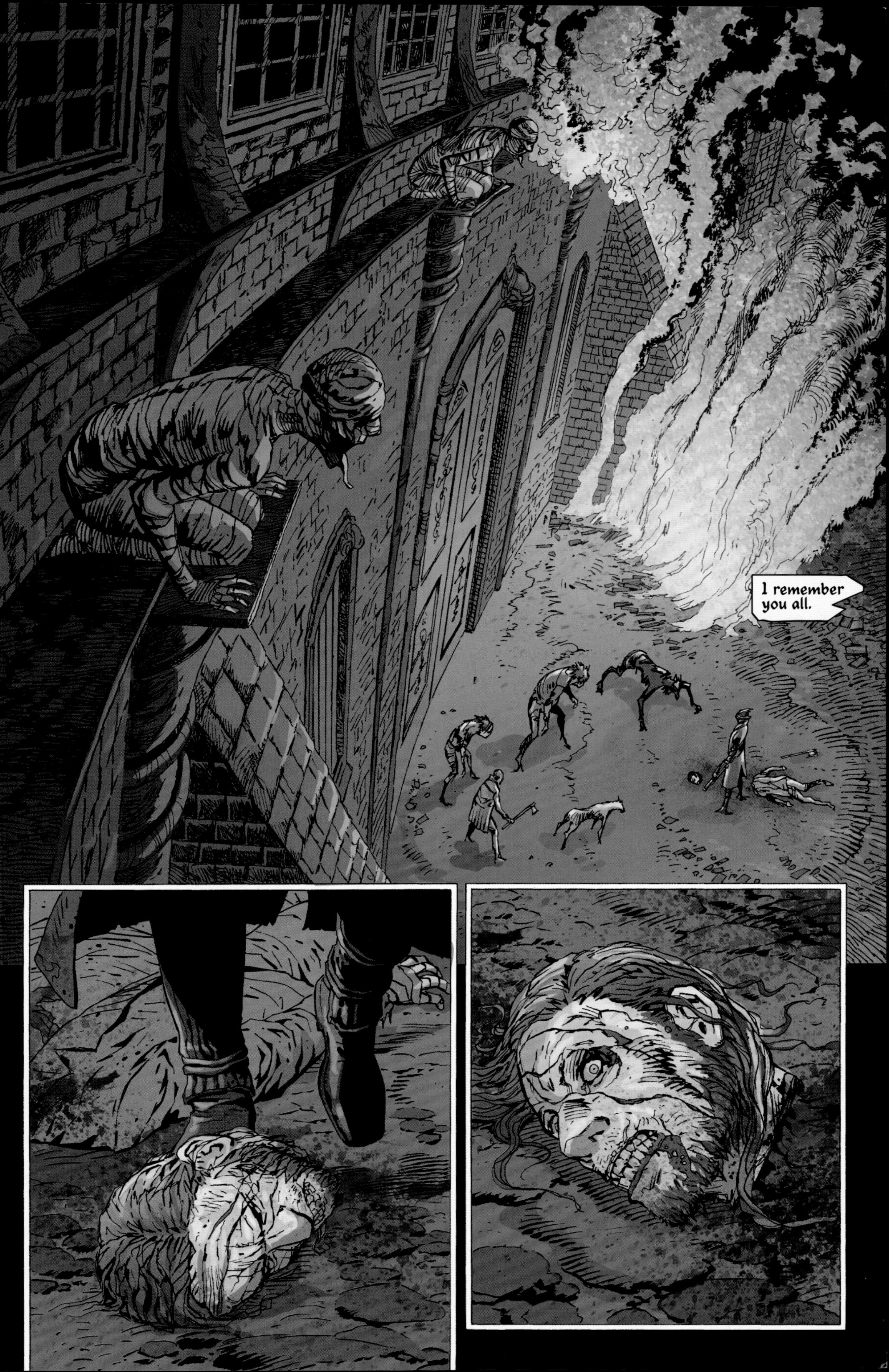
I remember you all.

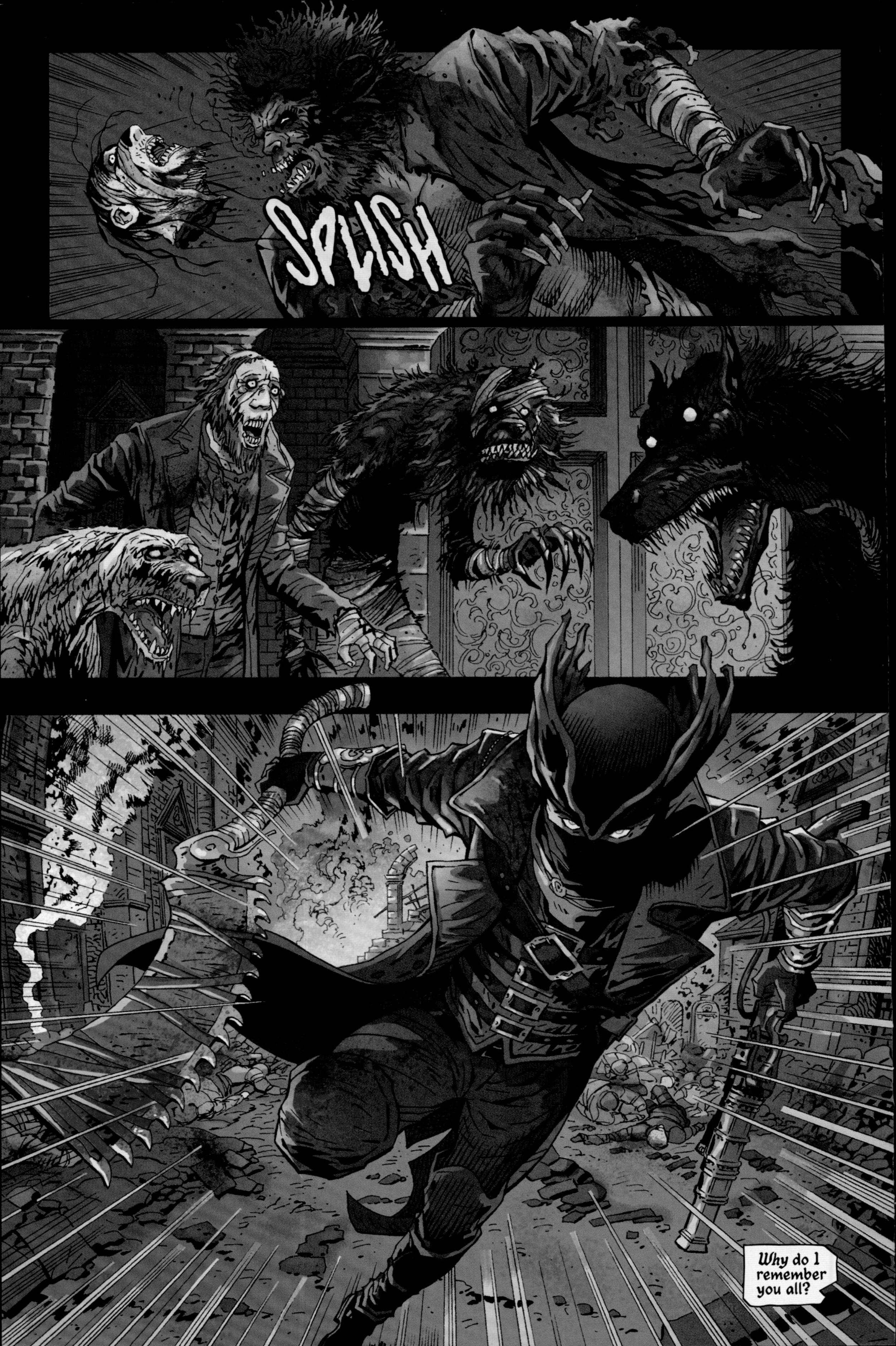
SPLISH
Why do I remember you all?

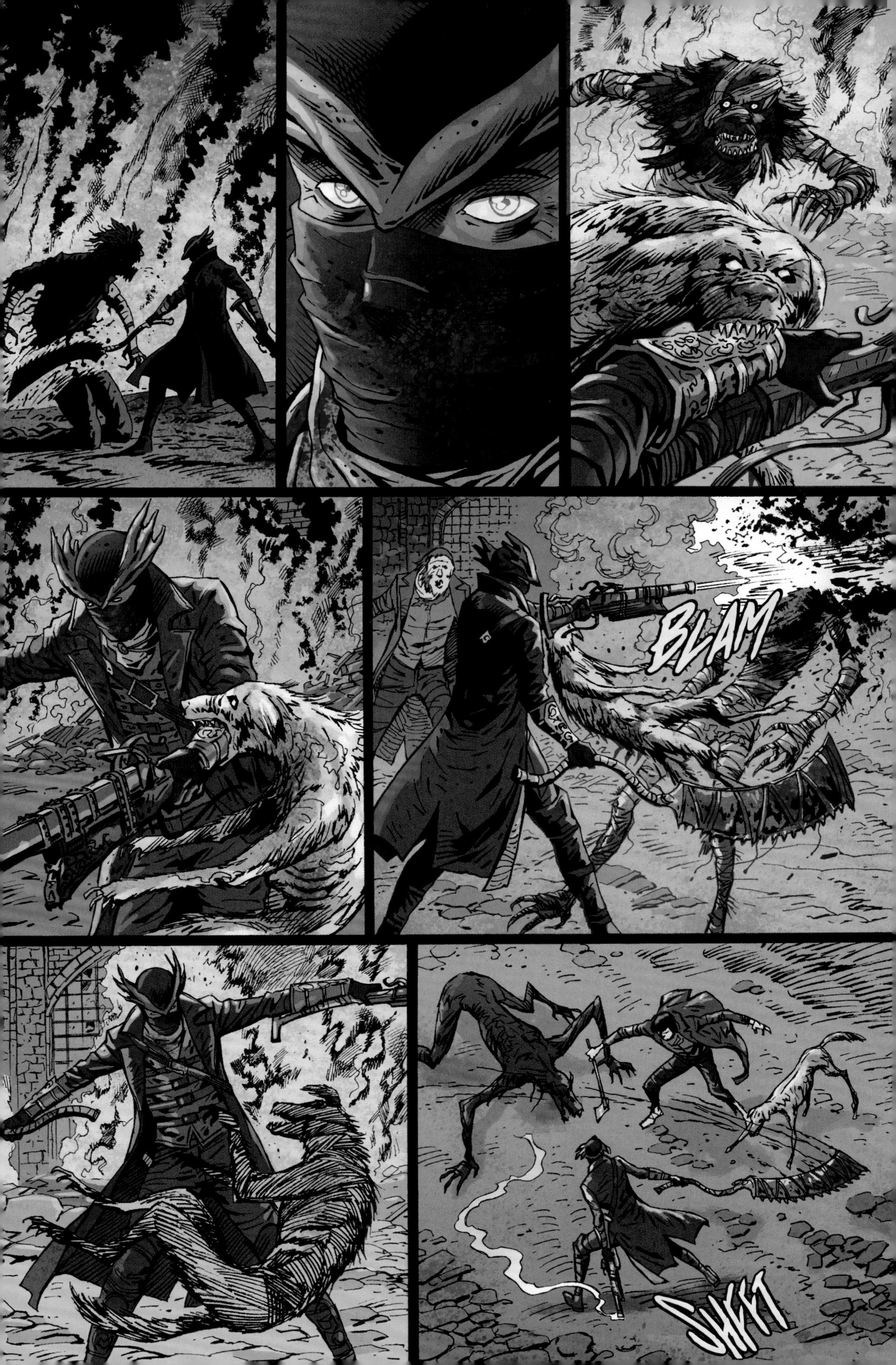
BLAM
SHKT

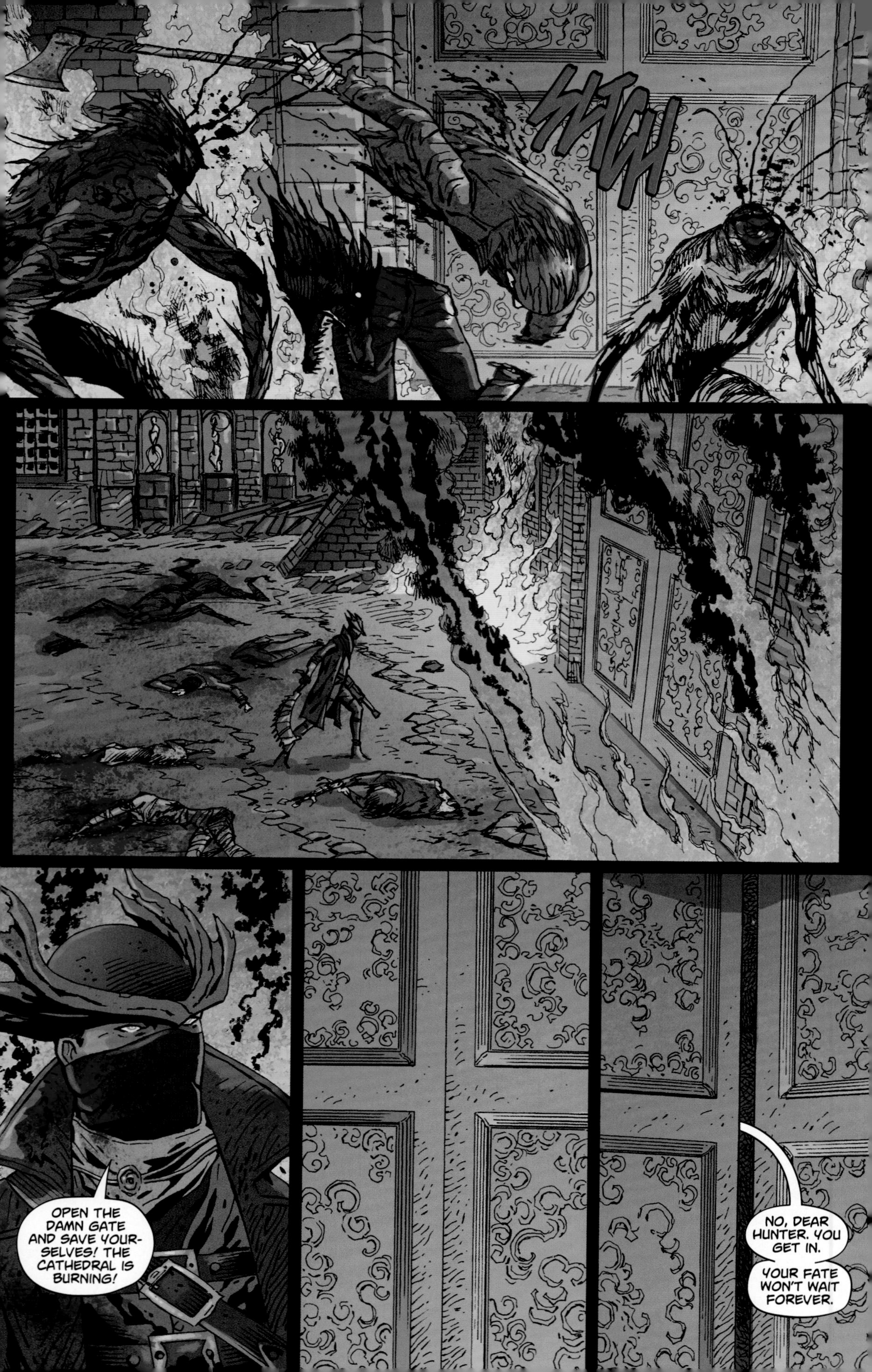
OPEN THE DAMN GATE AND SAVE YOUR-SELVES! THE CATHEDRAL IS BURNING!
NO, DEAR HUNTER. YOU GET IN.
YOUR FATE WON'T WAIT FOREVER.

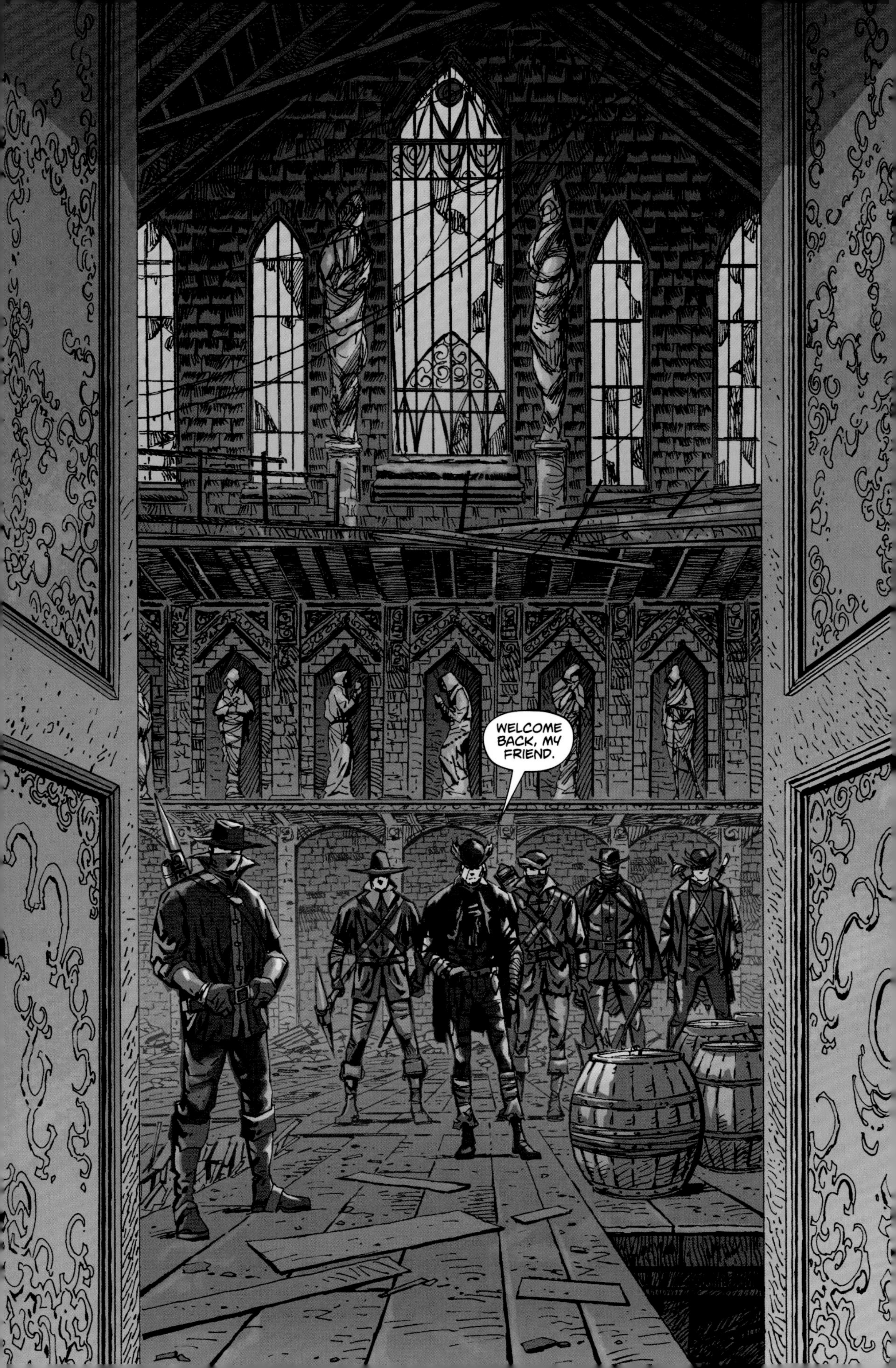
WELCOME BACK, MY FRIEND.

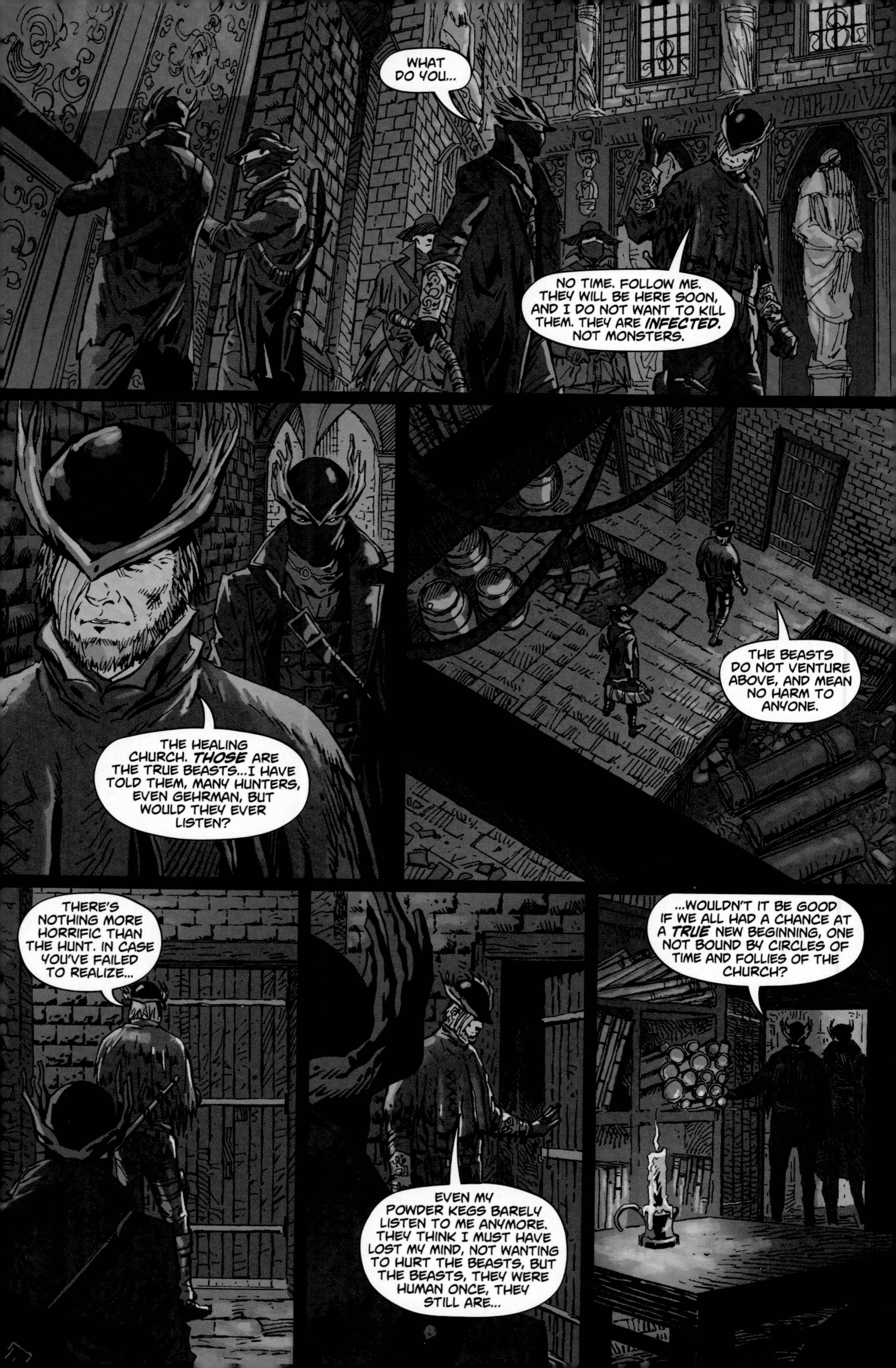
WHAT DO YOU...
NO TIME. FOLLOW ME. THEY WILL BE HERE SOON, AND I DO NOT WANT TO KILL THEM. THEY ARE *INFECTED*. NOT MONSTERS.
THE HEALING CHURCH. *THOSE* ARE THE TRUE BEASTS...I HAVE TOLD THEM, MANY HUNTERS, EVEN GEHRMAN, BUT WOULD THEY EVER LISTEN?
THE BEASTS DO NOT VENTURE ABOVE, AND MEAN NO HARM TO ANYONE.
THERE'S NOTHING MORE HORRIFIC THAN THE HUNT. IN CASE YOU'VE FAILED TO REALIZE...
EVEN MY POWDER KEGS BARELY LISTEN TO ME ANYMORE. THEY THINK I MUST HAVE LOST MY MIND, NOT WANTING TO HURT THE BEASTS, BUT THE BEASTS, THEY WERE HUMAN ONCE, THEY STILL ARE...
...WOULDN'T IT BE GOOD IF WE ALL HAD A CHANCE AT A *TRUE* NEW BEGINNING, ONE NOT BOUND BY CIRCLES OF TIME AND FOLLIES OF THE CHURCH?

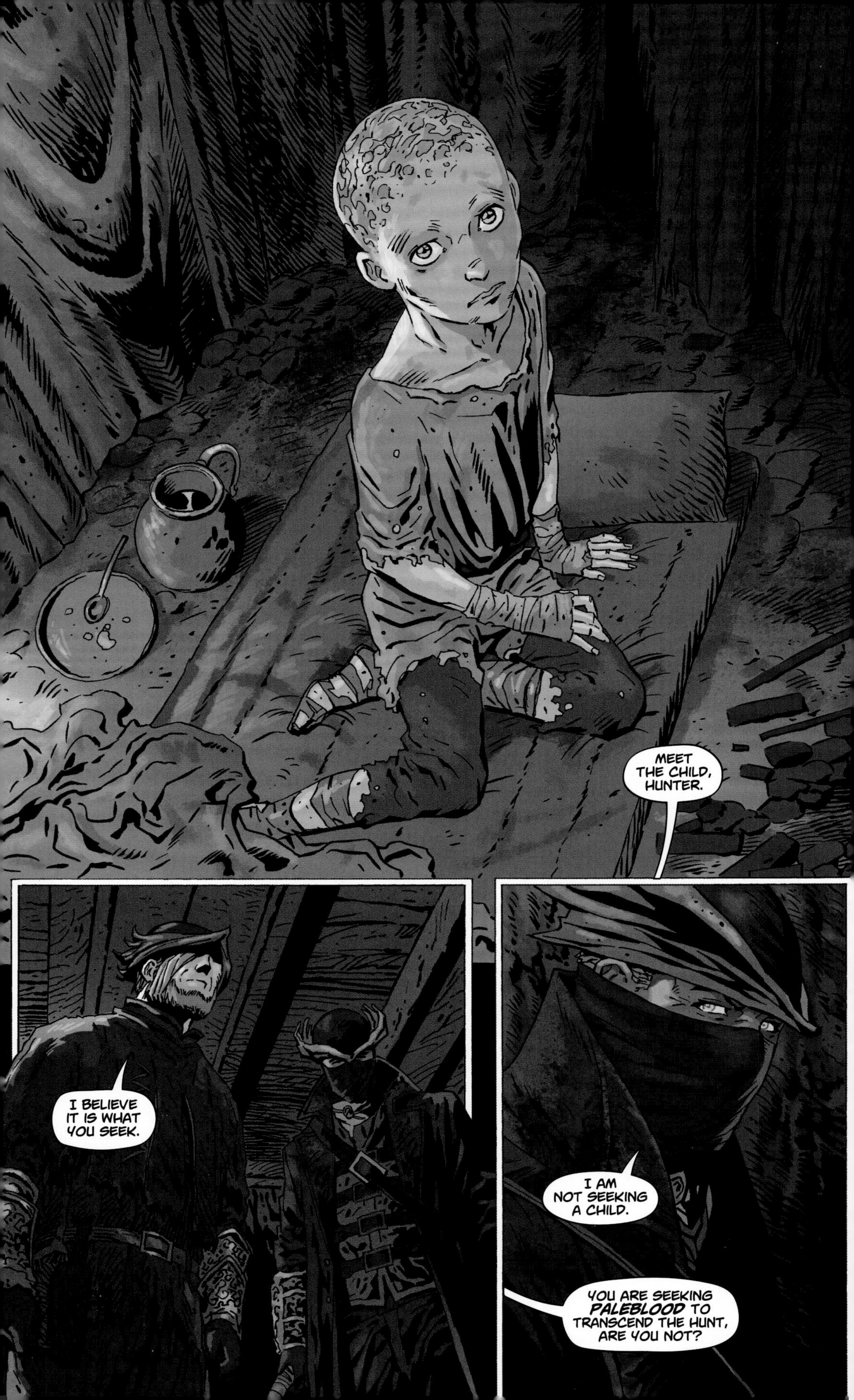
MEET THE CHILD, HUNTER.
I BELIEVE IT IS WHAT YOU SEEK.
I AM NOT SEEKING A CHILD.
YOU ARE SEEKING PALEBLOOD TO TRANSCEND THE HUNT, ARE YOU NOT?

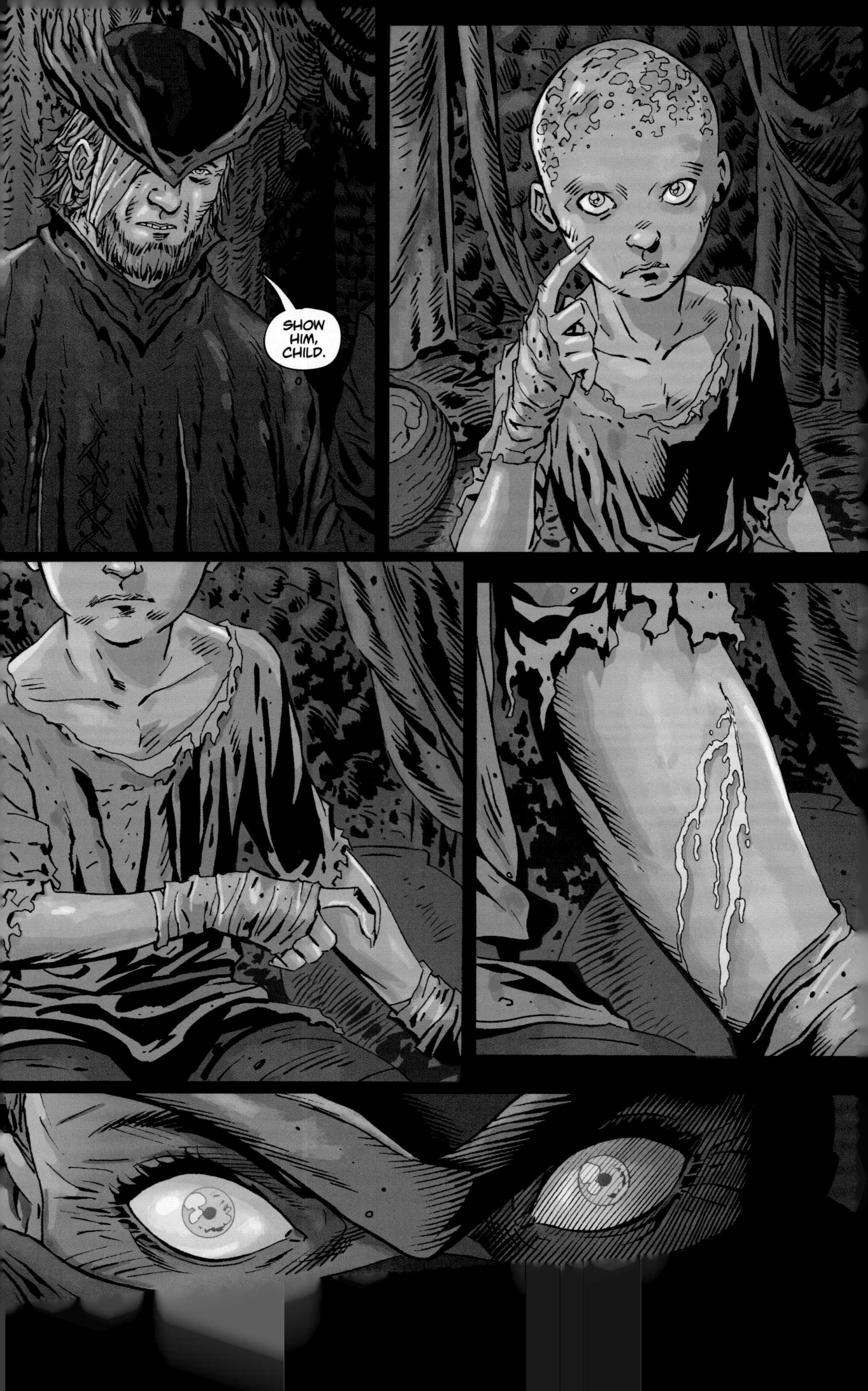
SHOW HIM, CHILD.

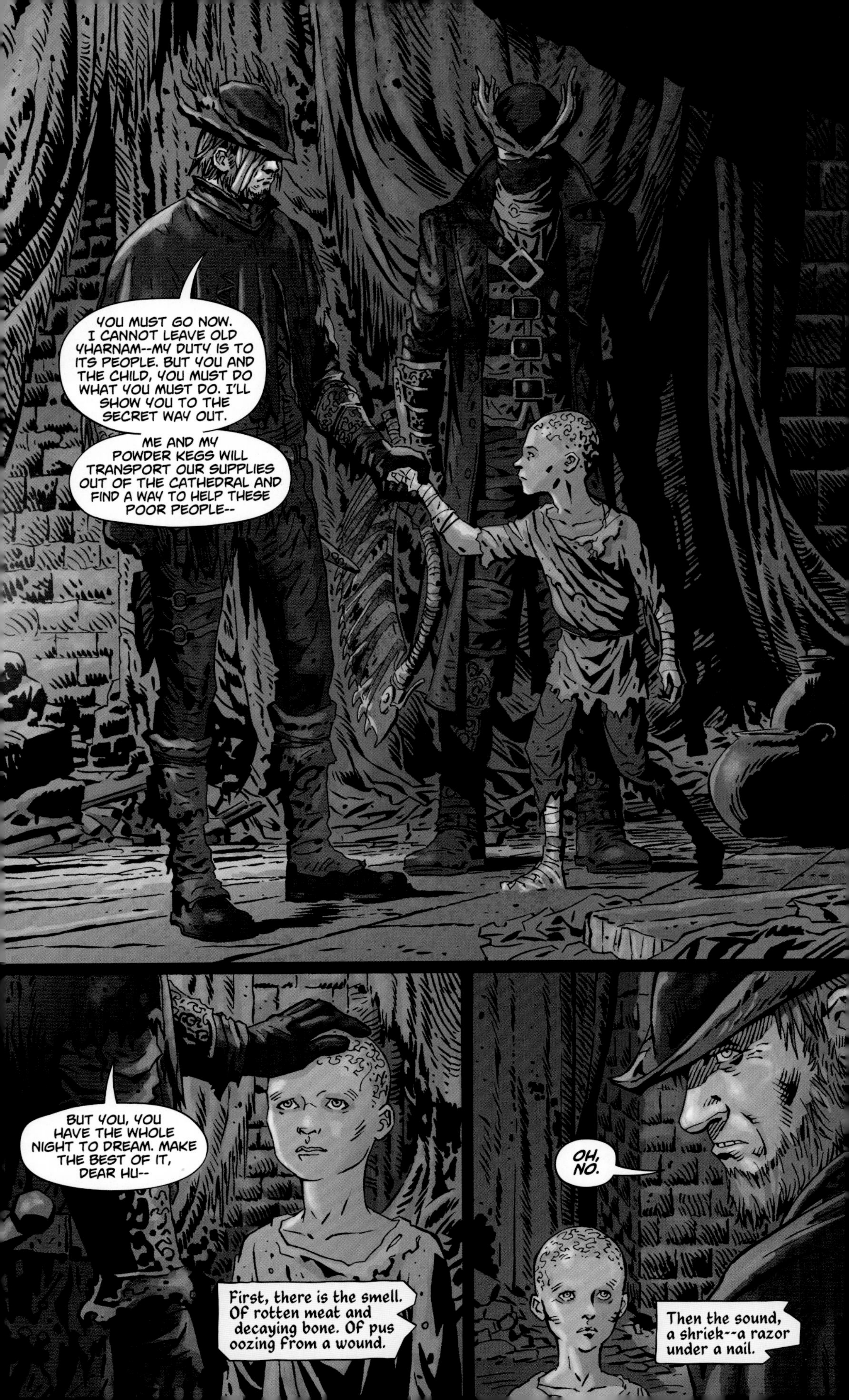
YOU MUST GO NOW. I CANNOT LEAVE OLD YHARNAM--MY DUTY IS TO ITS PEOPLE. BUT YOU AND THE CHILD, YOU MUST DO WHAT YOU MUST DO. I'LL SHOW YOU TO THE SECRET WAY OUT.
ME AND MY POWDER KEGS WILL TRANSPORT OUR SUPPLIES OUT OF THE CATHEDRAL AND FIND A WAY TO HELP THESE POOR PEOPLE--
BUT YOU, YOU HAVE THE WHOLE NIGHT TO DREAM. MAKE THE BEST OF IT, DEAR HU--
First, there is the smell. Of rotten meat and decaying bone. Of pus oozing from a wound.
OH, NO.
Then the sound, a shriek--a razor under a nail.

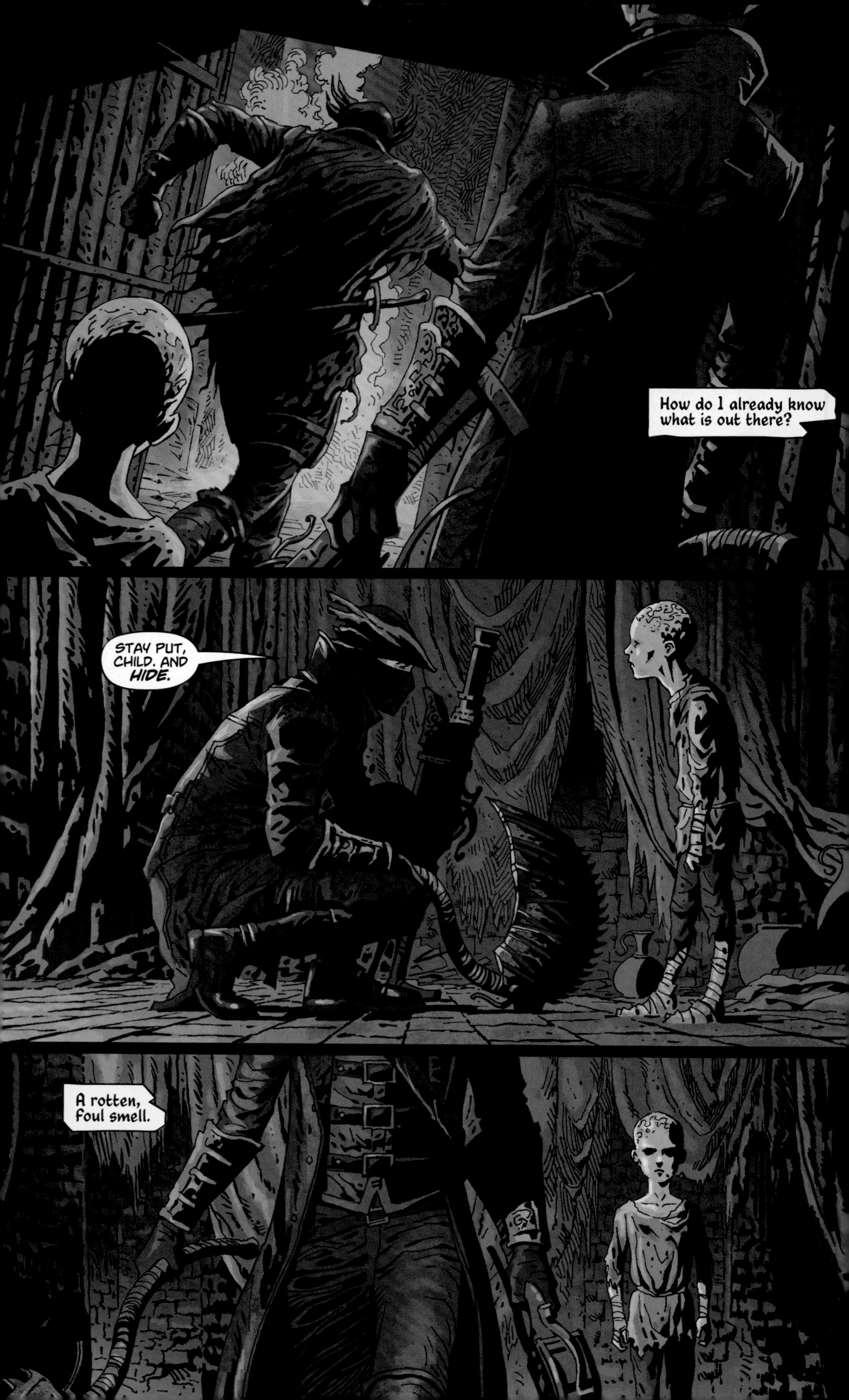
How do I already know what is out there?
STAY PUT, CHILD. AND HIDE.
A rotten, foul smell.

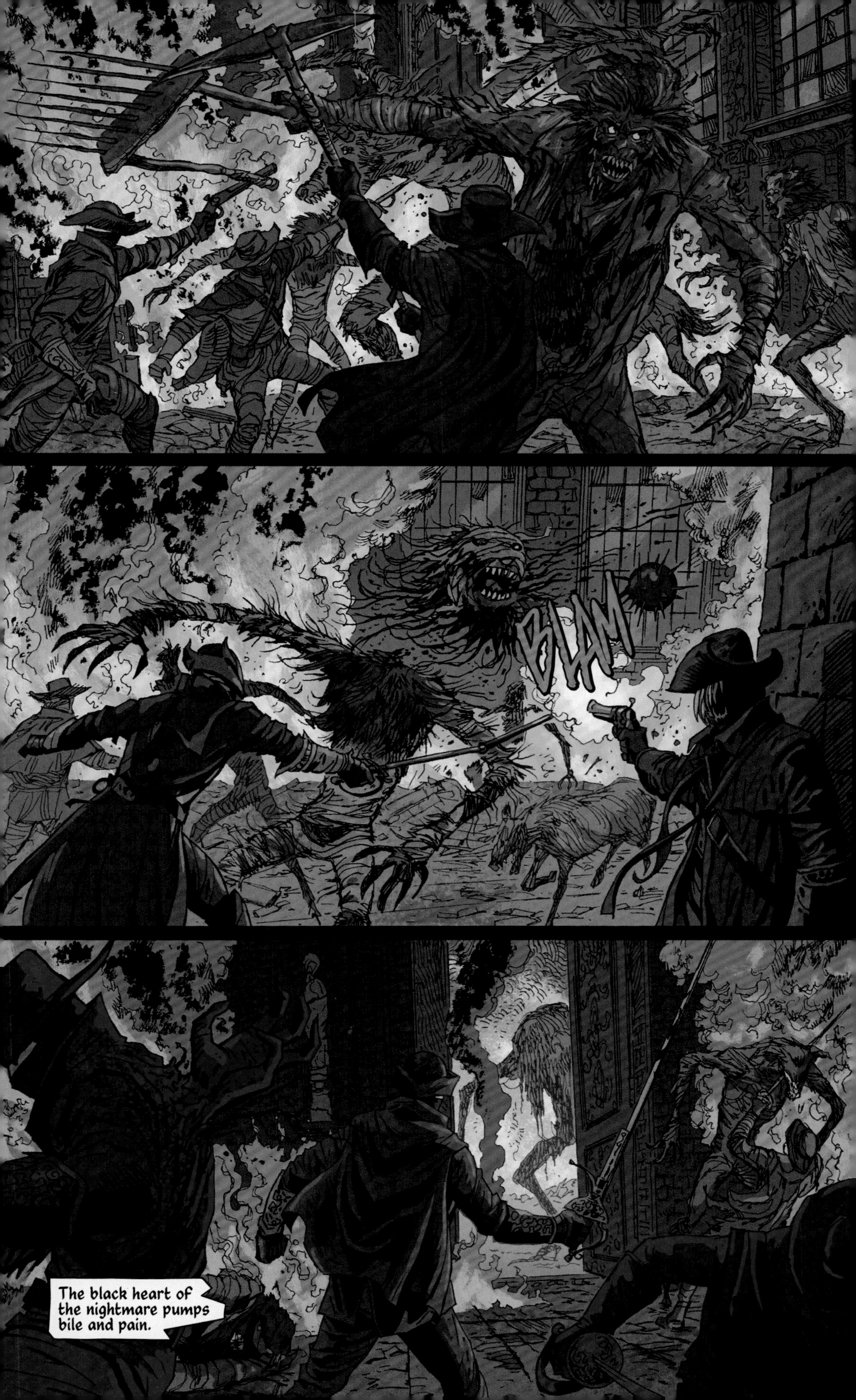
BLAM
The black heart of the nightmare pumps bile and pain.

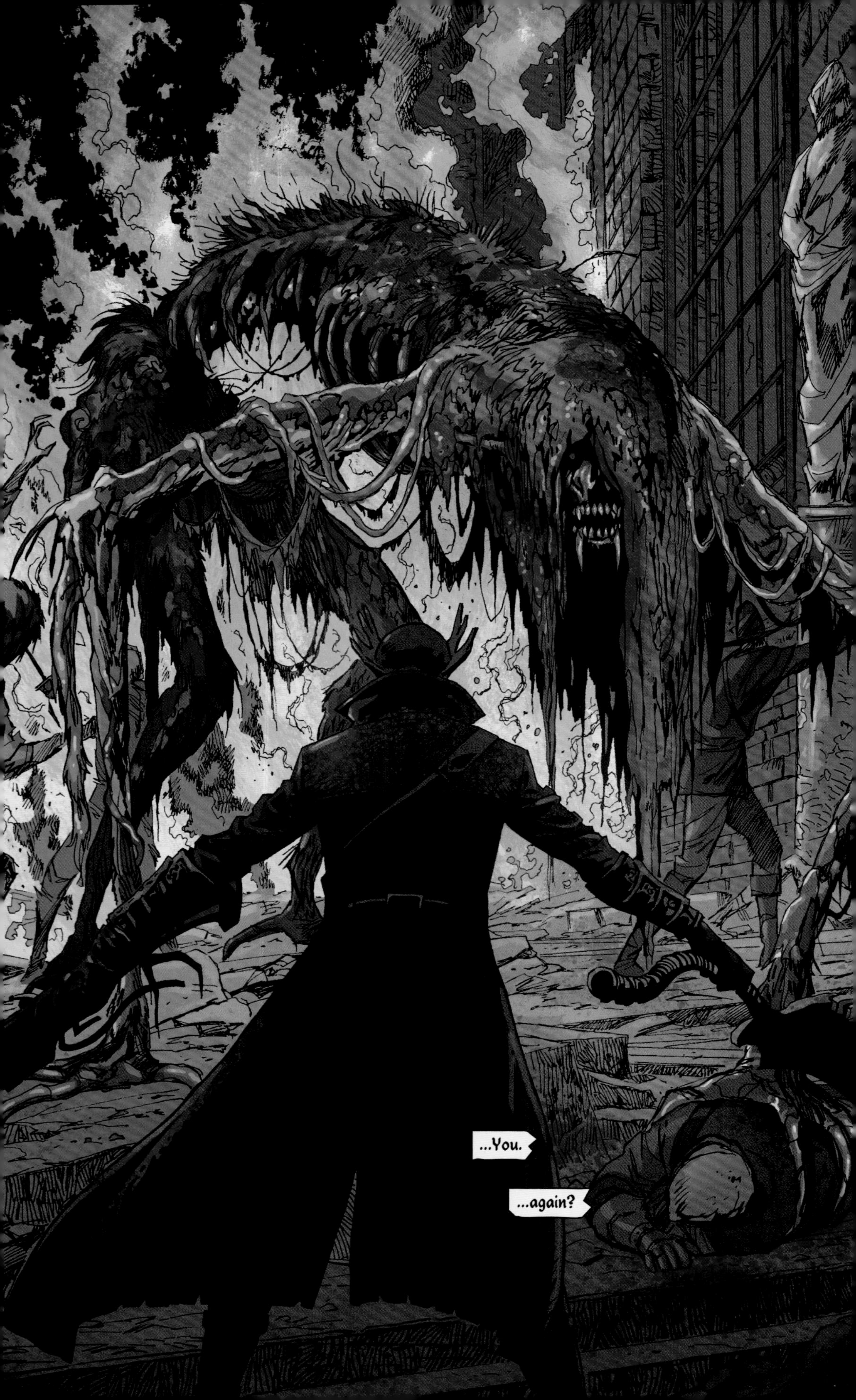
...You.
...again?

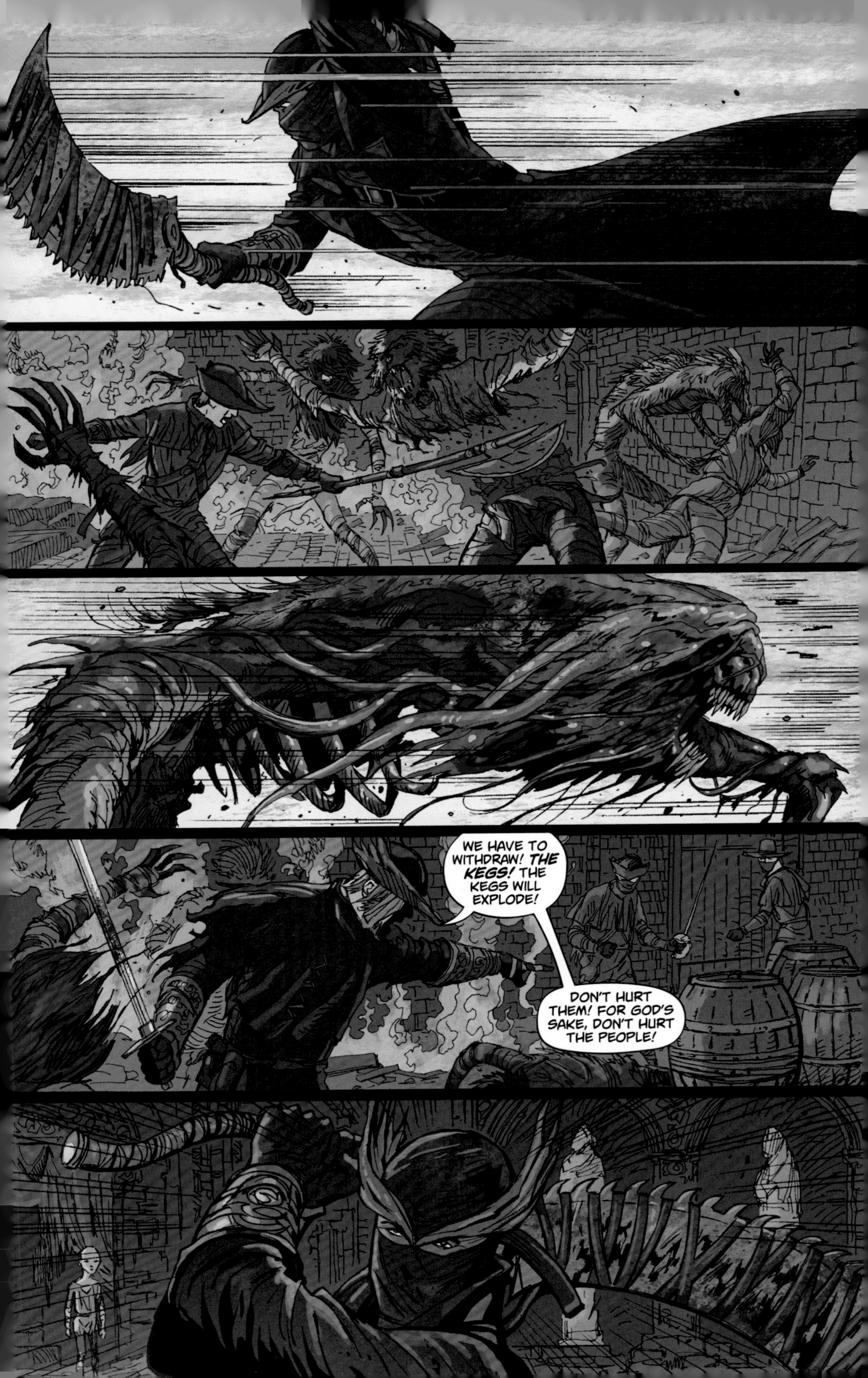
WE HAVE TO WITHDRAW! THE KEGS! THE KEGS WILL EXPLODE!
DON'T HURT THEM! FOR GOD'S SAKE, DON'T HURT THE PEOPLE!

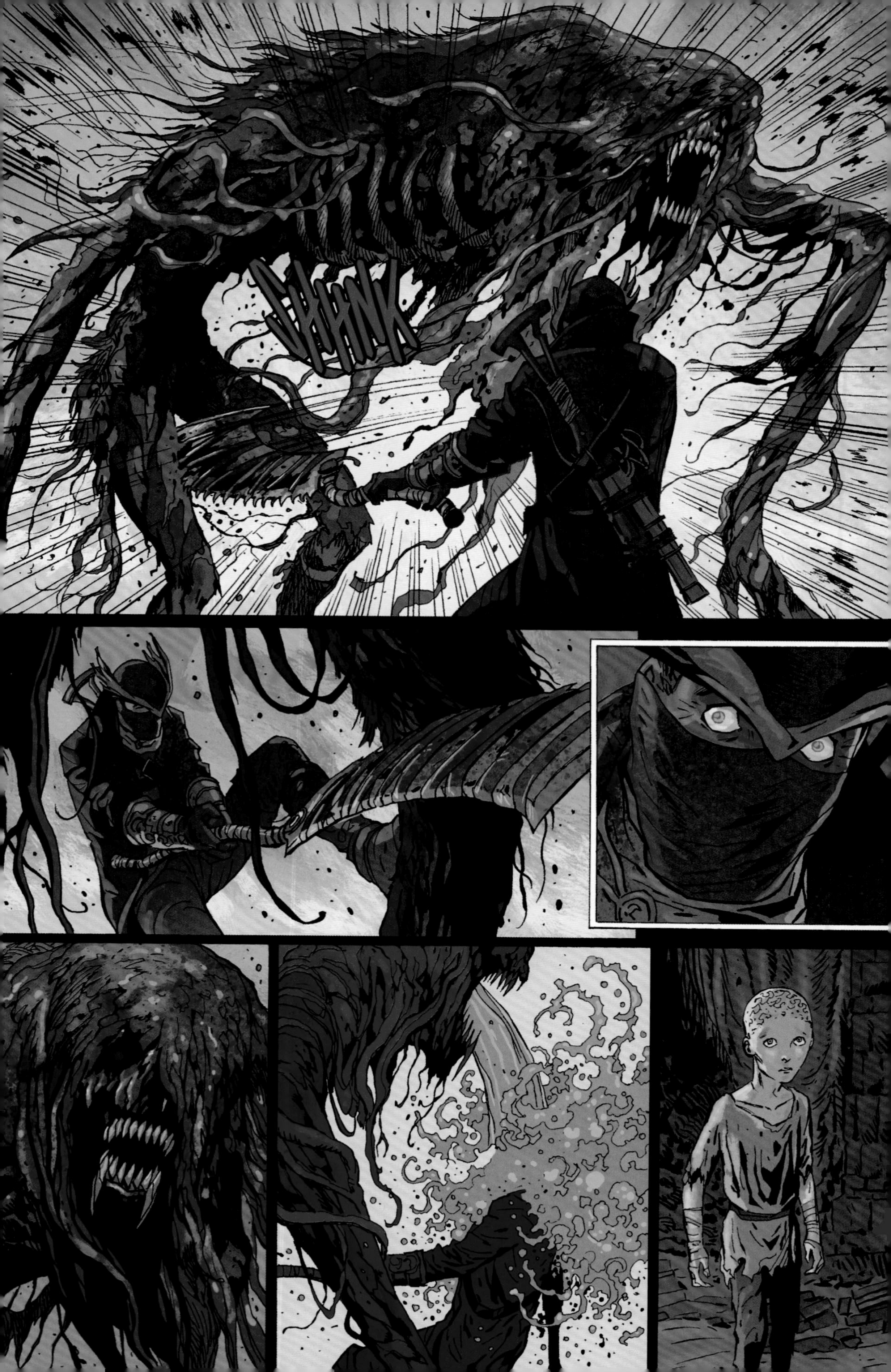
CHUNK

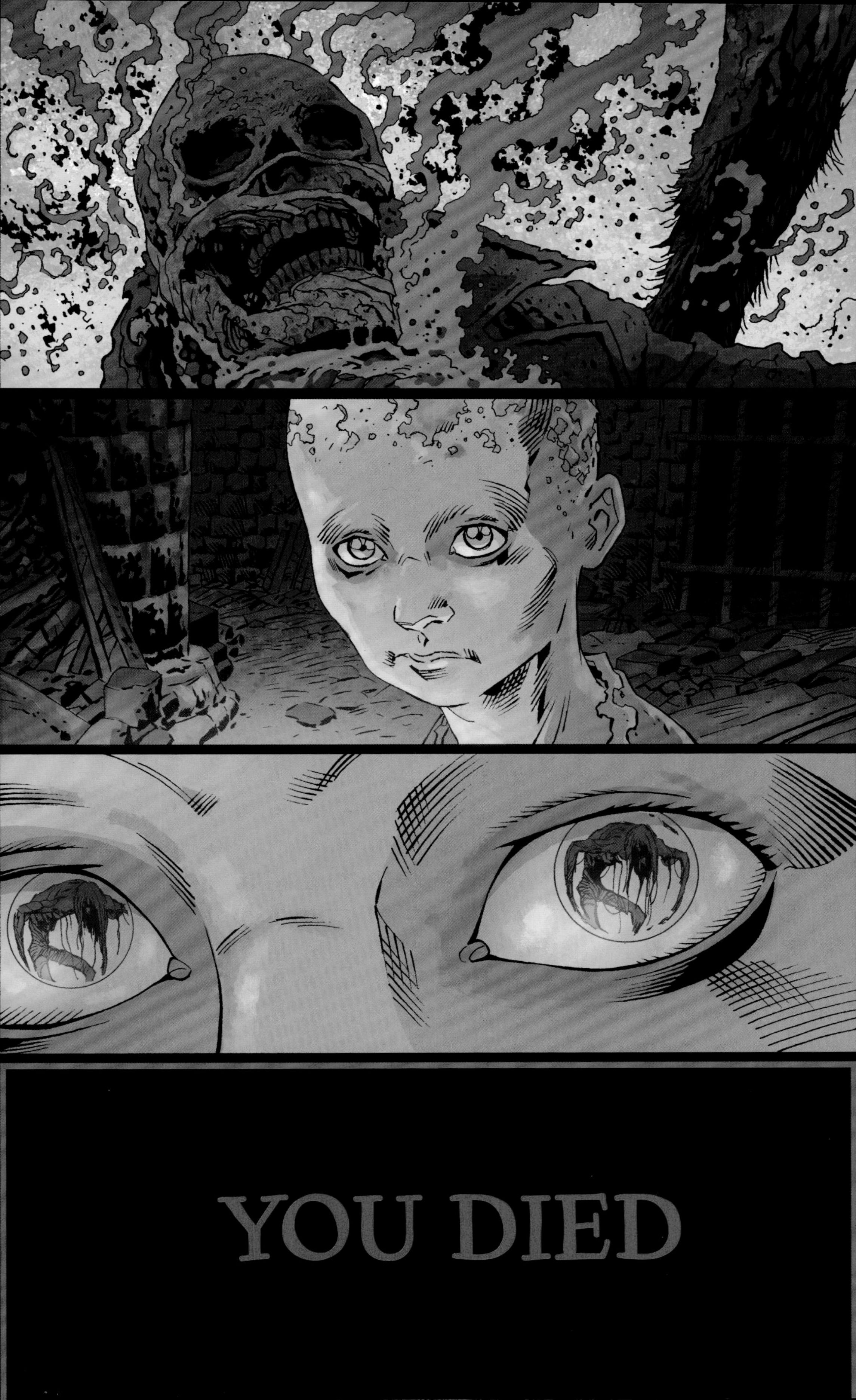
YOU DIED

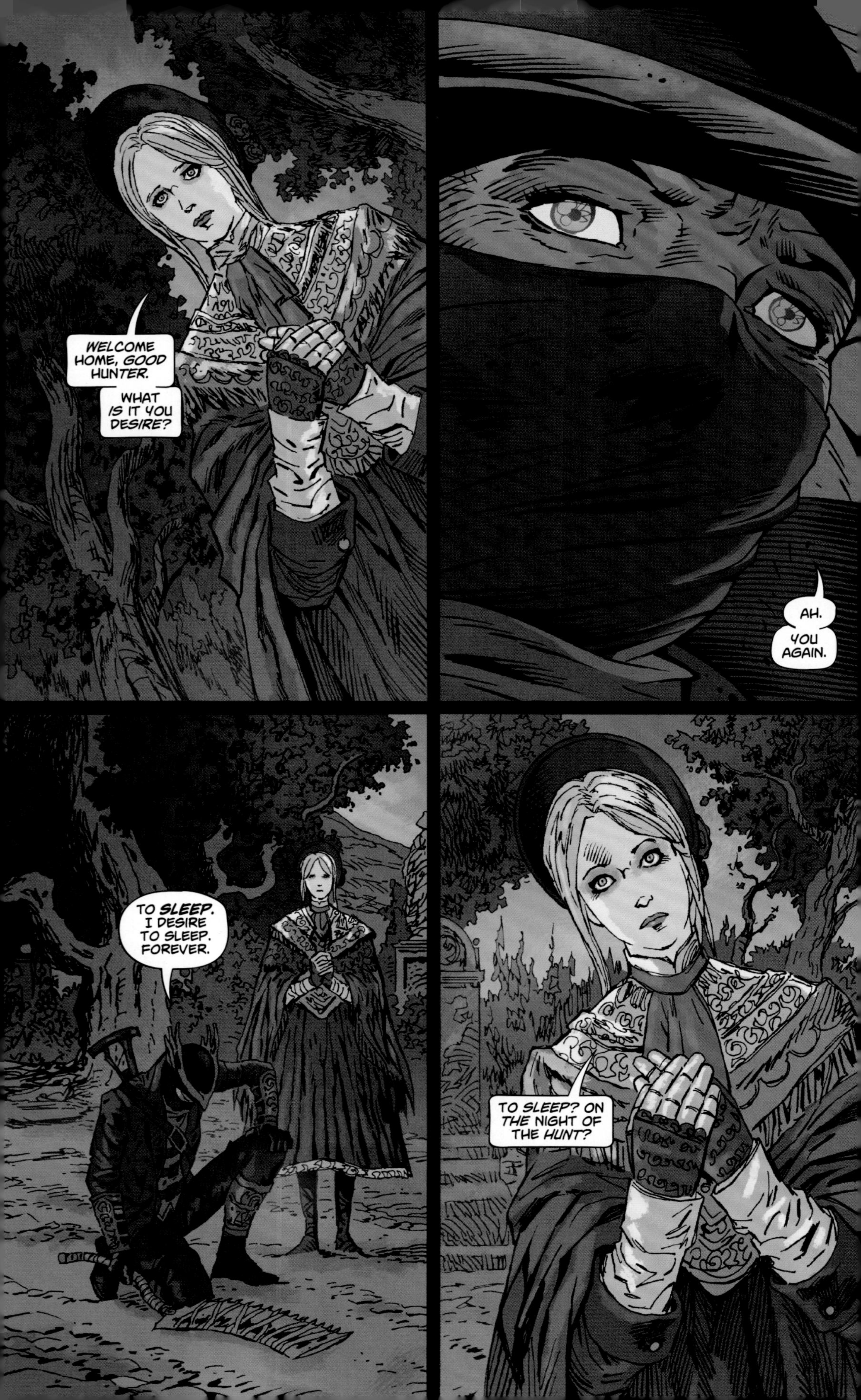
WELCOME HOME, GOOD HUNTER.
WHAT IS IT YOU DESIRE?
AH. YOU AGAIN.
TO SLEEP. I DESIRE TO SLEEP. FOREVER.
TO SLEEP? ON THE NIGHT OF THE HUNT?

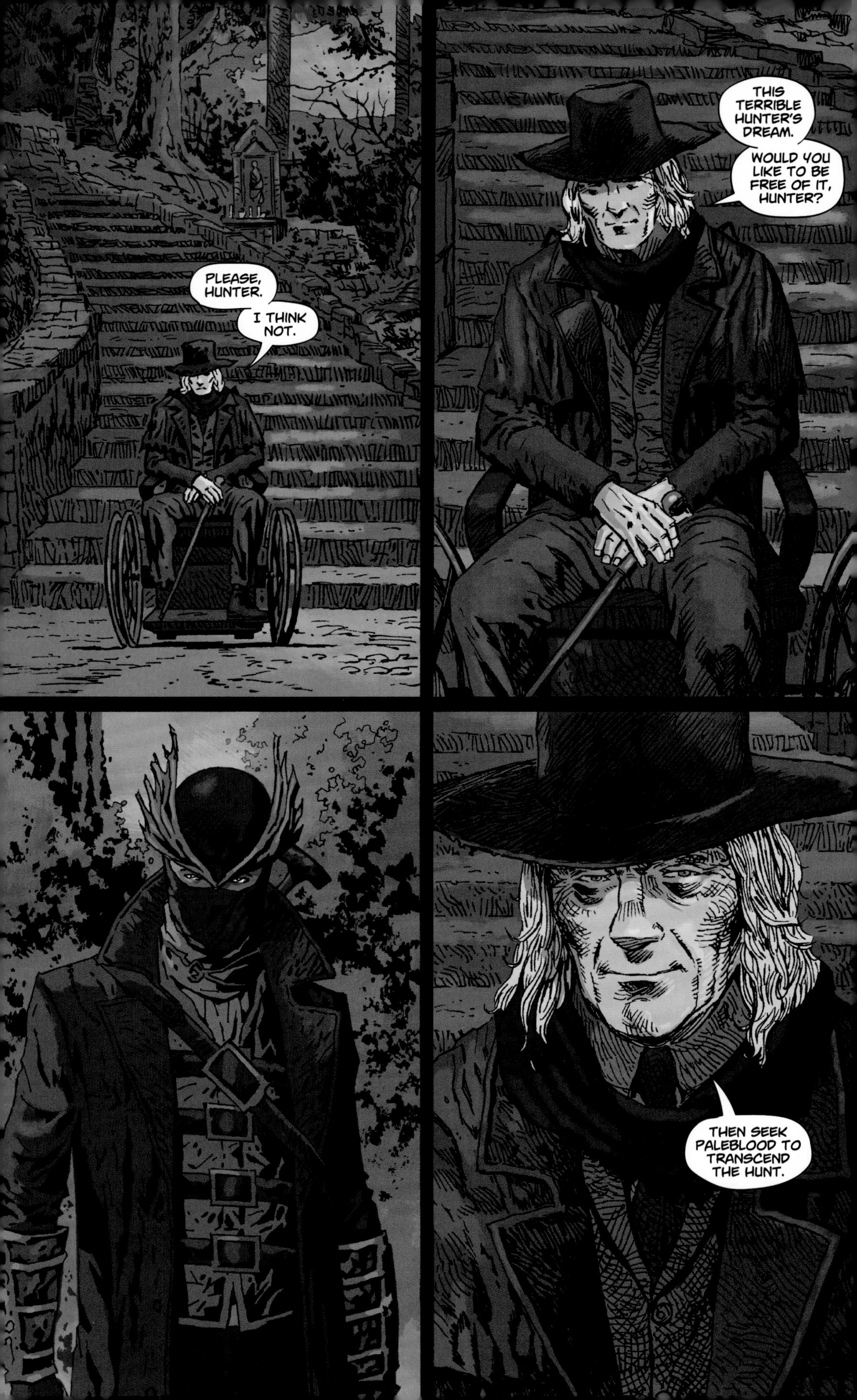
PLEASE, HUNTER.
I THINK NOT.
THIS TERRIBLE HUNTER'S DREAM.
WOULD YOU LIKE TO BE FREE OF IT, HUNTER?
THEN SEEK PALEBLOOD TO TRANSCEND THE HUNT.

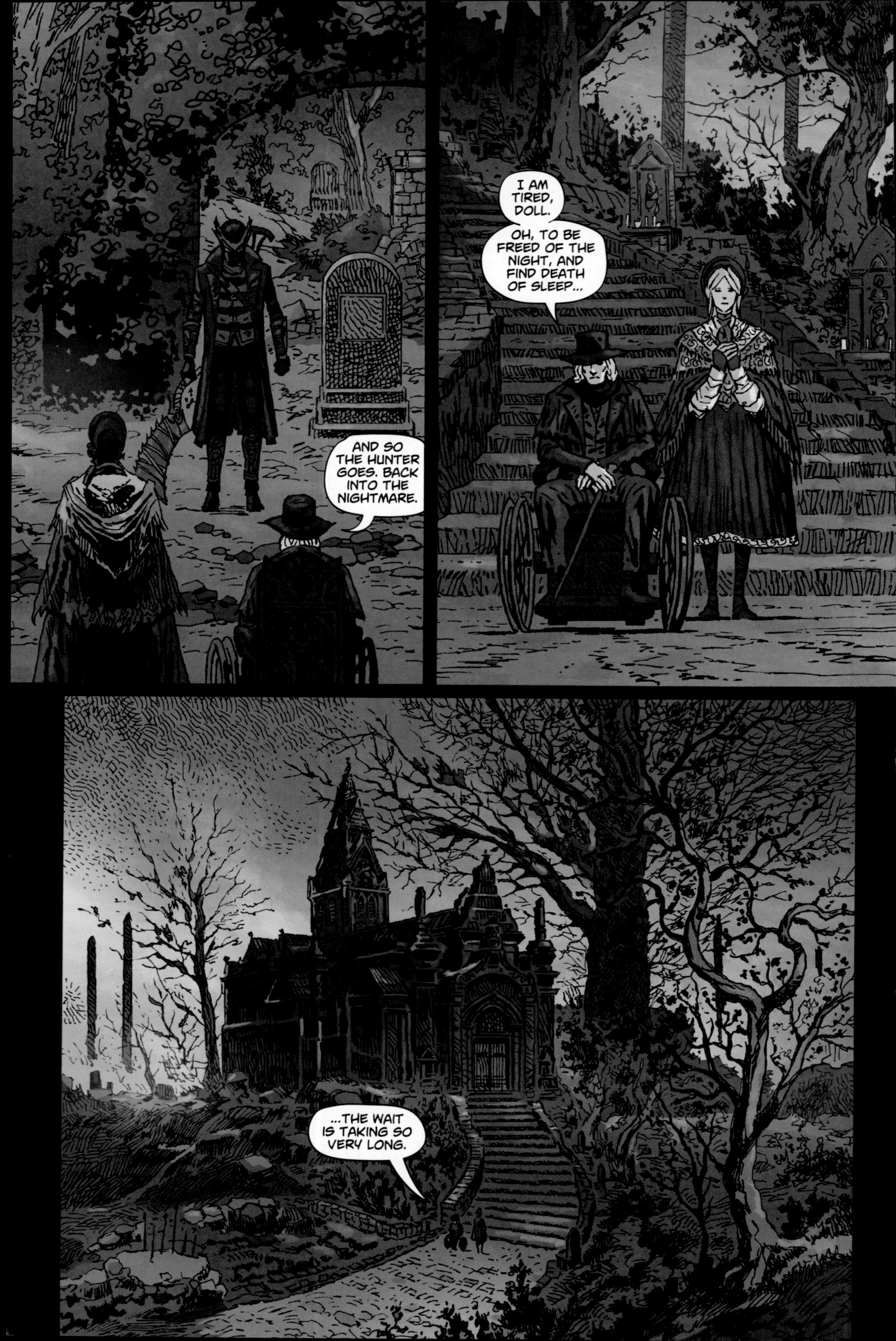
AND SO THE HUNTER GOES. BACK INTO THE NIGHTMARE.
I AM TIRED, DOLL.
OH, TO BE FREED OF THE NIGHT, AND FIND DEATH OF SLEEP...
...THE WAIT IS TAKING SO VERY LONG.

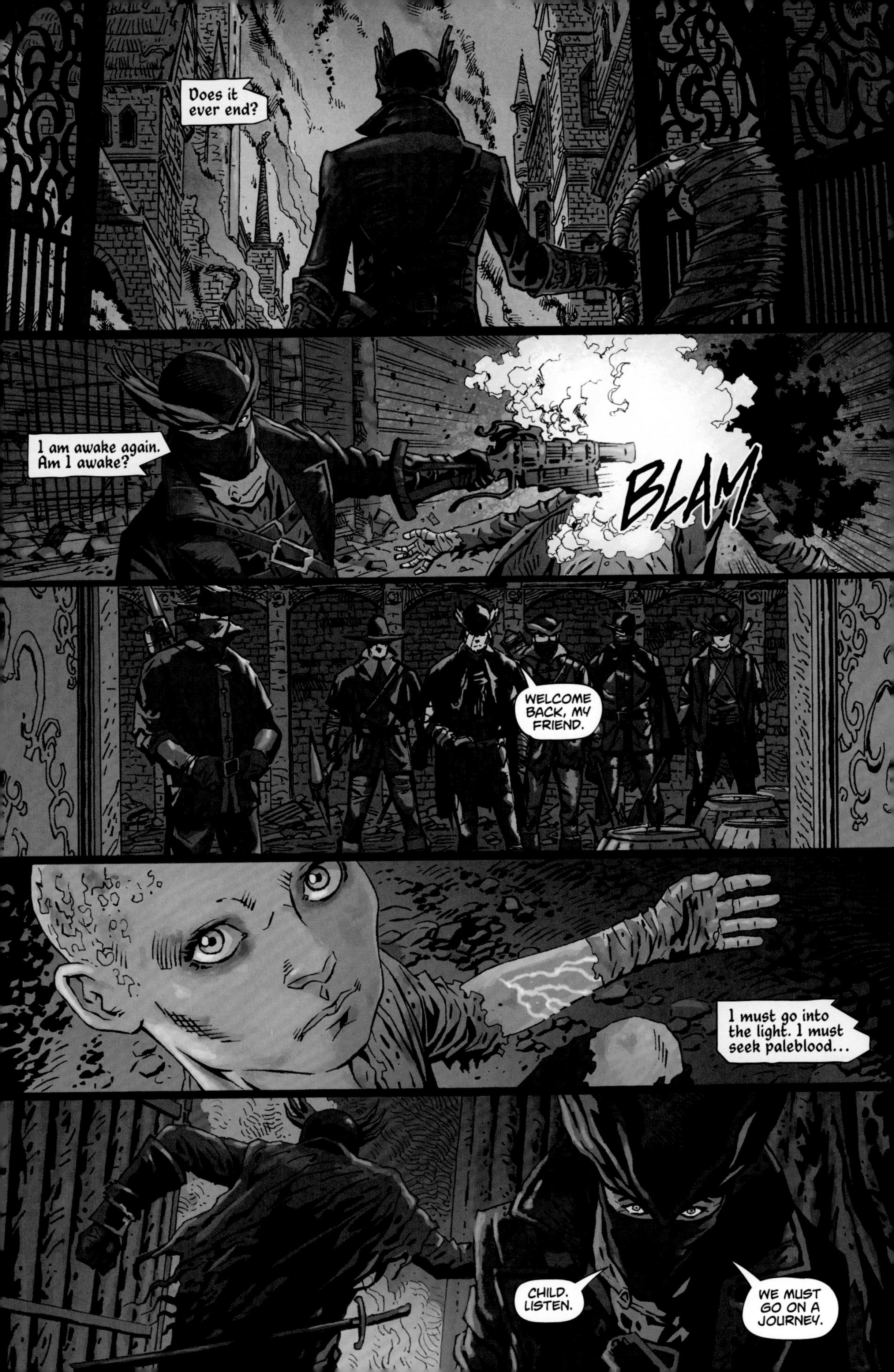
Does it ever end?
I am awake again. Am I awake?
BLAM
WELCOME BACK, MY FRIEND.
I must go into the light. I must seek paleblood...
CHILD. LISTEN.
WE MUST GO ON A JOURNEY.

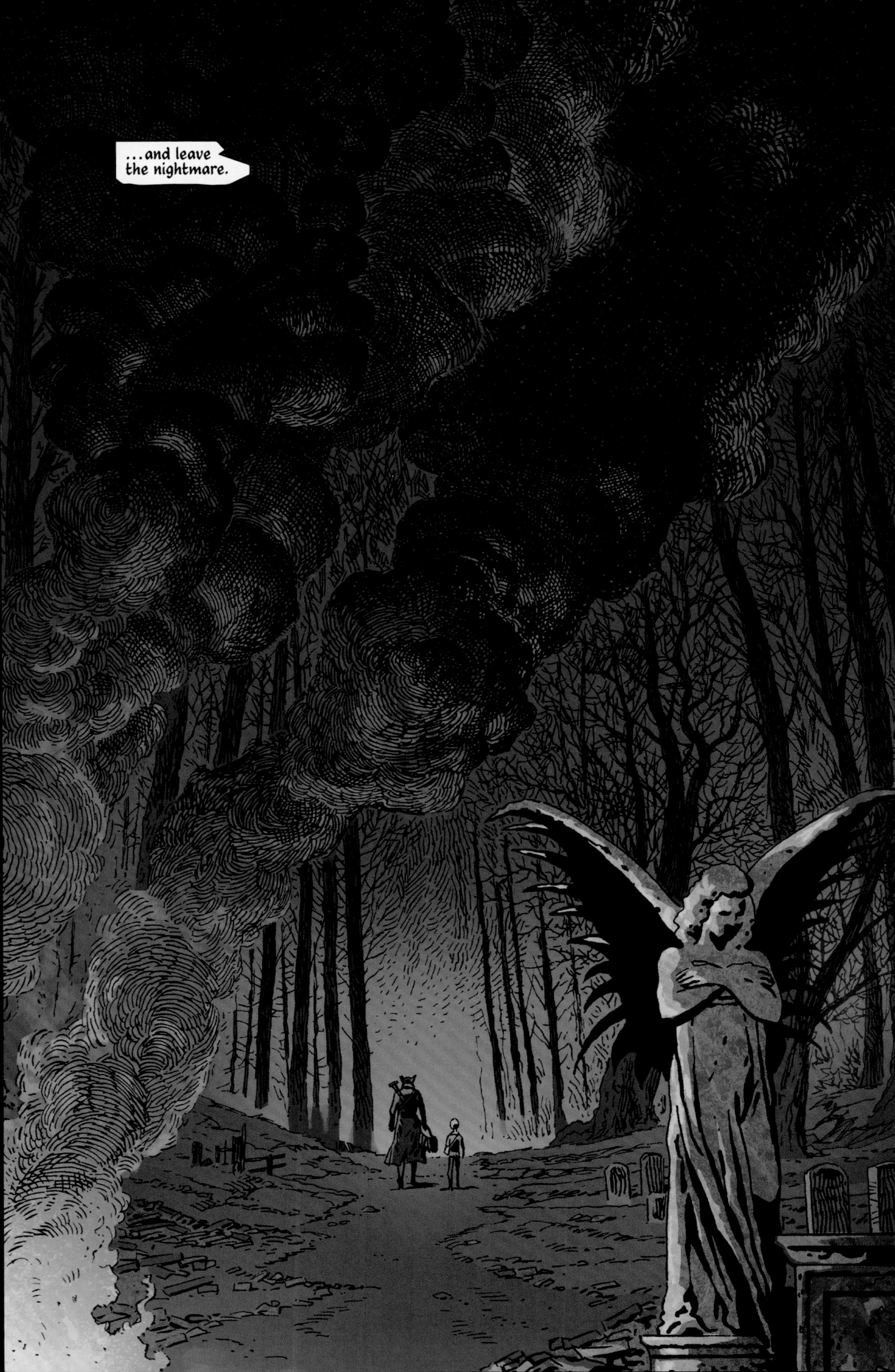
...and leave the nightmare.

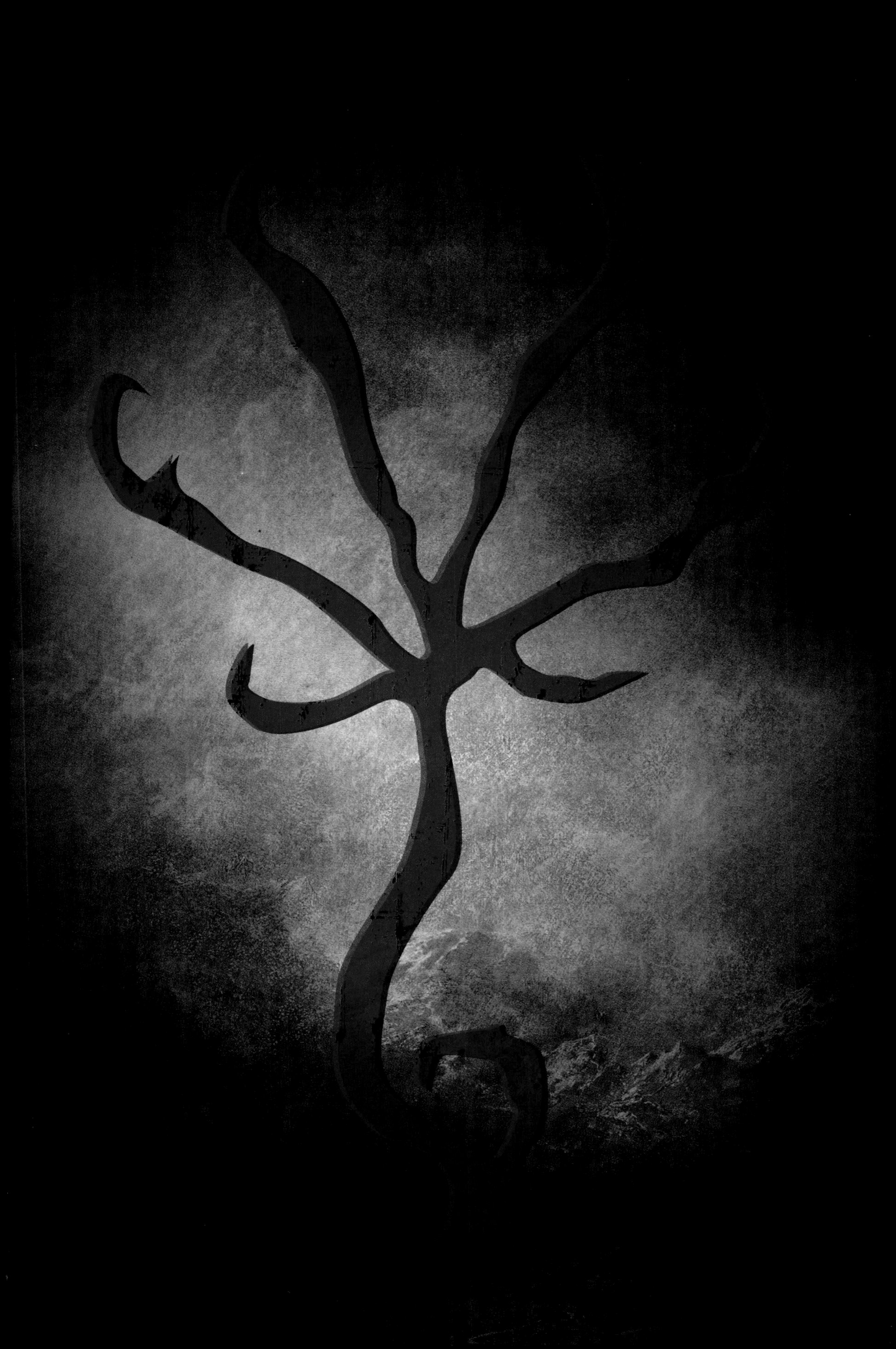

#2 COVER A
BY
DAMIEN WORM

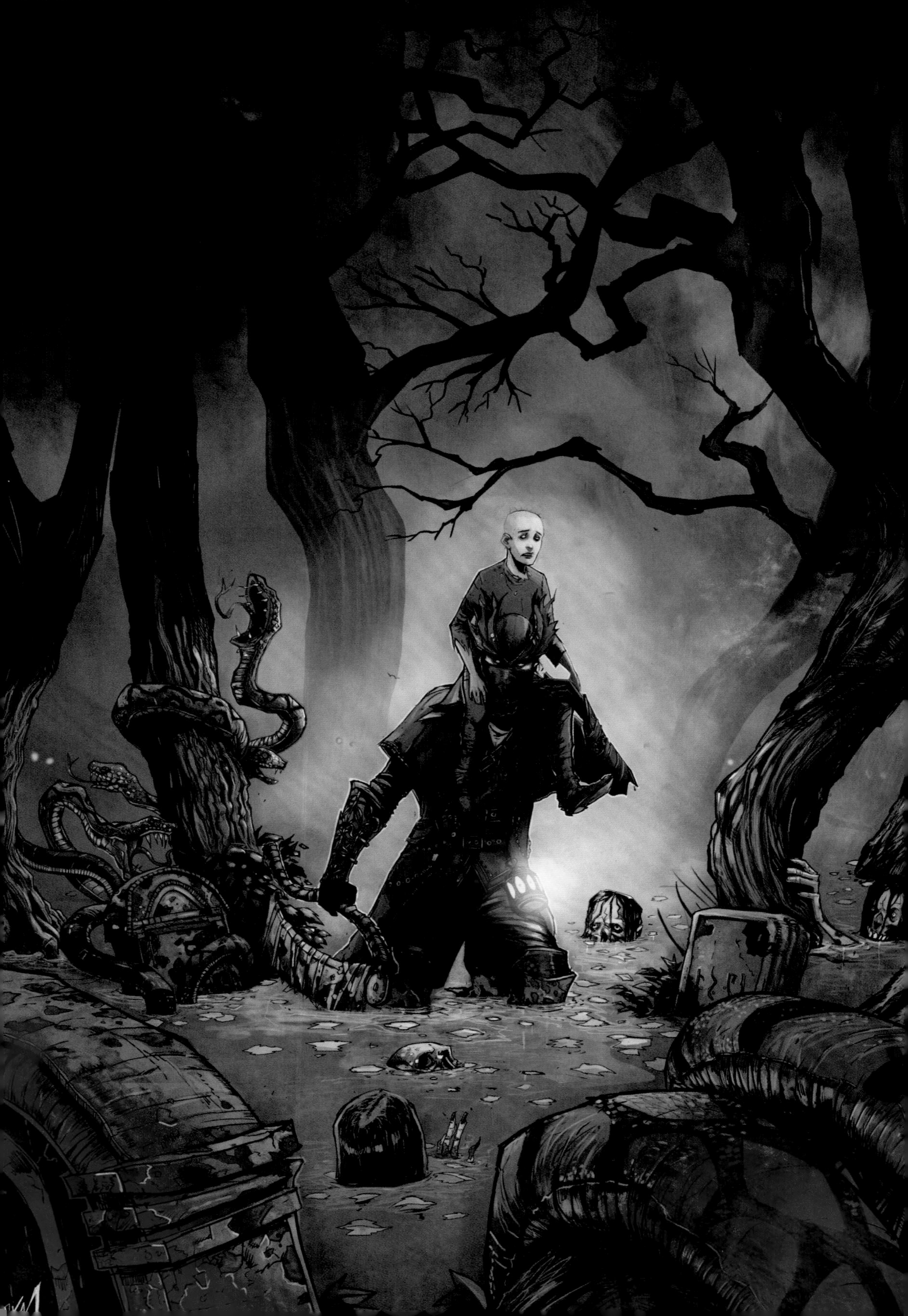

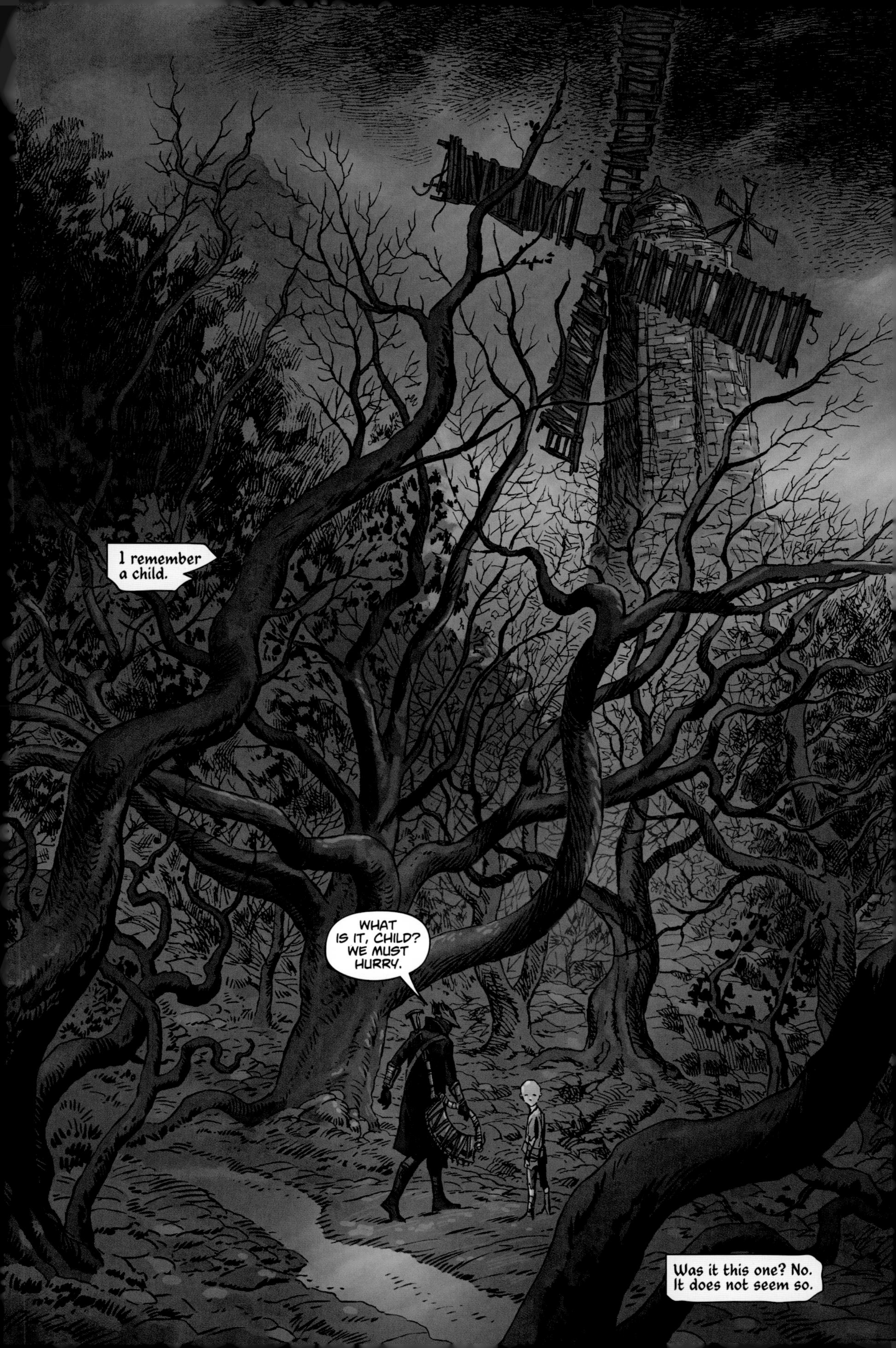
I remember a child.
WHAT IS IT, CHILD? WE MUST HURRY.
Was it this one? No. It does not seem so.

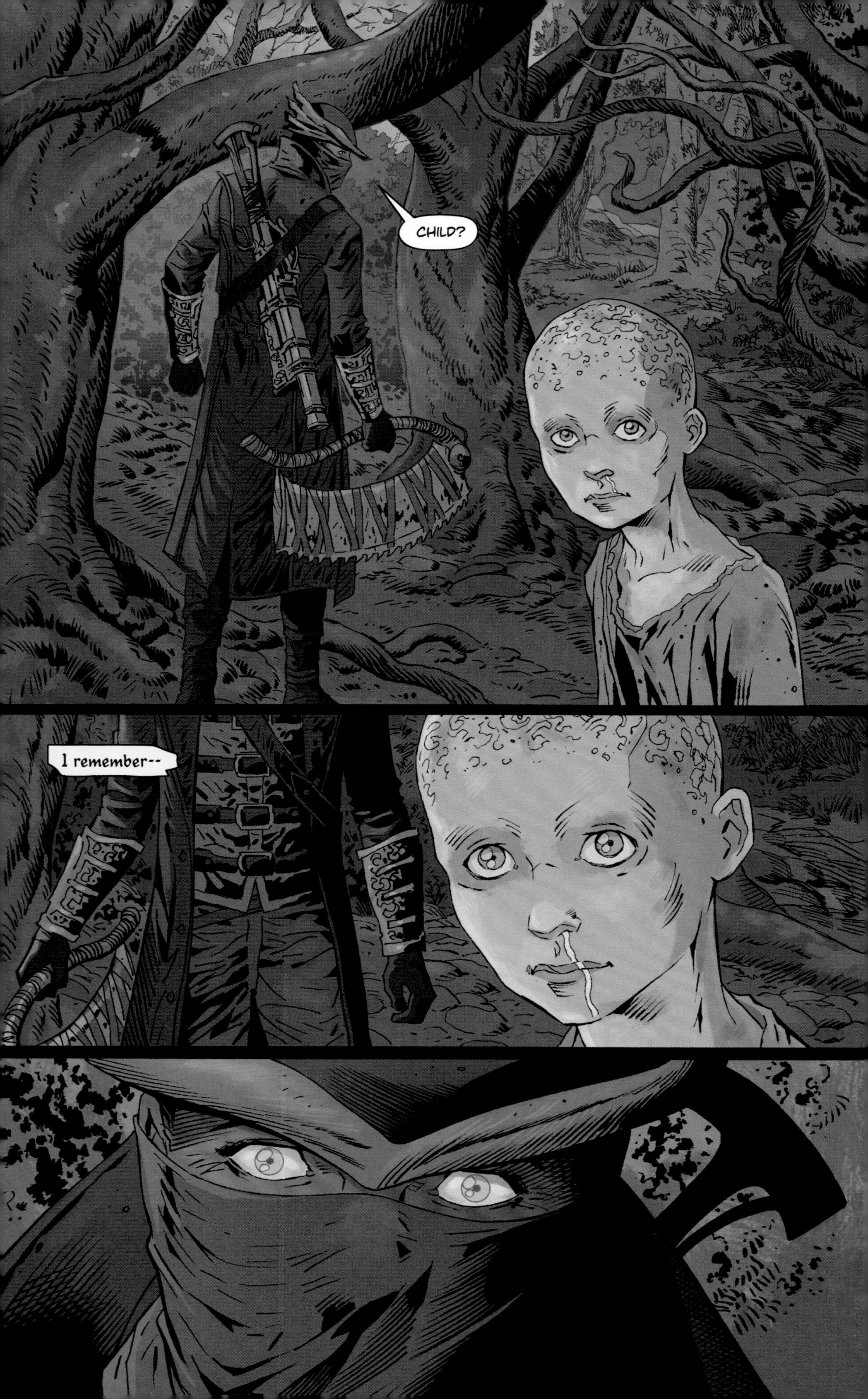
CHILD?
I remember--

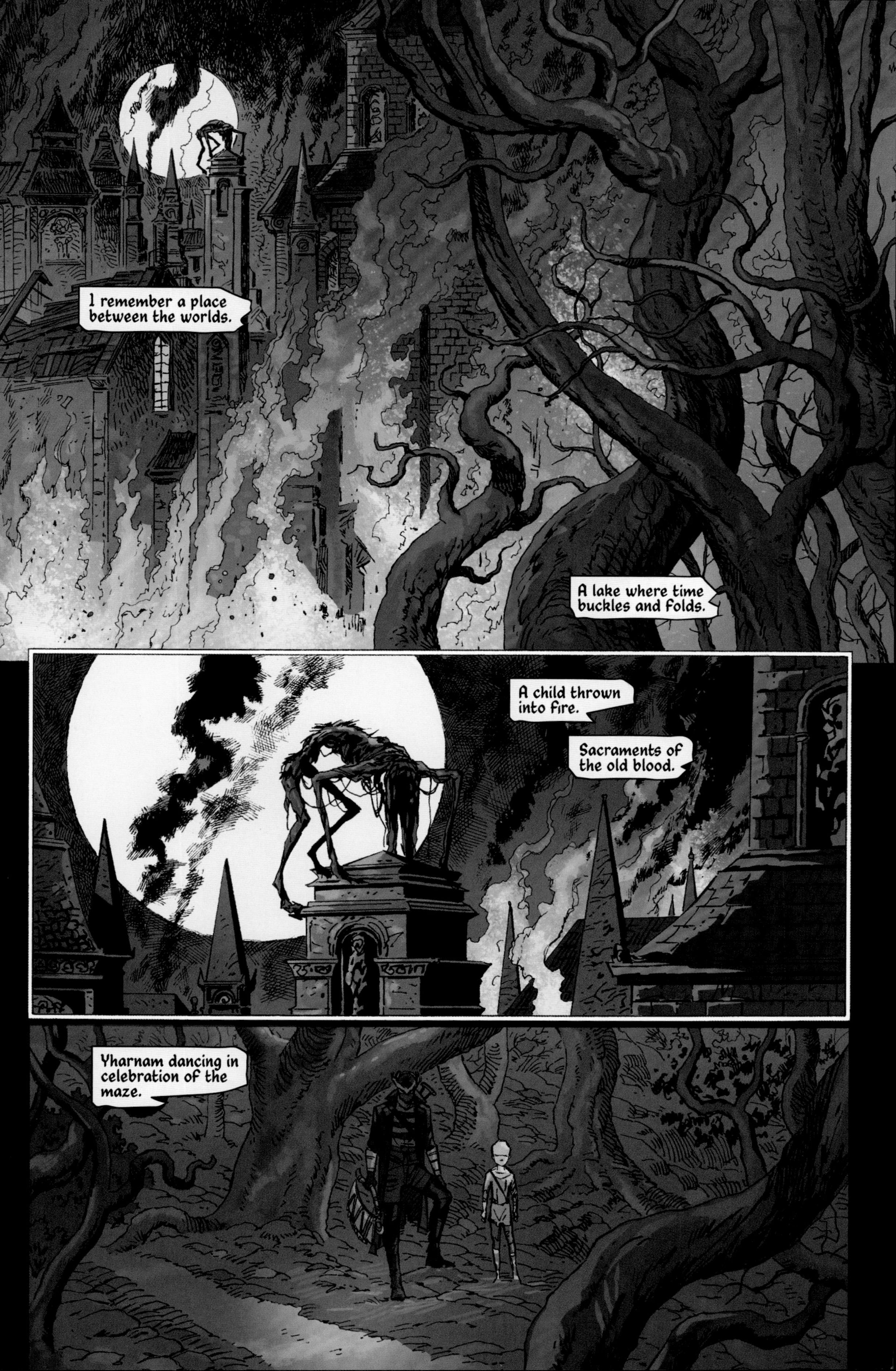
I remember a place between the worlds.
A lake where time buckles and folds.
A child thrown into fire.
Sacraments of the old blood.
Yharnam dancing in celebration of the maze.

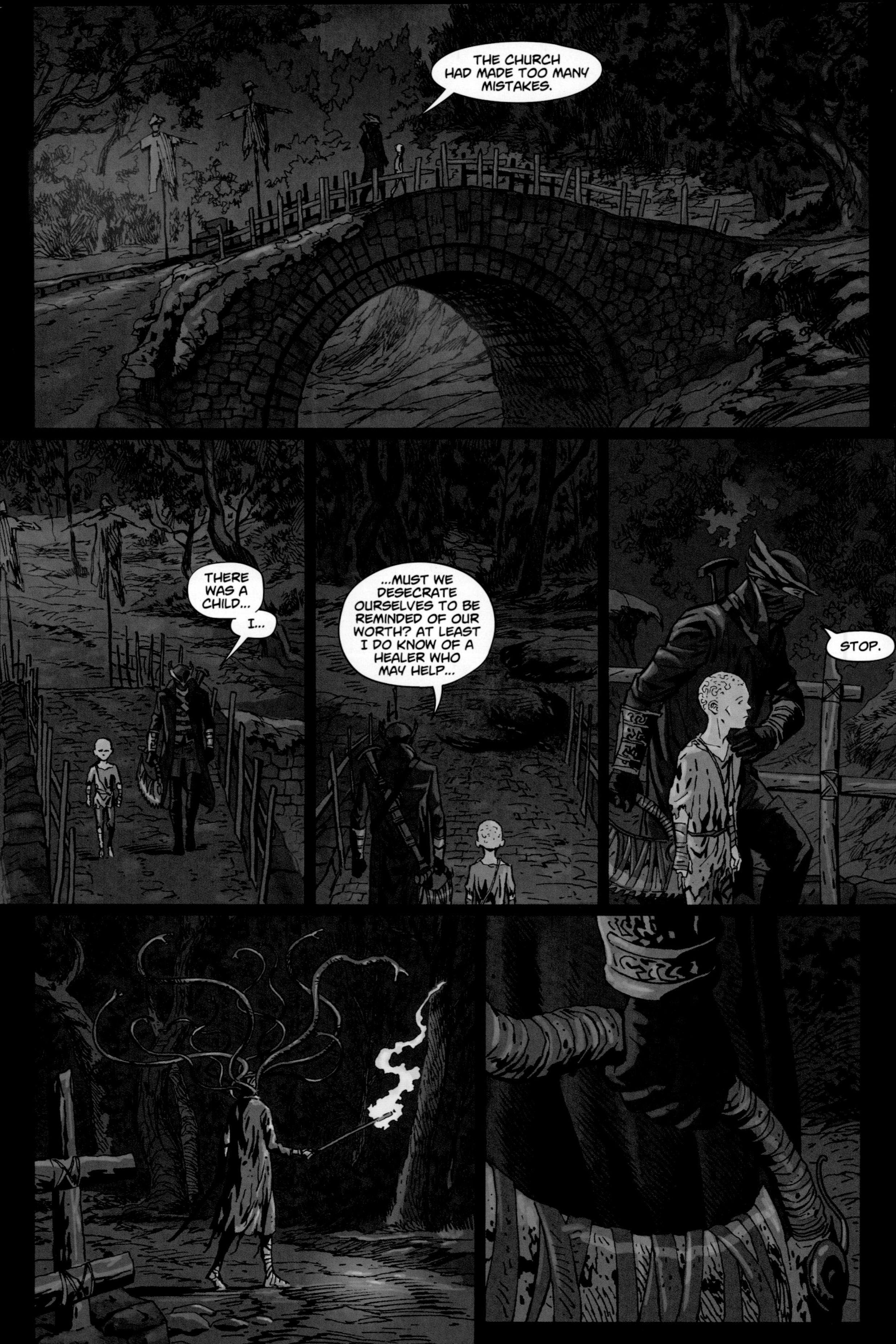
THE CHURCH HAD MADE TOO MANY MISTAKES.
THERE WAS A CHILD...
I...
...MUST WE DESECRATE OURSELVES TO BE REMINDED OF OUR WORTH? AT LEAST I DO KNOW OF A HEALER WHO MAY HELP...
STOP.

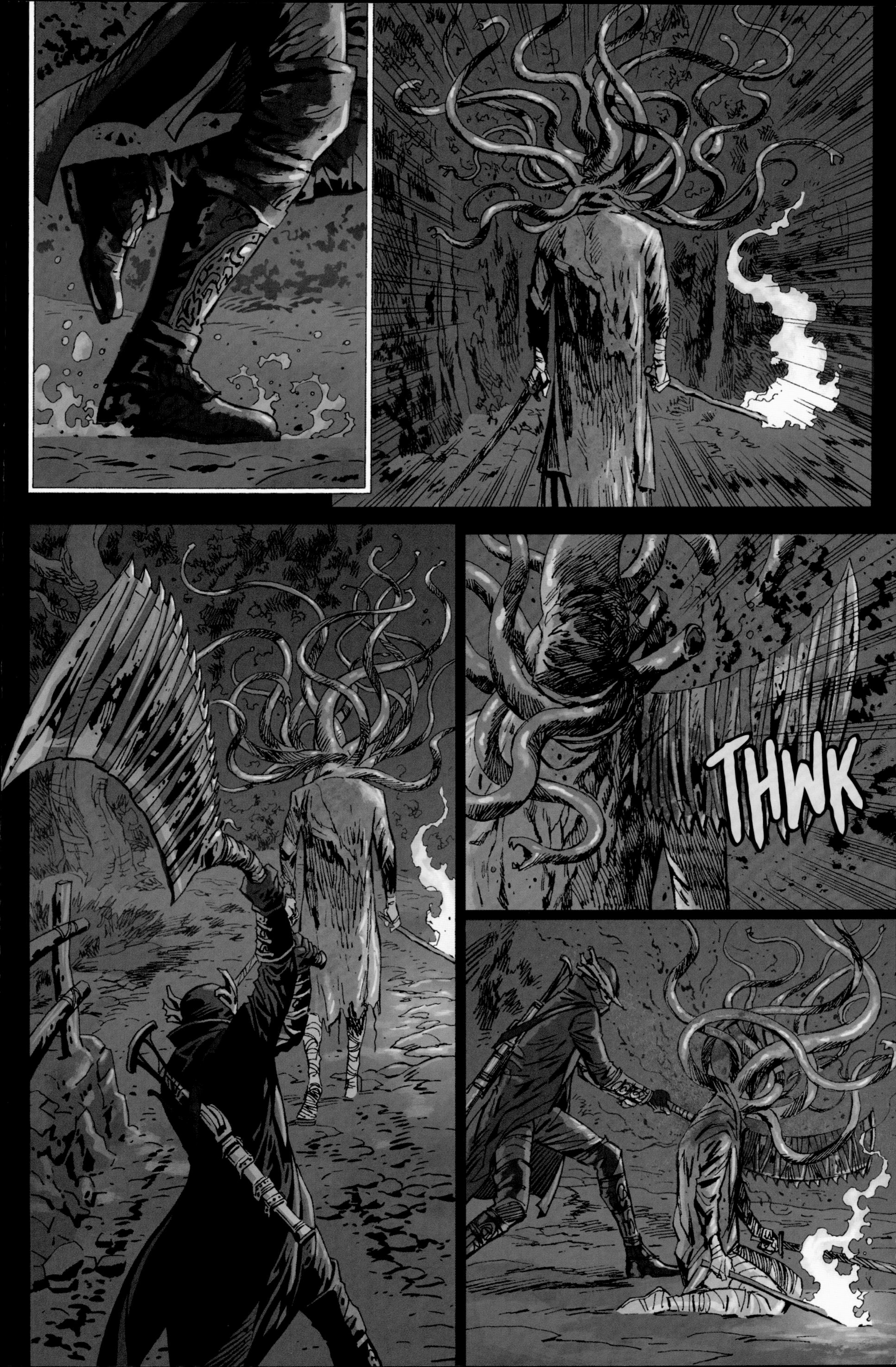
THWK

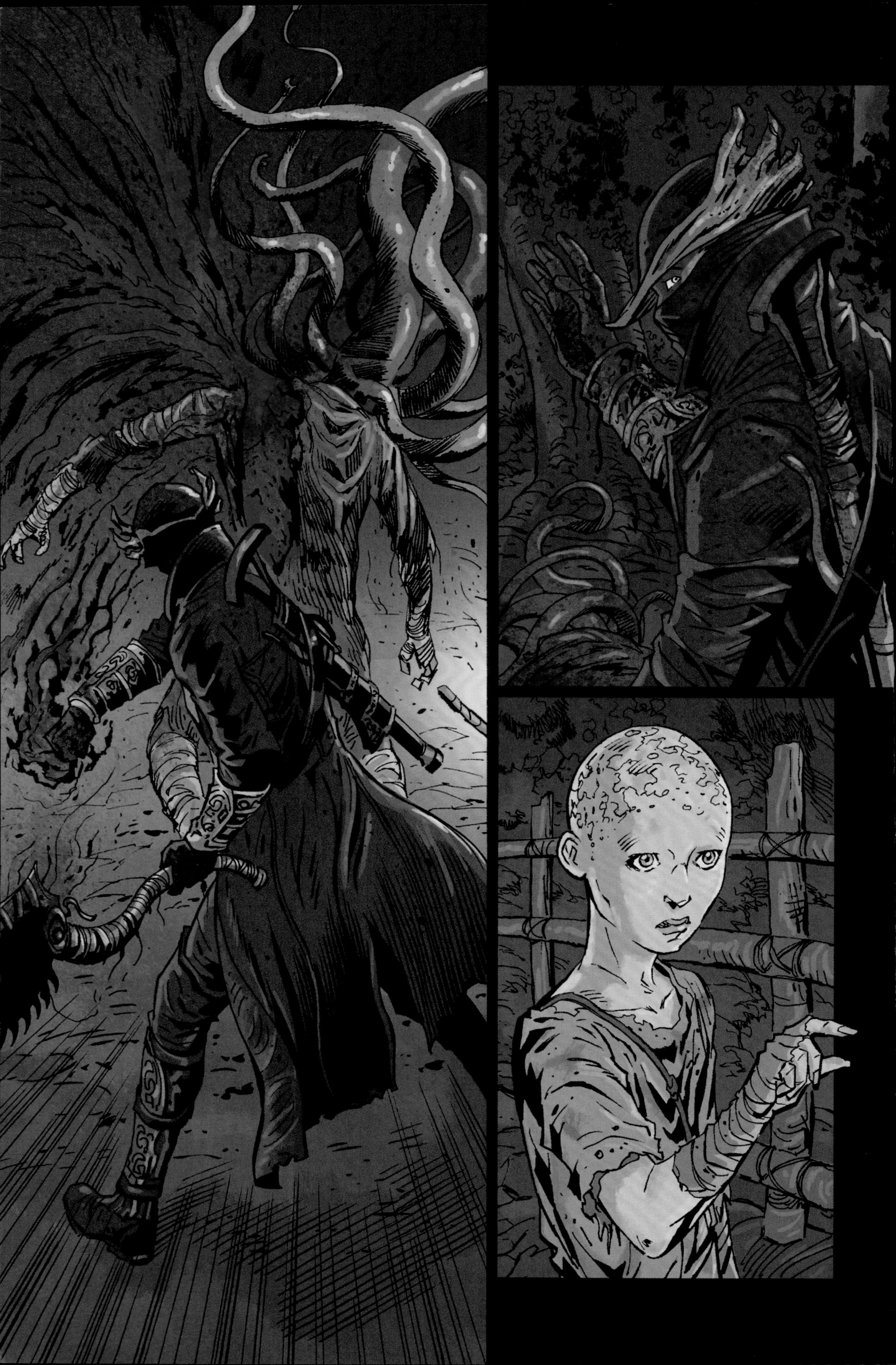

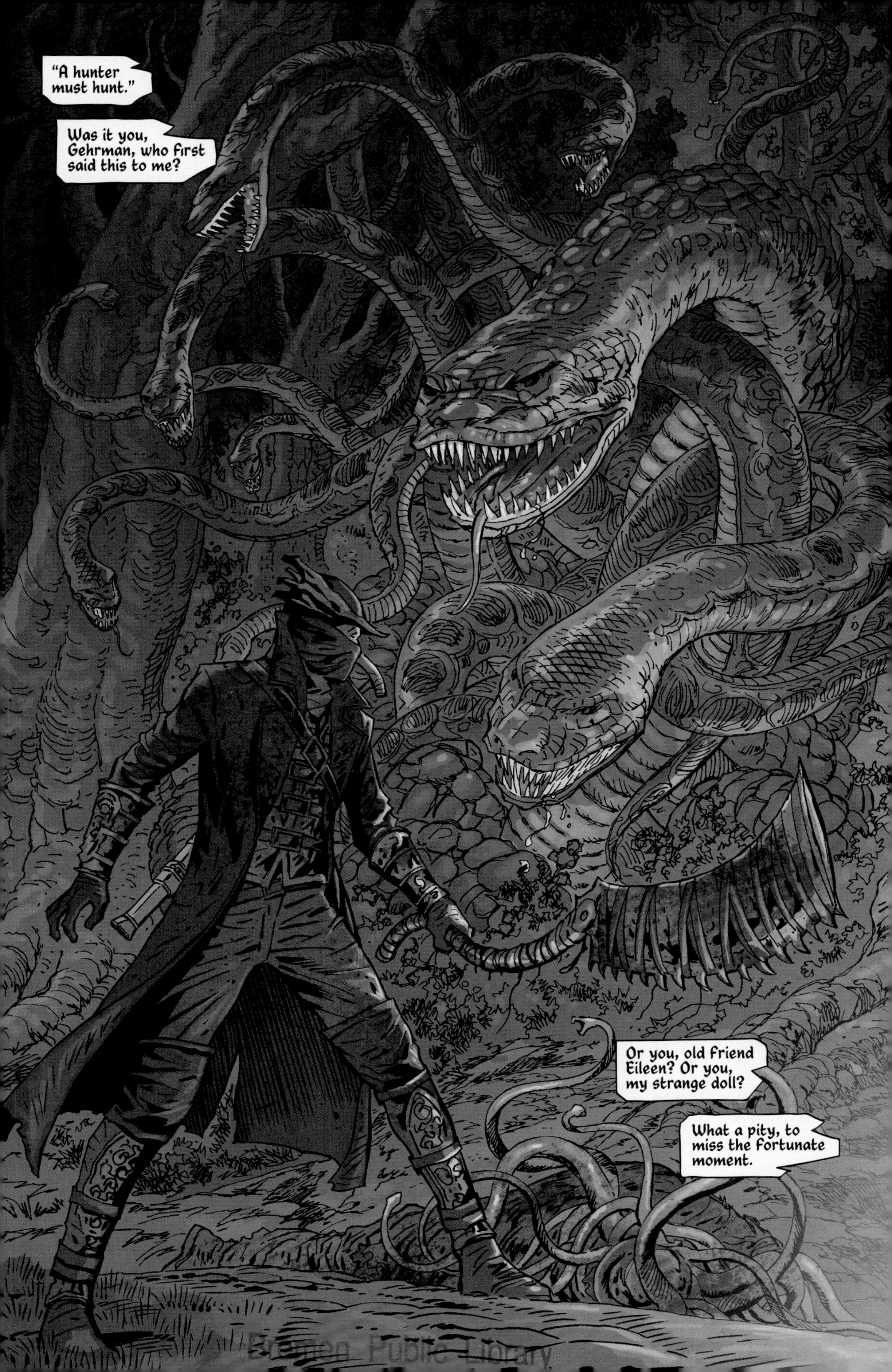
"A hunter must hunt."
Was it you, Gehrman, who first said this to me?
Or you, old friend Eileen? Or you, my strange doll?
What a pity, to miss the fortunate moment.

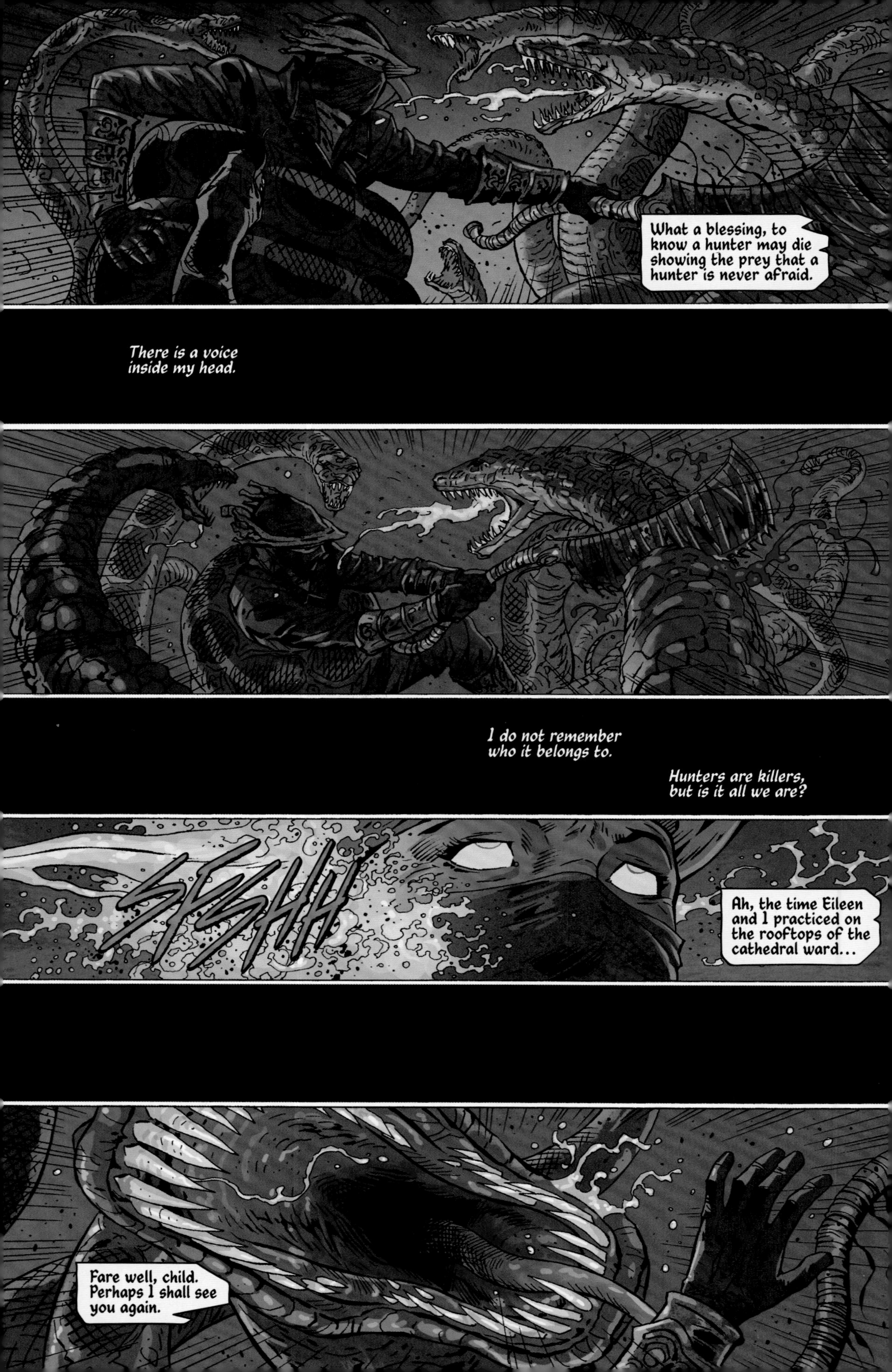
What a blessing, to know a hunter may die showing the prey that a hunter is never afraid.
There is a voice inside my head.
I do not remember who it belongs to.
Hunters are killers, but is it all we are?
SFSHH
Ah, the time Eileen and I practiced on the rooftops of the cathedral ward...
Fare well, child. Perhaps I shall see you again.

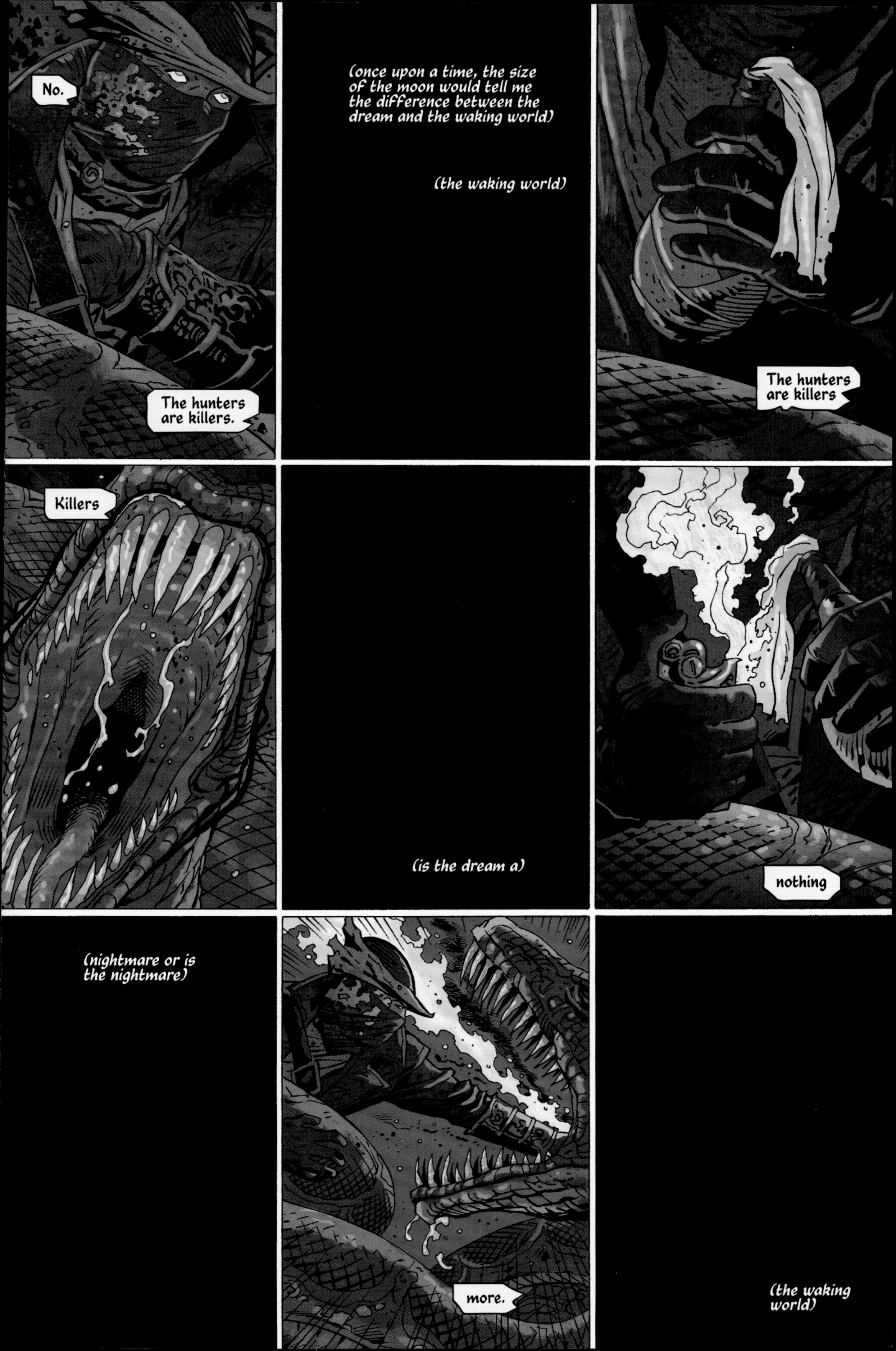
No.
The hunters are killers.
(once upon a time, the size of the moon would tell me the difference between the dream and the waking world)
(the waking world)
The hunters are killers
Killers
(is the dream a)
nothing
(nightmare or is the nightmare)
more.
(the waking world)

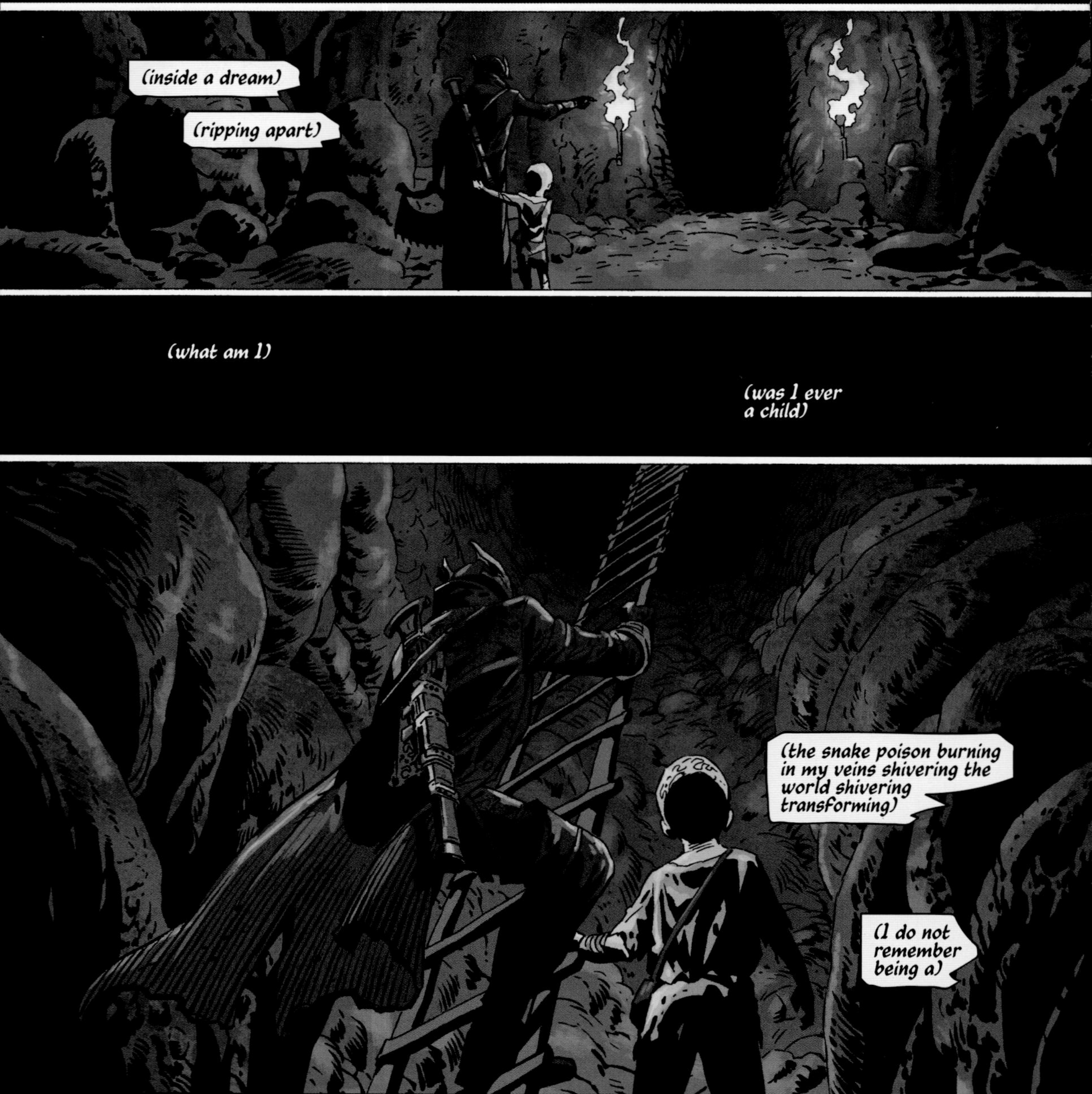
(inside a dream)
(ripping apart)
(what am I)
(was I ever a child)
(the snake poison burning in my veins shivering the world shivering transforming)
(I do not remember being a)

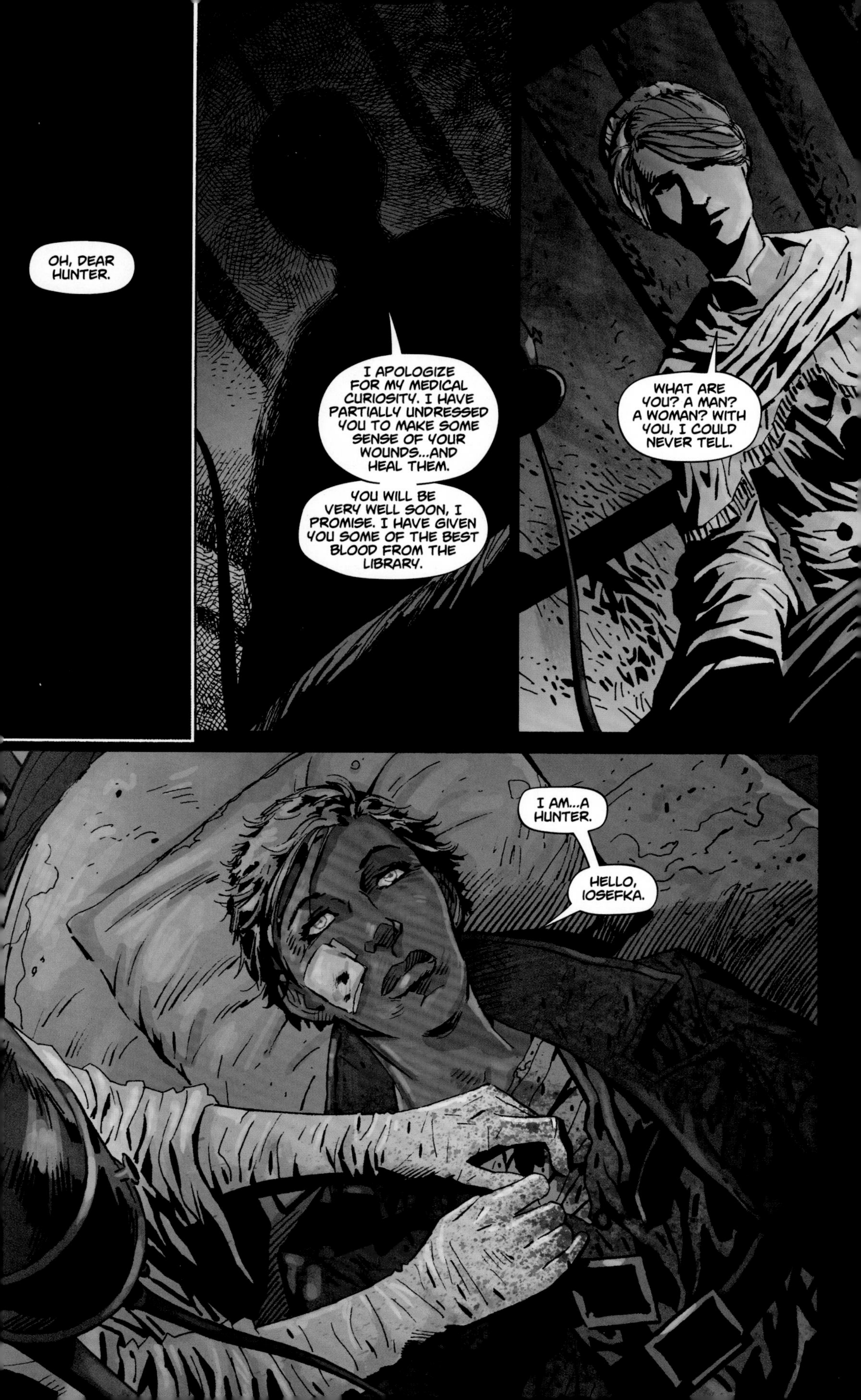
OH, DEAR HUNTER.
I APOLOGIZE FOR MY MEDICAL CURIOSITY. I HAVE PARTIALLY UNDRESSED YOU TO MAKE SOME SENSE OF YOUR WOUNDS...AND HEAL THEM.
YOU WILL BE VERY WELL SOON, I PROMISE. I HAVE GIVEN YOU SOME OF THE BEST BLOOD FROM THE LIBRARY.
WHAT ARE YOU? A MAN? A WOMAN? WITH YOU, I COULD NEVER TELL.
I AM...A HUNTER.
HELLO, IOSEFKA.

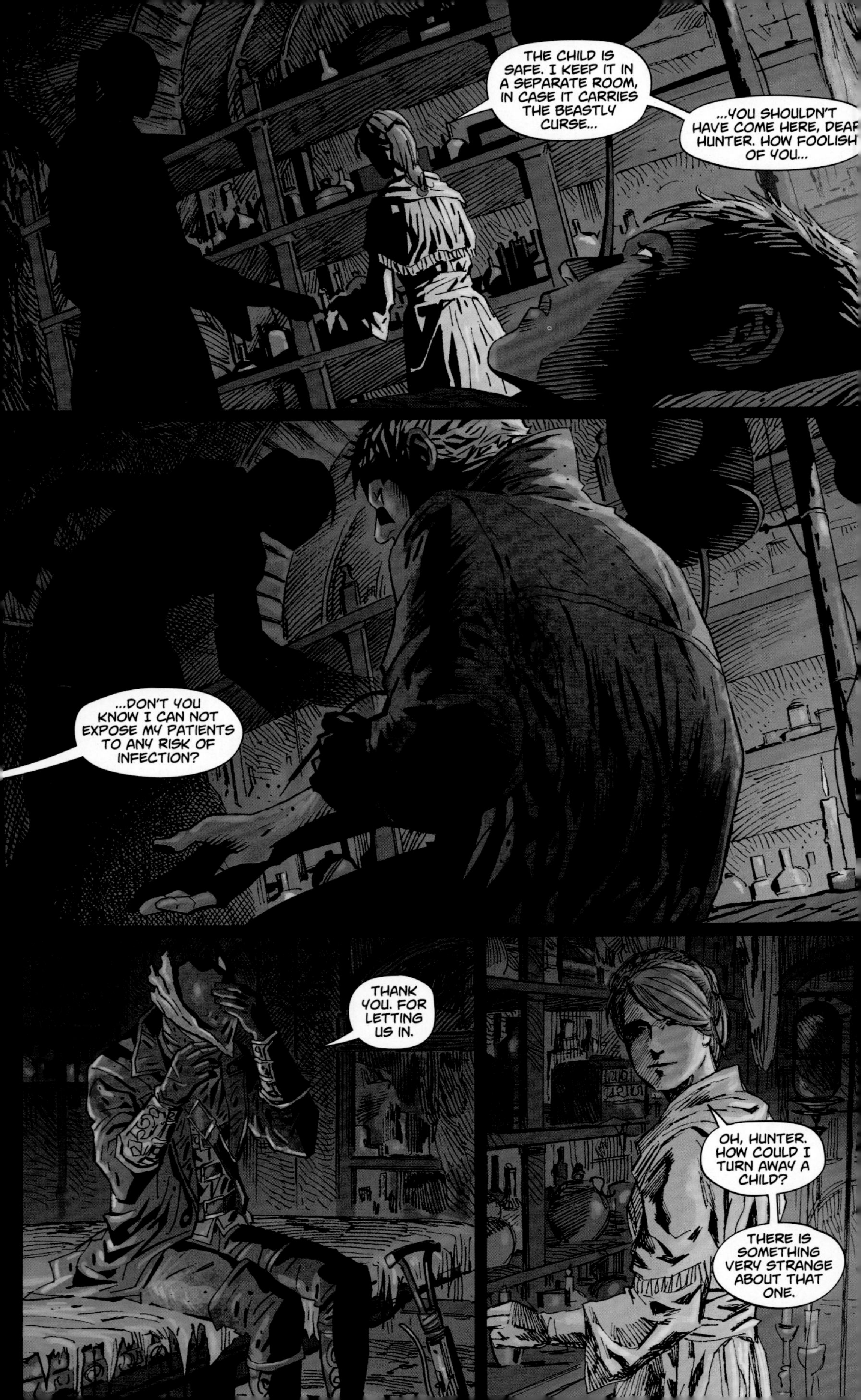
THE CHILD IS SAFE. I KEEP IT IN A SEPARATE ROOM, IN CASE IT CARRIES THE BEASTLY CURSE...
...YOU SHOULDN'T HAVE COME HERE, DEAR HUNTER. HOW FOOLISH OF YOU...
...DON'T YOU KNOW I CAN NOT EXPOSE MY PATIENTS TO ANY RISK OF INFECTION?
THANK YOU. FOR LETTING US IN.
OH, HUNTER. HOW COULD I TURN AWAY A CHILD?
THERE IS SOMETHING VERY STRANGE ABOUT THAT ONE.

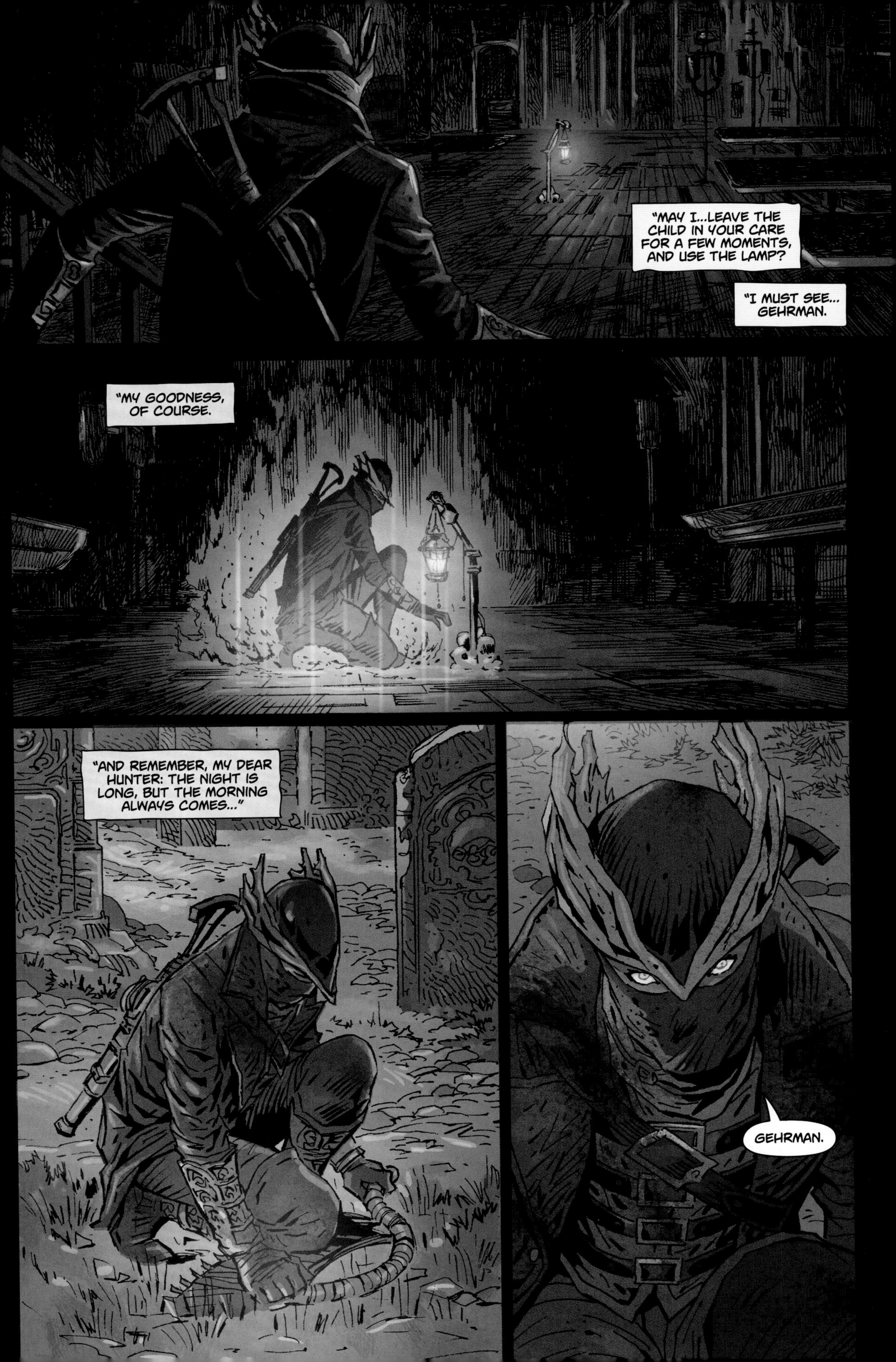
"MAY I...LEAVE THE CHILD IN YOUR CARE FOR A FEW MOMENTS, AND USE THE LAMP?
"I MUST SEE... GEHRMAN.
"MY GOODNESS, OF COURSE.
"AND REMEMBER, MY DEAR HUNTER: THE NIGHT IS LONG, BUT THE MORNING ALWAYS COMES..."
GEHRMAN.

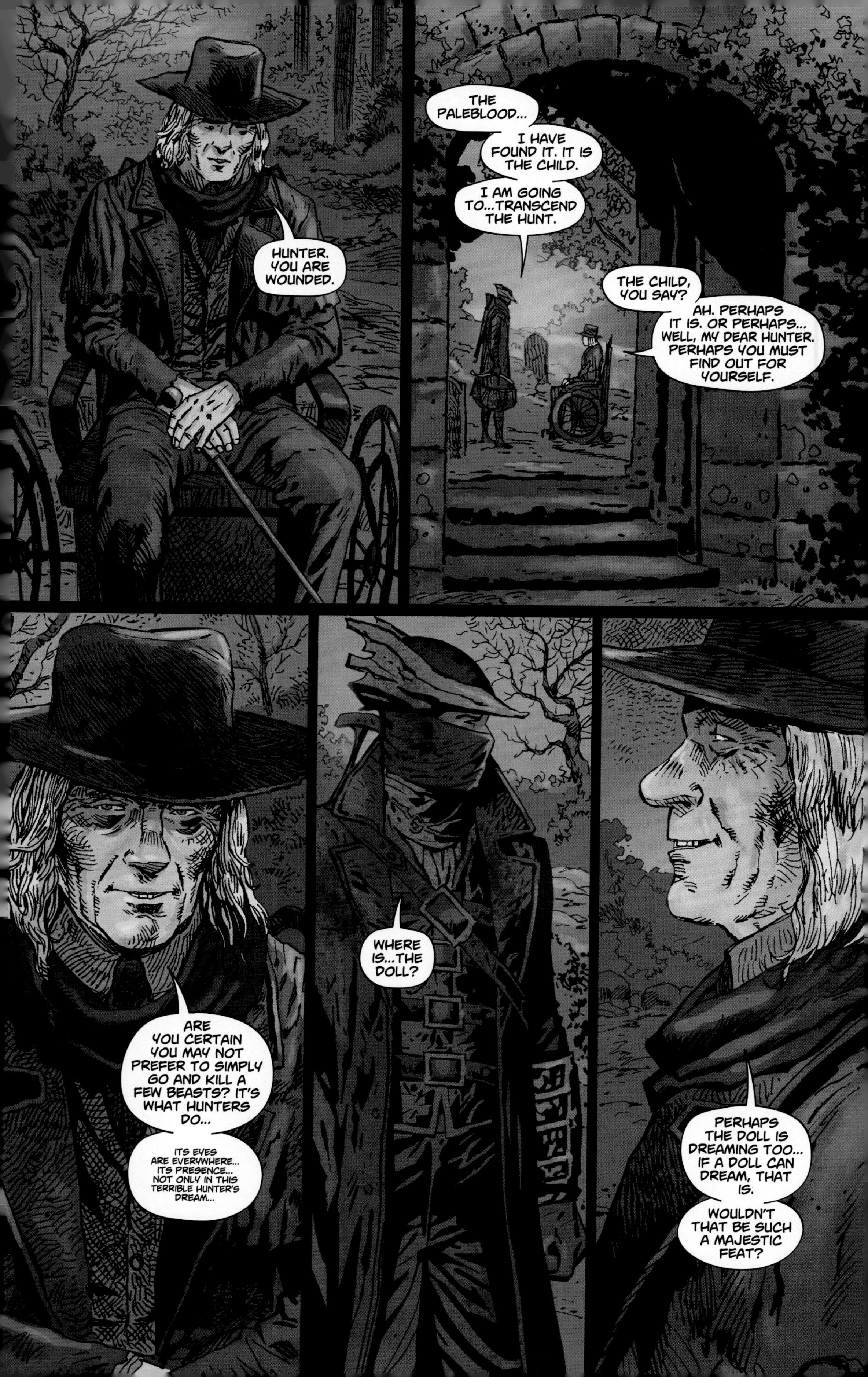
HUNTER. YOU ARE WOUNDED.
THE PALEBLOOD...
I HAVE FOUND IT. IT IS THE CHILD.
I AM GOING TO...TRANSCEND THE HUNT.
THE CHILD, YOU SAY?
AH. PERHAPS IT IS. OR PERHAPS... WELL, MY DEAR HUNTER. PERHAPS YOU MUST FIND OUT FOR YOURSELF.
ARE YOU CERTAIN YOU MAY NOT PREFER TO SIMPLY GO AND KILL A FEW BEASTS? IT'S WHAT HUNTERS DO...
ITS EYES ARE EVERYWHERE... ITS PRESENCE... NOT ONLY IN THIS TERRIBLE HUNTER'S DREAM...
WHERE IS...THE DOLL?
PERHAPS THE DOLL IS DREAMING TOO... IF A DOLL CAN DREAM, THAT IS.
WOULDN'T THAT BE SUCH A MAJESTIC FEAT?

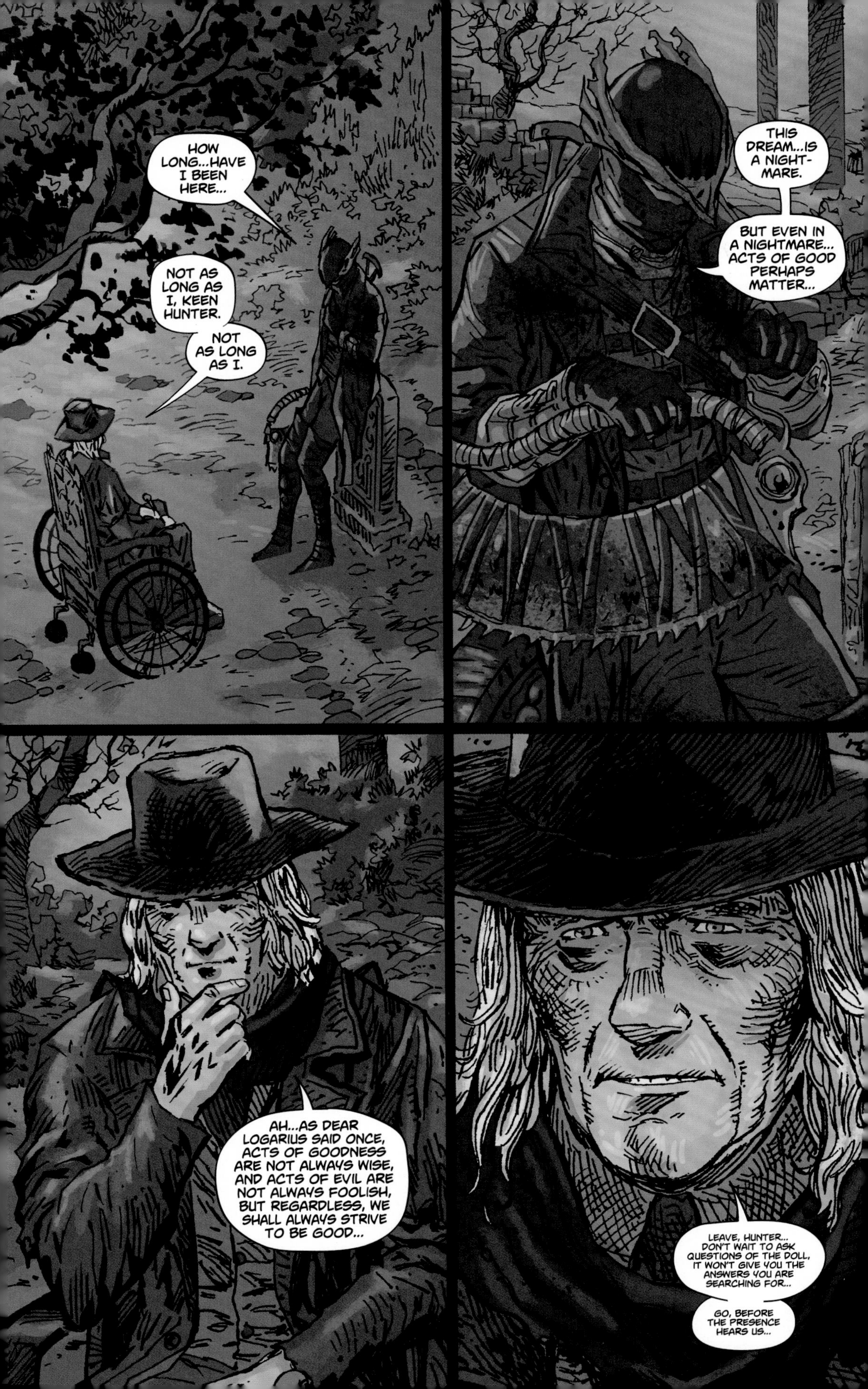
HOW LONG...HAVE I BEEN HERE...
NOT AS LONG AS I, KEEN HUNTER.
NOT AS LONG AS I.
THIS DREAM...IS A NIGHT-MARE.
BUT EVEN IN A NIGHTMARE... ACTS OF GOOD PERHAPS MATTER...
AH...AS DEAR LOGARIUS SAID ONCE, ACTS OF GOODNESS ARE NOT ALWAYS WISE, AND ACTS OF EVIL ARE NOT ALWAYS FOOLISH, BUT REGARDLESS, WE SHALL ALWAYS STRIVE TO BE GOOD...
LEAVE, HUNTER... DON'T WAIT TO ASK QUESTIONS OF THE DOLL, IT WON'T GIVE YOU THE ANSWERS YOU ARE SEARCHING FOR...
GO, BEFORE THE PRESENCE HEARS US...

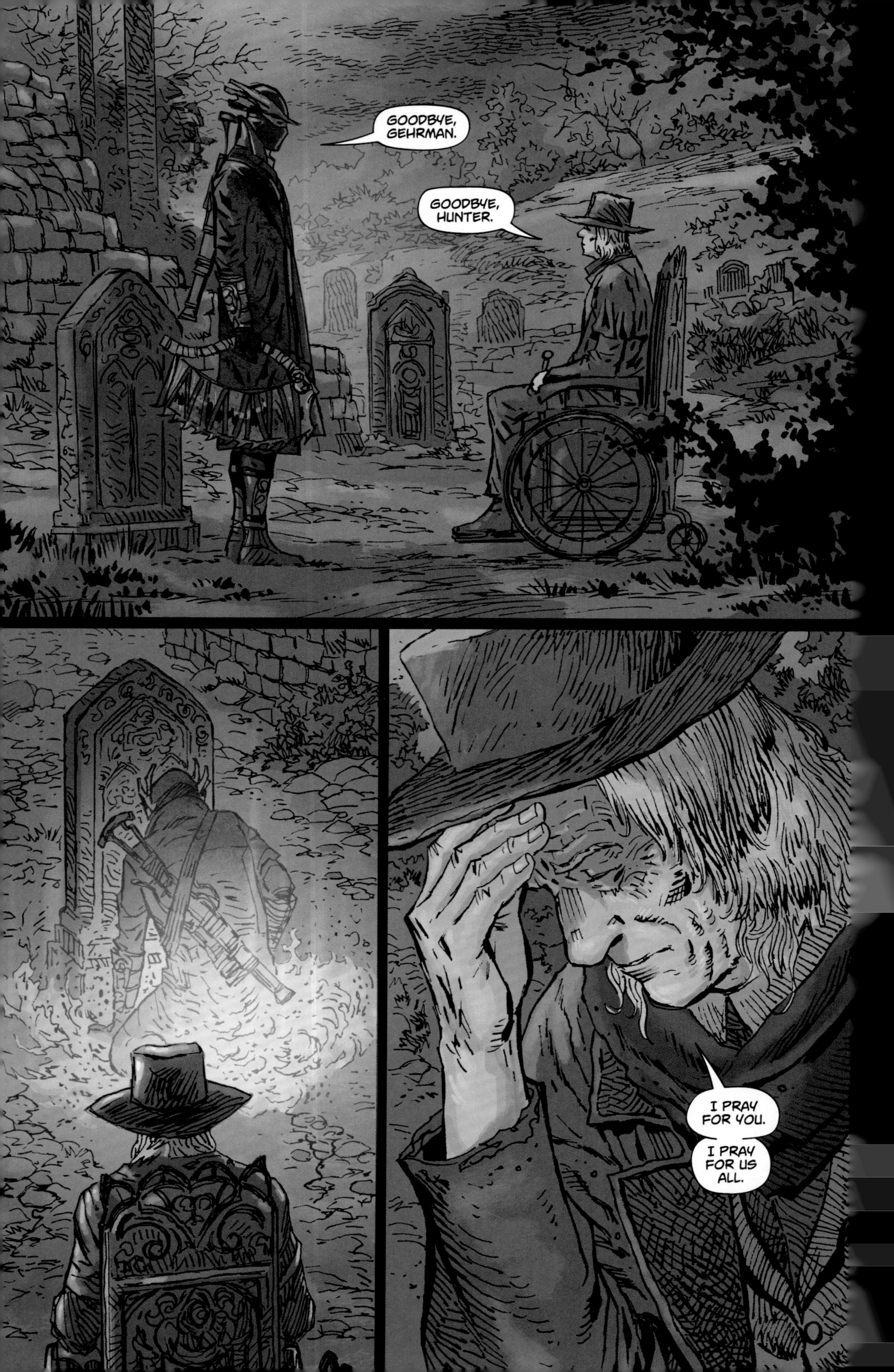
GOODBYE, GEHRMAN.
GOODBYE, HUNTER.
I PRAY FOR YOU.
I PRAY FOR US ALL.

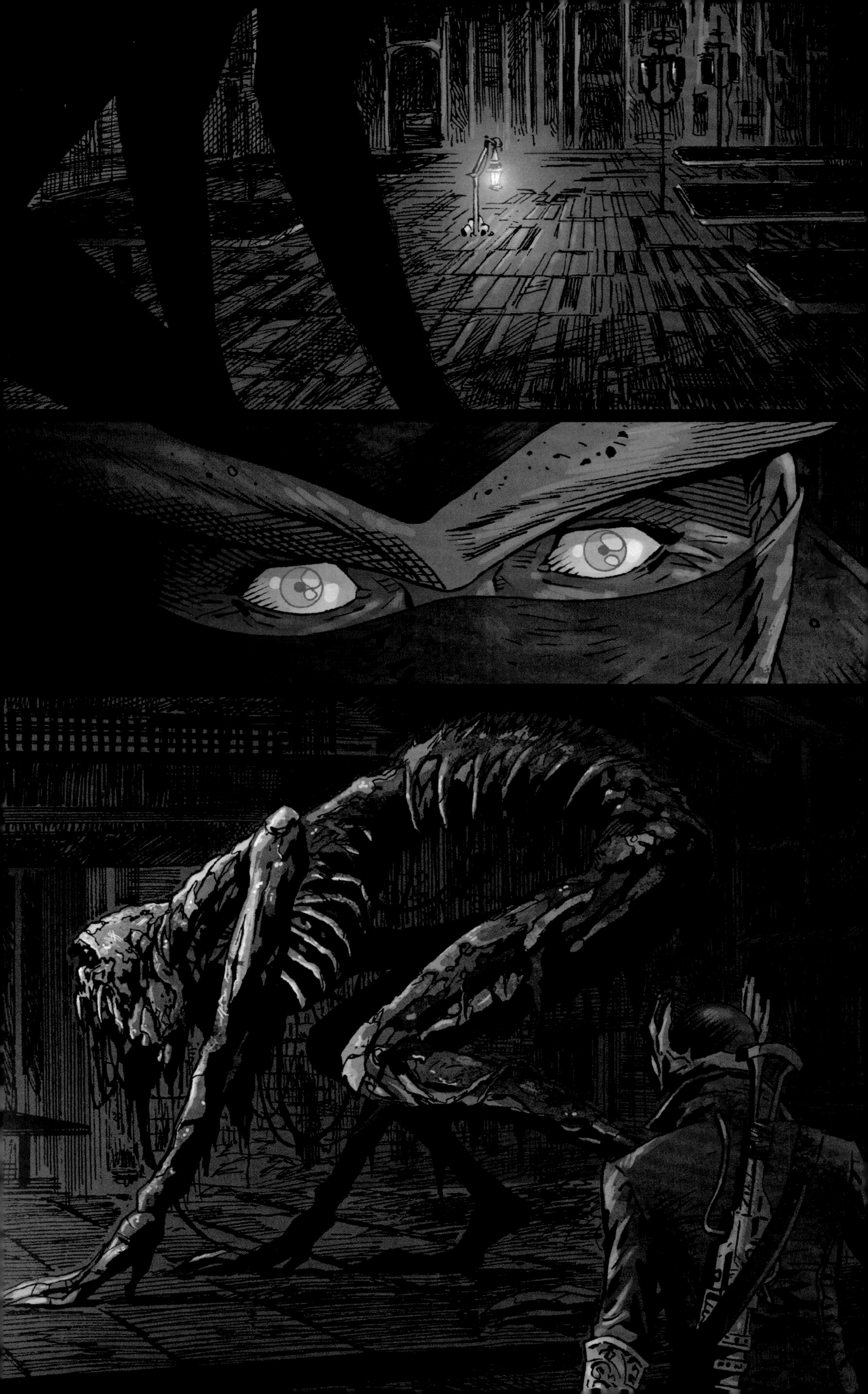

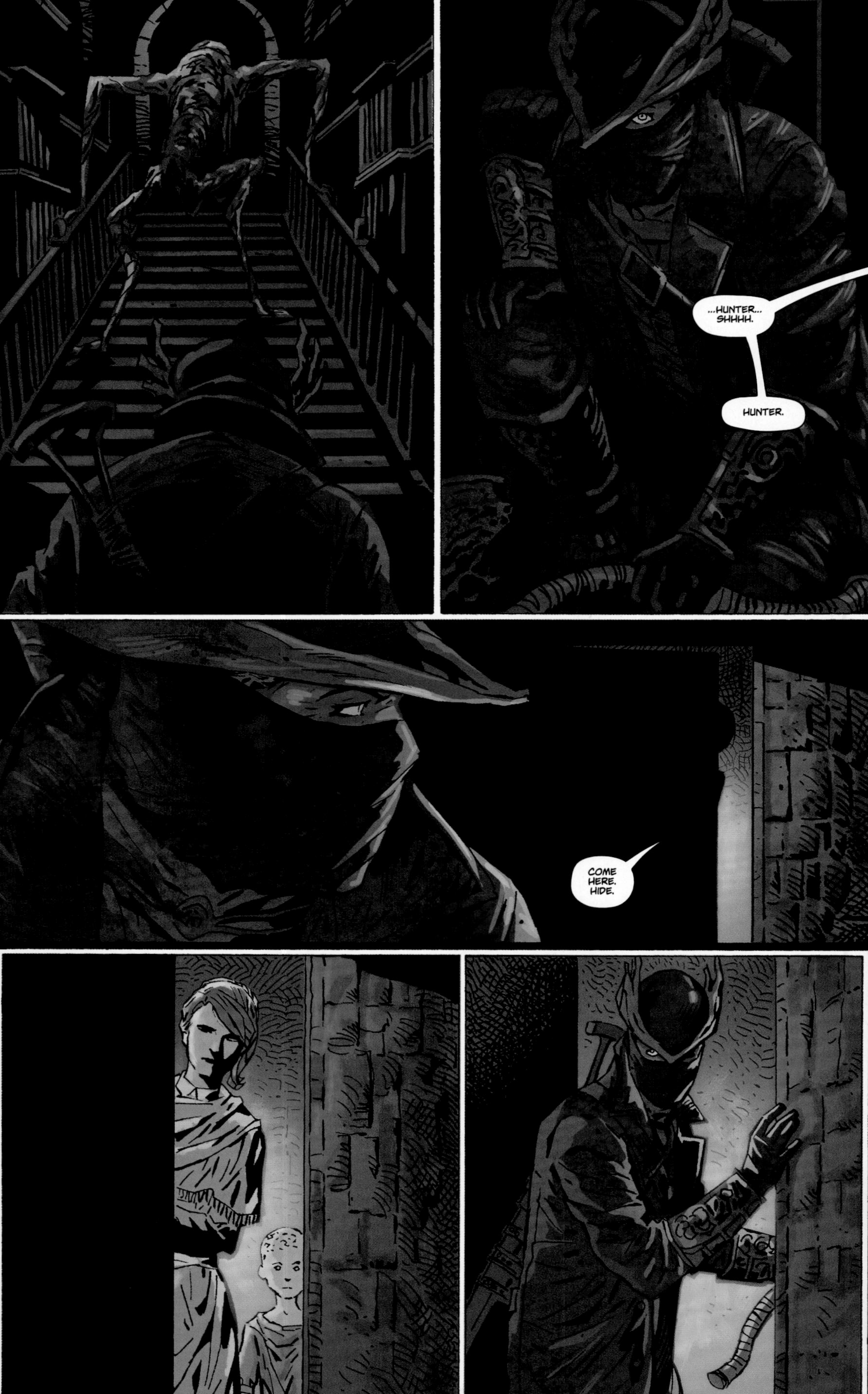
...HUNTER... SHHHH.
HUNTER.
COME HERE. HIDE.

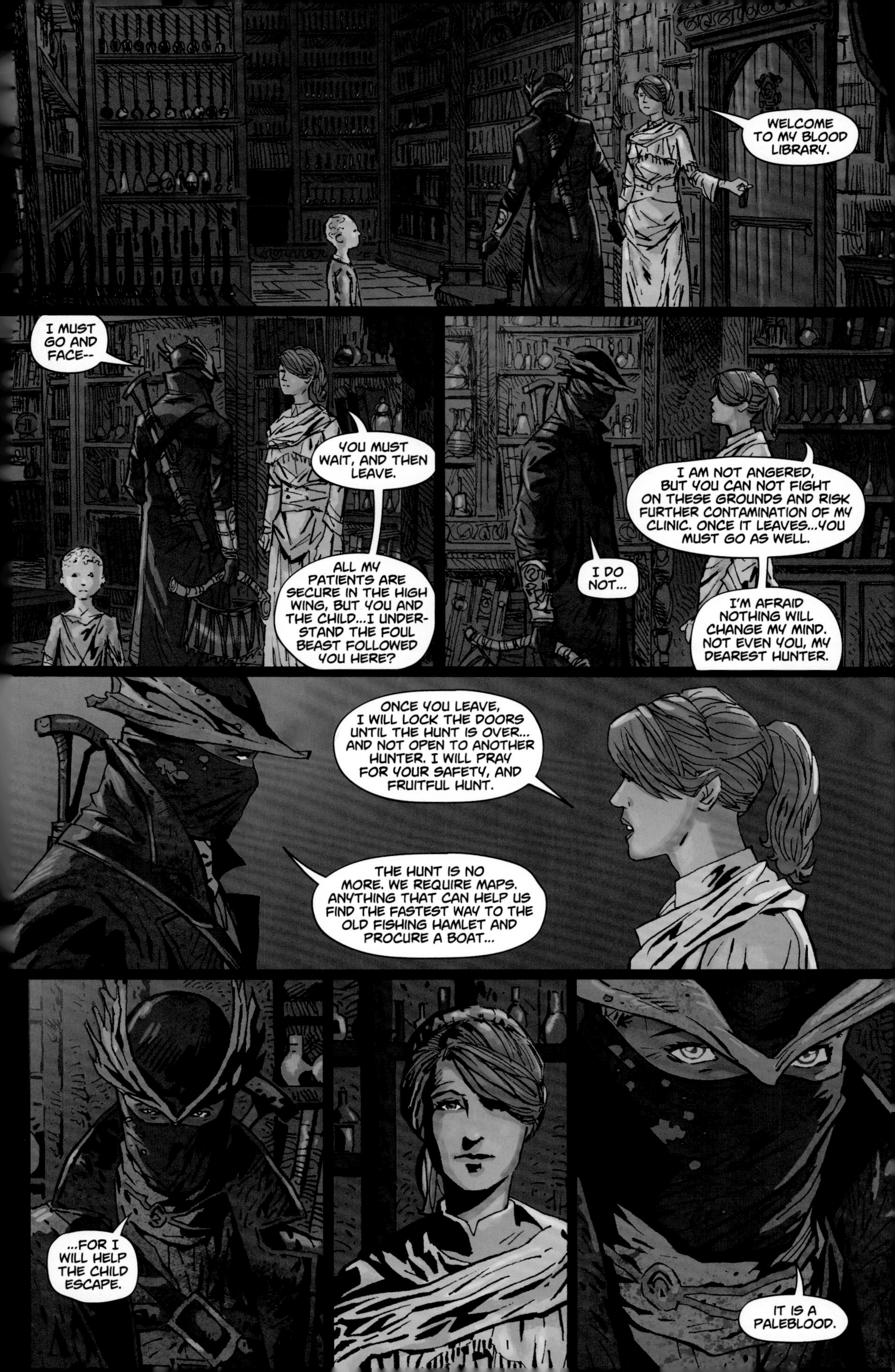
WELCOME TO MY BLOOD LIBRARY.
I MUST GO AND FACE--
YOU MUST WAIT, AND THEN LEAVE.
ALL MY PATIENTS ARE SECURE IN THE HIGH WING, BUT YOU AND THE CHILD...I UNDERSTAND THE FOUL BEAST FOLLOWED YOU HERE?
I DO NOT...
I AM NOT ANGERED, BUT YOU CAN NOT FIGHT ON THESE GROUNDS AND RISK FURTHER CONTAMINATION OF MY CLINIC. ONCE IT LEAVES...YOU MUST GO AS WELL.
I'M AFRAID NOTHING WILL CHANGE MY MIND. NOT EVEN YOU, MY DEAREST HUNTER.
ONCE YOU LEAVE, I WILL LOCK THE DOORS UNTIL THE HUNT IS OVER... AND NOT OPEN TO ANOTHER HUNTER. I WILL PRAY FOR YOUR SAFETY, AND FRUITFUL HUNT.
THE HUNT IS NO MORE. WE REQUIRE MAPS. ANYTHING THAT CAN HELP US FIND THE FASTEST WAY TO THE OLD FISHING HAMLET AND PROCURE A BOAT...
...FOR I WILL HELP THE CHILD ESCAPE.
IT IS A PALEBLOOD.

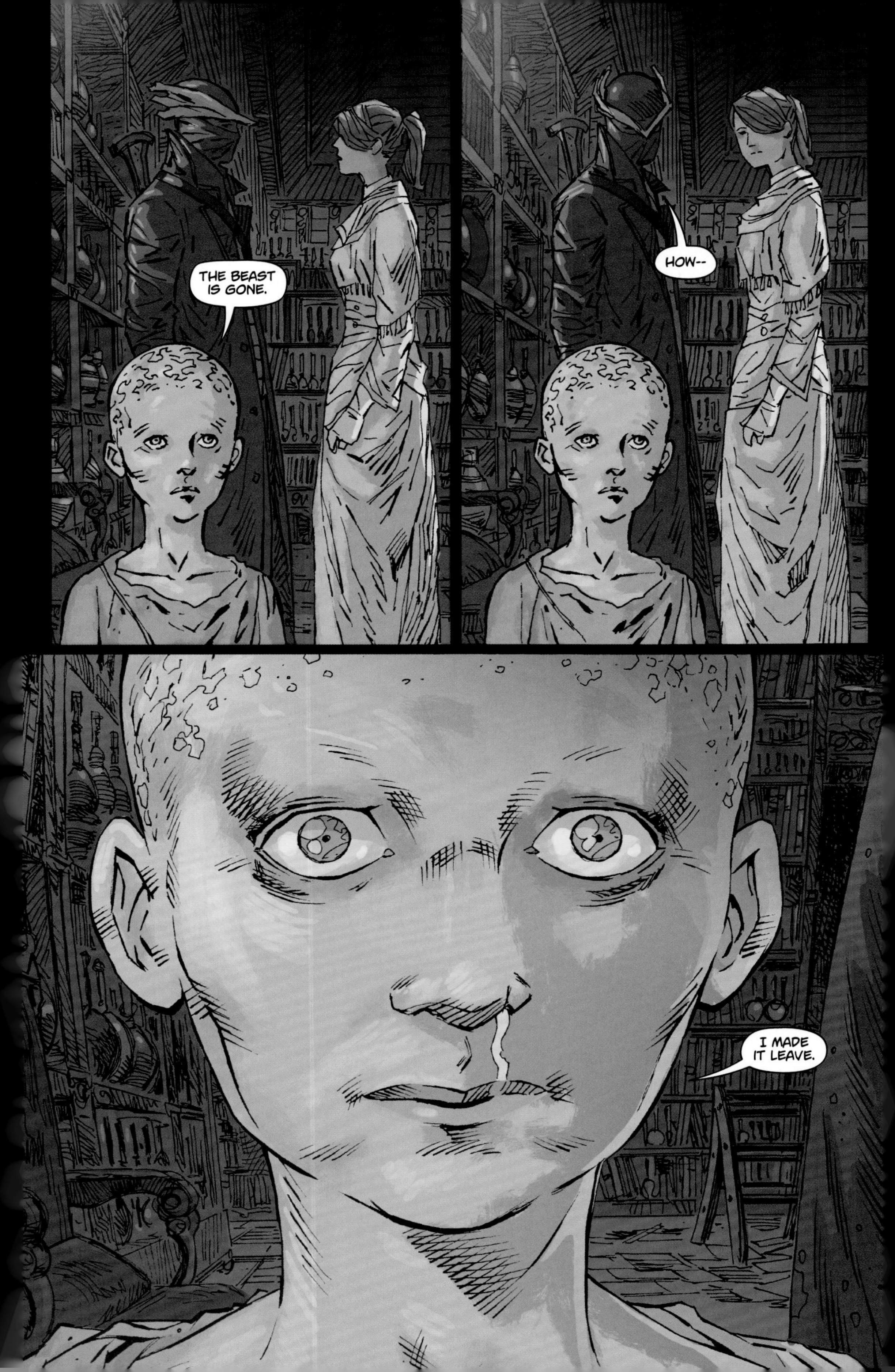
THE BEAST IS GONE.
HOW--
I MADE IT LEAVE.

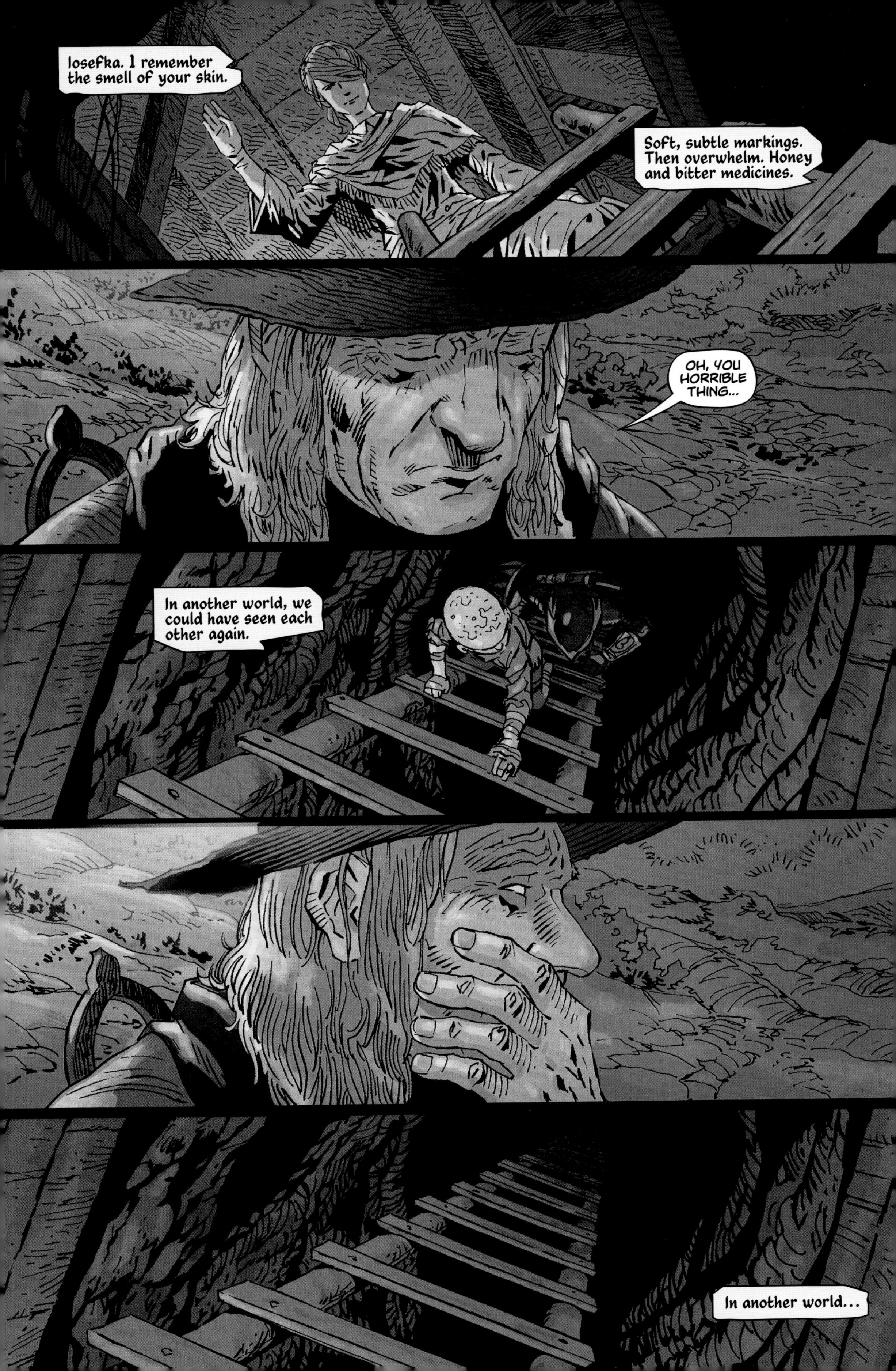
Iosefka. I remember the smell of your skin.
Soft, subtle markings. Then overwhelm. Honey and bitter medicines.
OH, YOU HORRIBLE THING...
In another world, we could have seen each other again.
In another world...

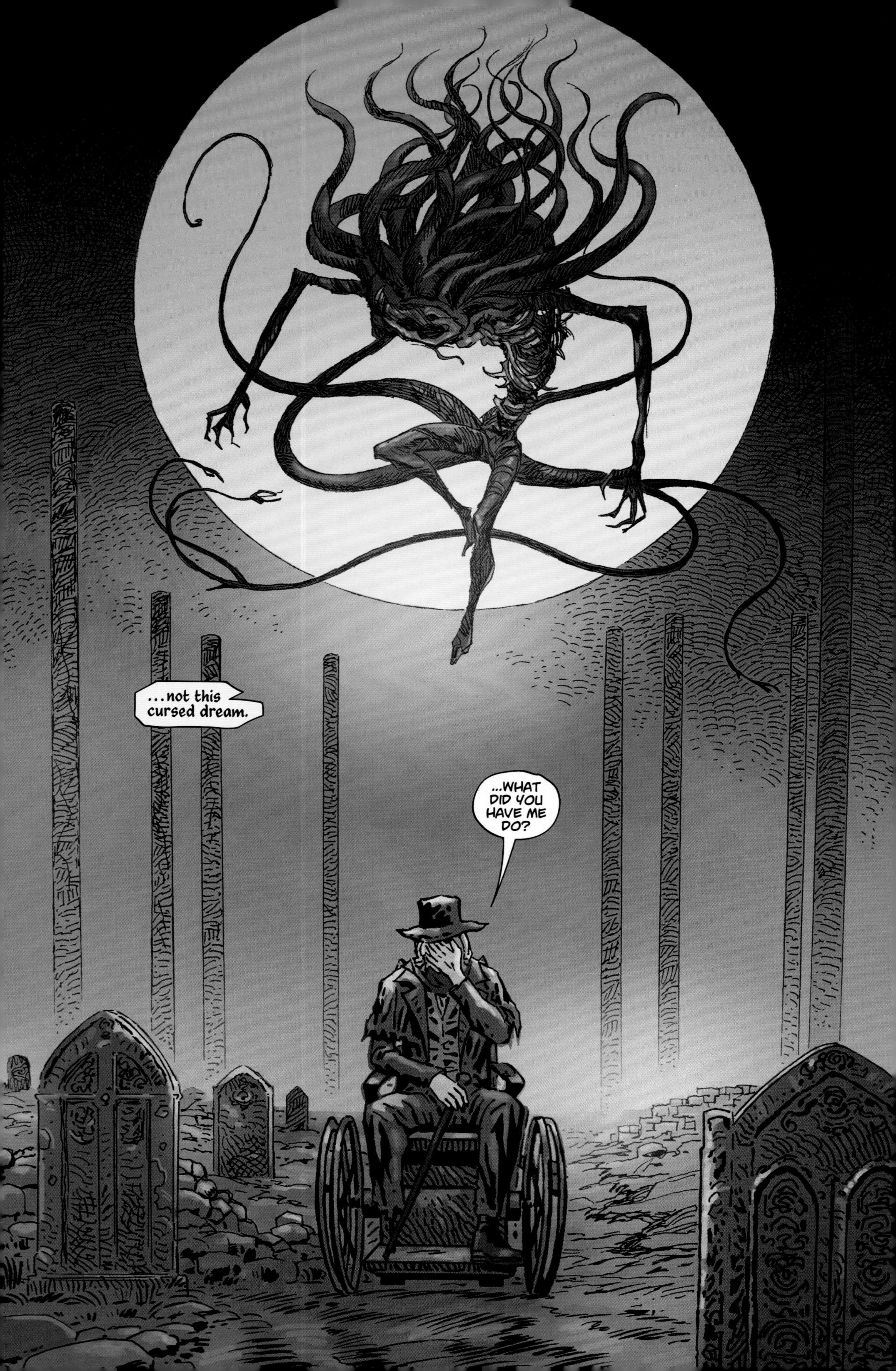
...not this cursed dream.
...WHAT DID YOU HAVE ME DO?

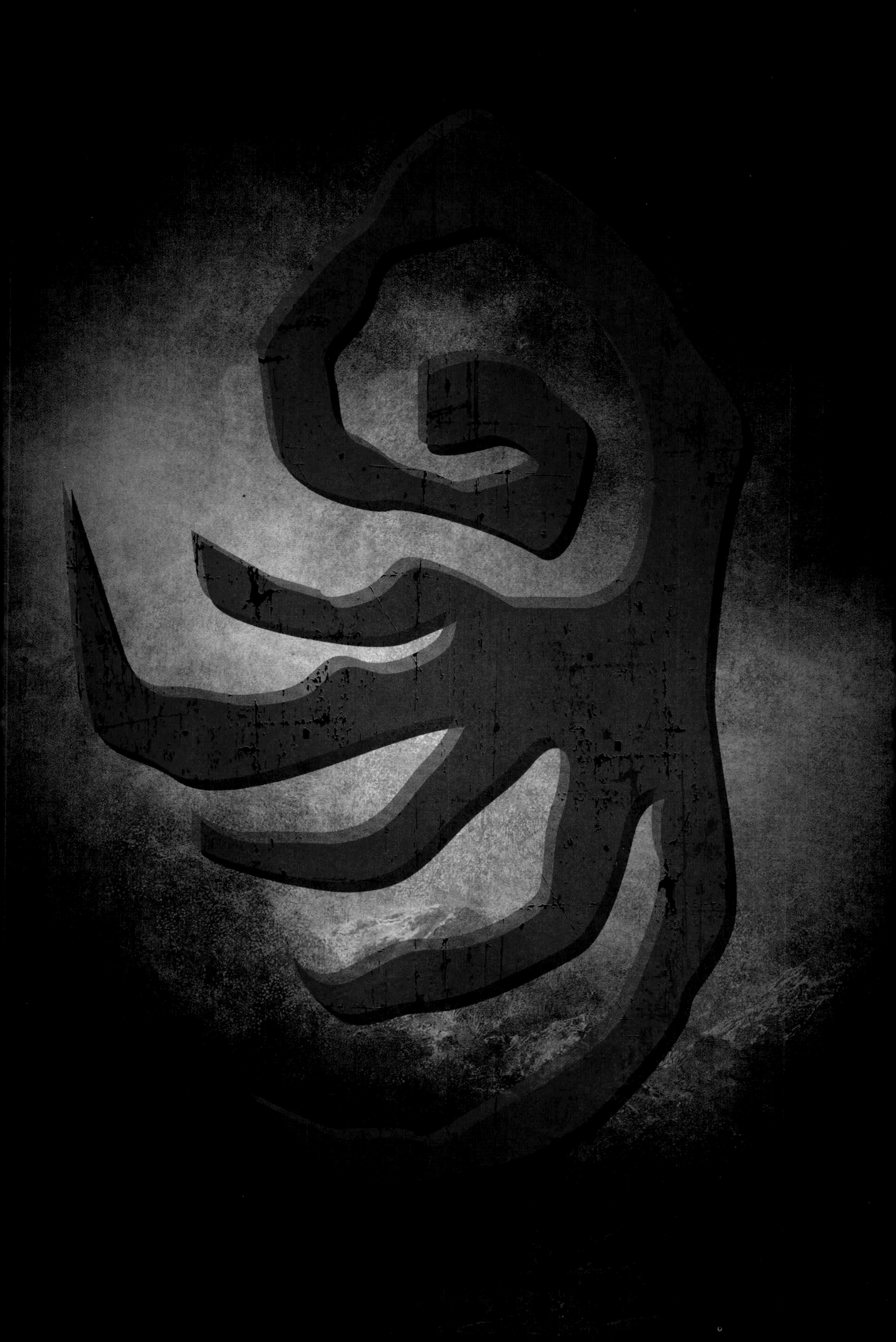

#3 COVER A
BY
PIOTR KOWALSKI
& BRAD SIMPSON

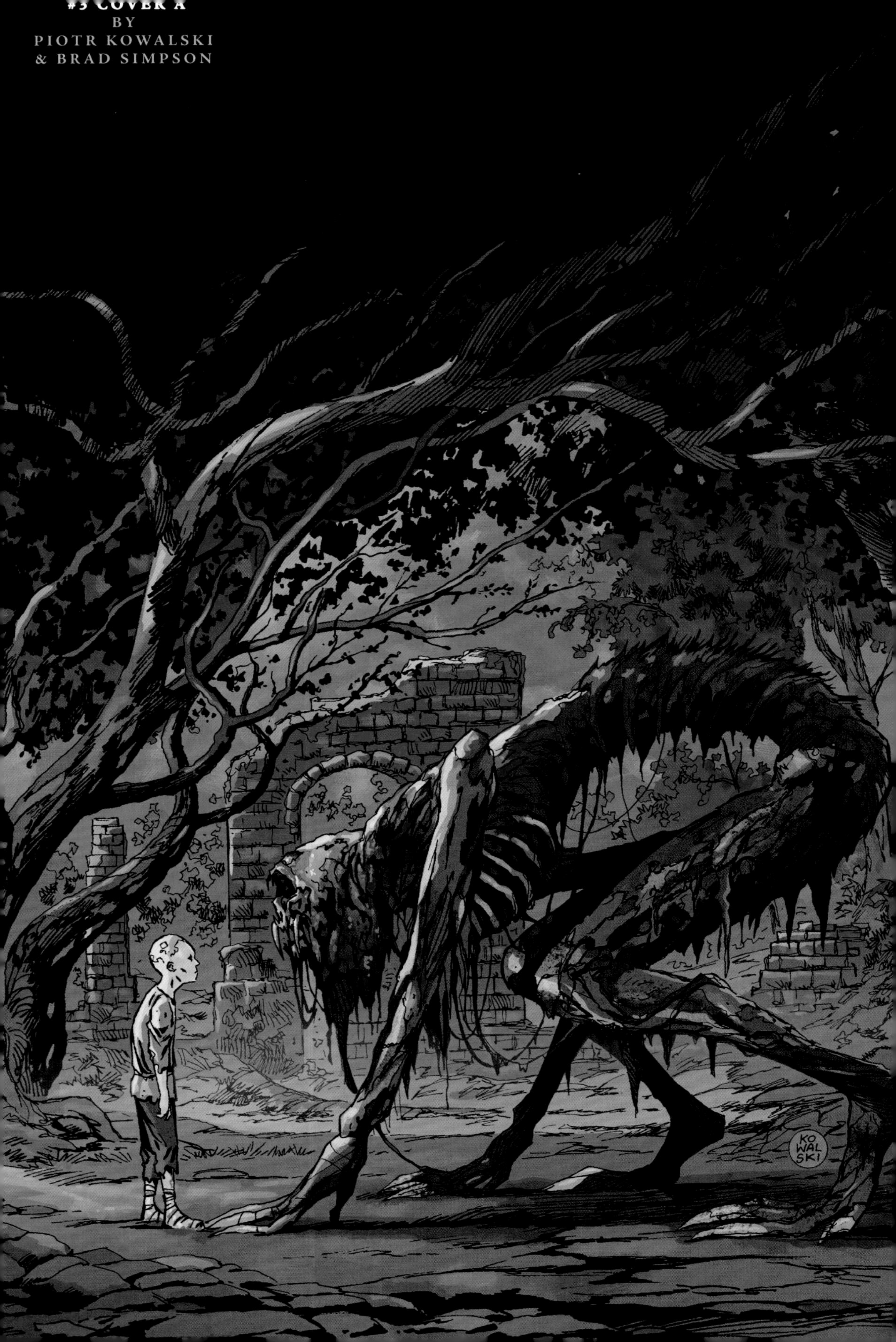
KO
WAL
SKI

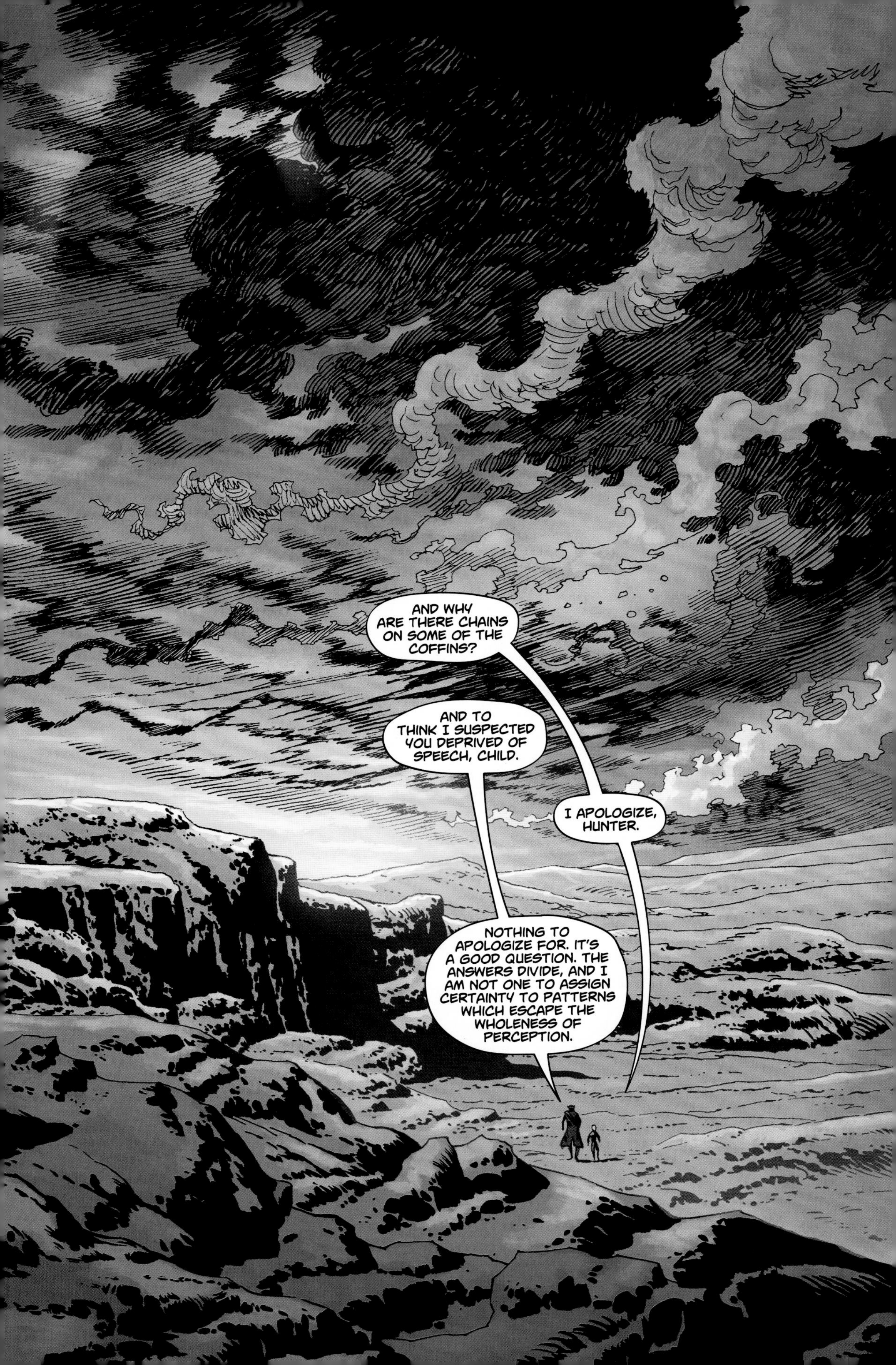
AND WHY ARE THERE CHAINS ON SOME OF THE COFFINS?
AND TO THINK I SUSPECTED YOU DEPRIVED OF SPEECH, CHILD.
I APOLOGIZE, HUNTER.
NOTHING TO APOLOGIZE FOR. IT'S A GOOD QUESTION. THE ANSWERS DIVIDE, AND I AM NOT ONE TO ASSIGN CERTAINTY TO PATTERNS WHICH ESCAPE THE WHOLENESS OF PERCEPTION.

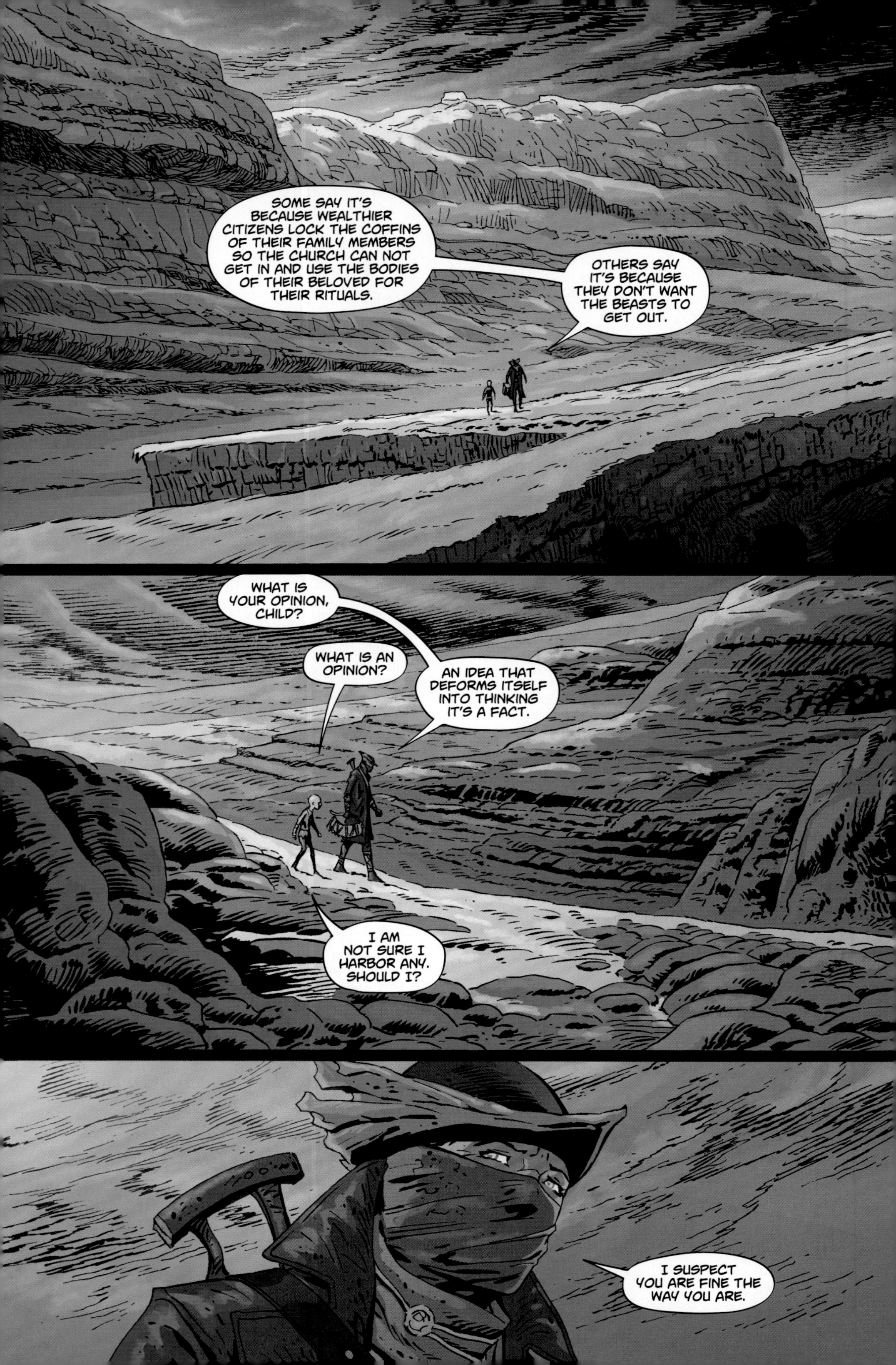
SOME SAY IT'S BECAUSE WEALTHIER CITIZENS LOCK THE COFFINS OF THEIR FAMILY MEMBERS SO THE CHURCH CAN NOT GET IN AND USE THE BODIES OF THEIR BELOVED FOR THEIR RITUALS.
OTHERS SAY IT'S BECAUSE THEY DON'T WANT THE BEASTS TO GET OUT.
WHAT IS YOUR OPINION, CHILD?
WHAT IS AN OPINION?
AN IDEA THAT DEFORMS ITSELF INTO THINKING IT'S A FACT.
I AM NOT SURE I HARBOR ANY. SHOULD I?
I SUSPECT YOU ARE FINE THE WAY YOU ARE.

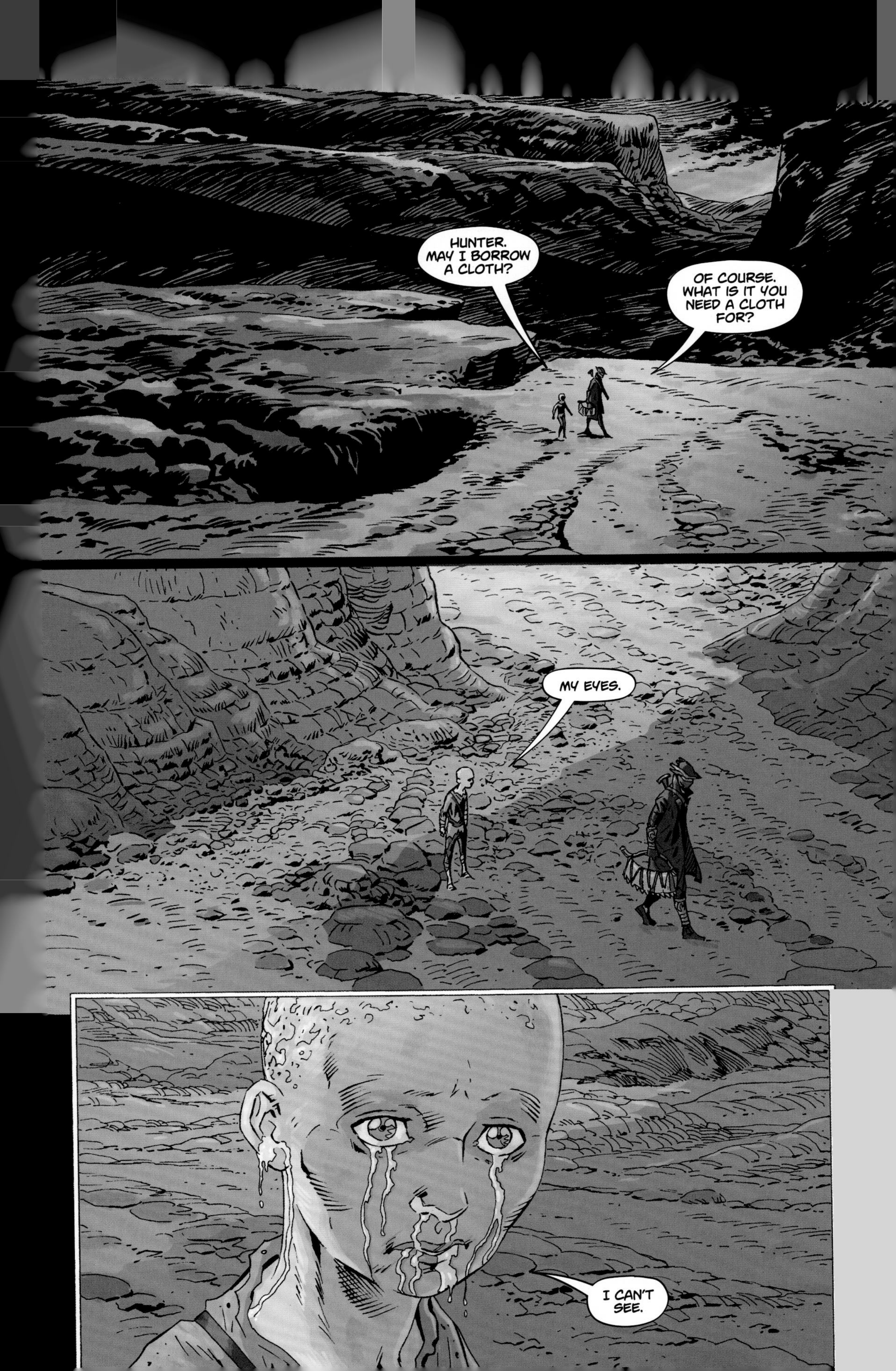
HUNTER. MAY I BORROW A CLOTH?
OF COURSE. WHAT IS IT YOU NEED A CLOTH FOR?
MY EYES.
I CAN'T SEE.

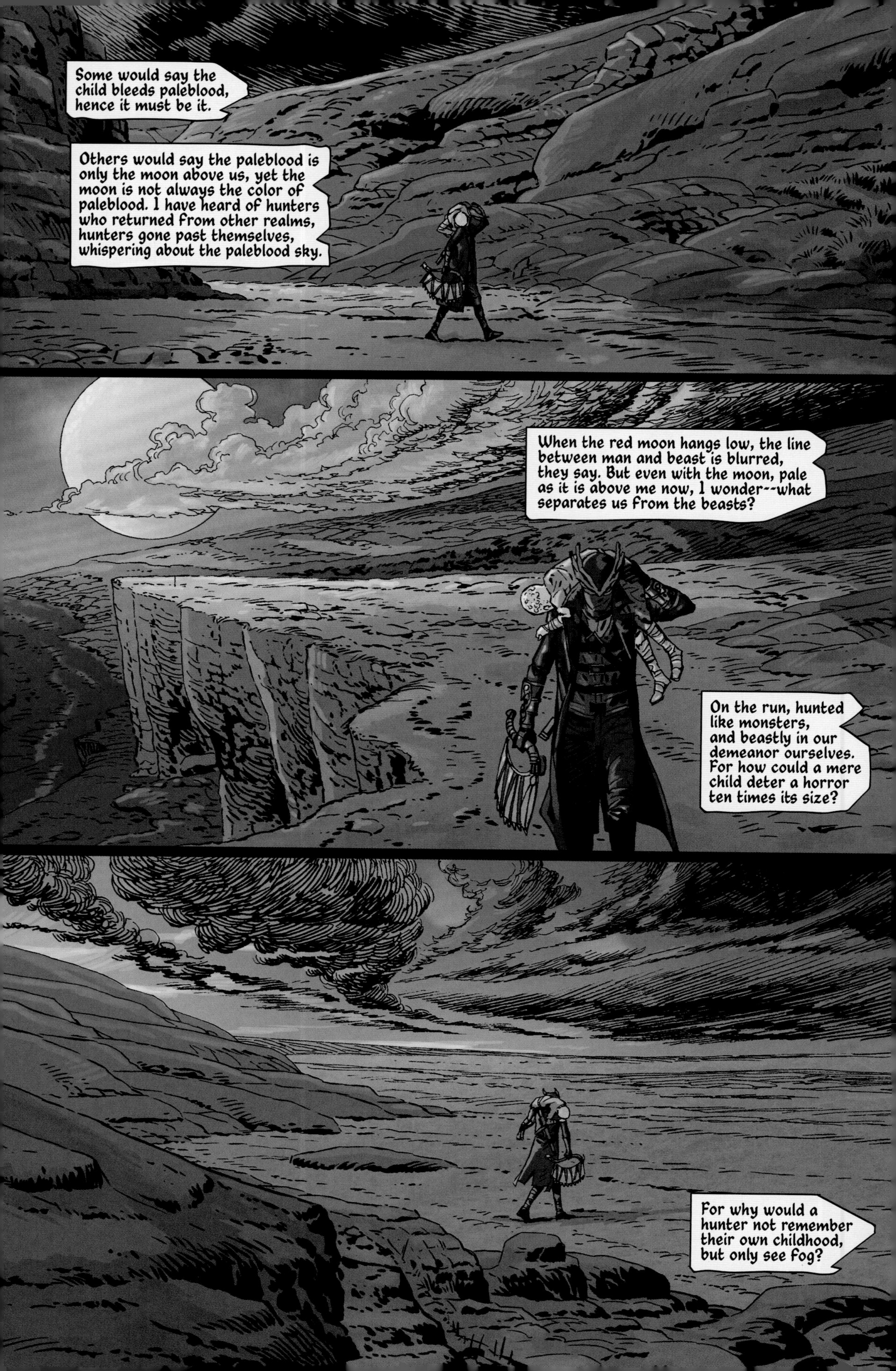
Some would say the child bleeds paleblood, hence it must be it.
Others would say the paleblood is only the moon above us, yet the moon is not always the color of paleblood. I have heard of hunters who returned from other realms, hunters gone past themselves, whispering about the paleblood sky.
When the red moon hangs low, the line between man and beast is blurred, they say. But even with the moon, pale as it is above me now, I wonder--what separates us from the beasts?
On the run, hunted like monsters, and beastly in our demeanor ourselves. For how could a mere child deter a horror ten times its size?
For why would a hunter not remember their own childhood, but only see fog?

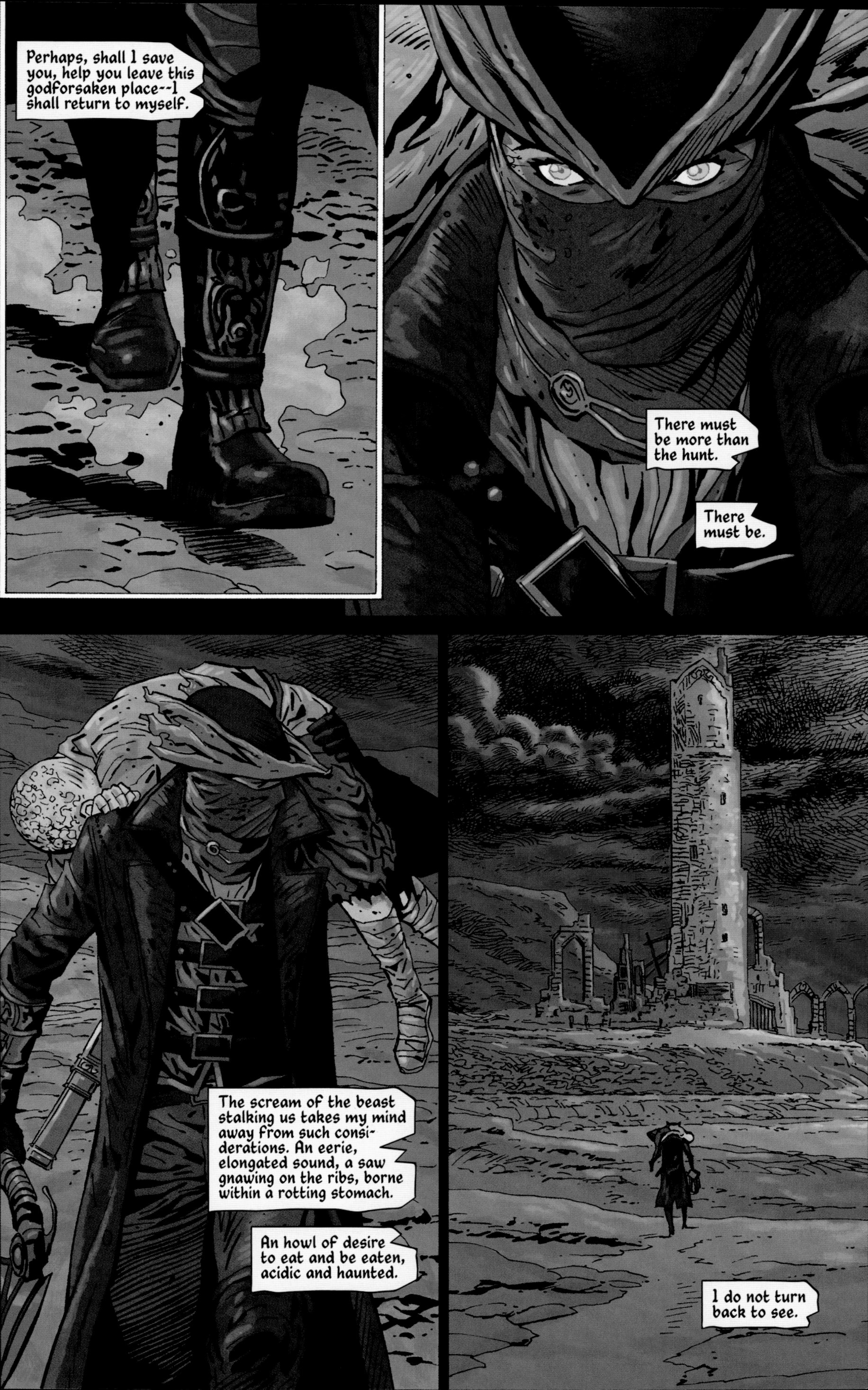
Perhaps, shall I save you, help you leave this godforsaken place--I shall return to myself.
There must be more than the hunt.
There must be.
The scream of the beast stalking us takes my mind away from such consi-derations. An eerie, elongated sound, a saw gnawing on the ribs, borne within a rotting stomach.
An howl of desire to eat and be eaten, acidic and haunted.
I do not turn back to see.

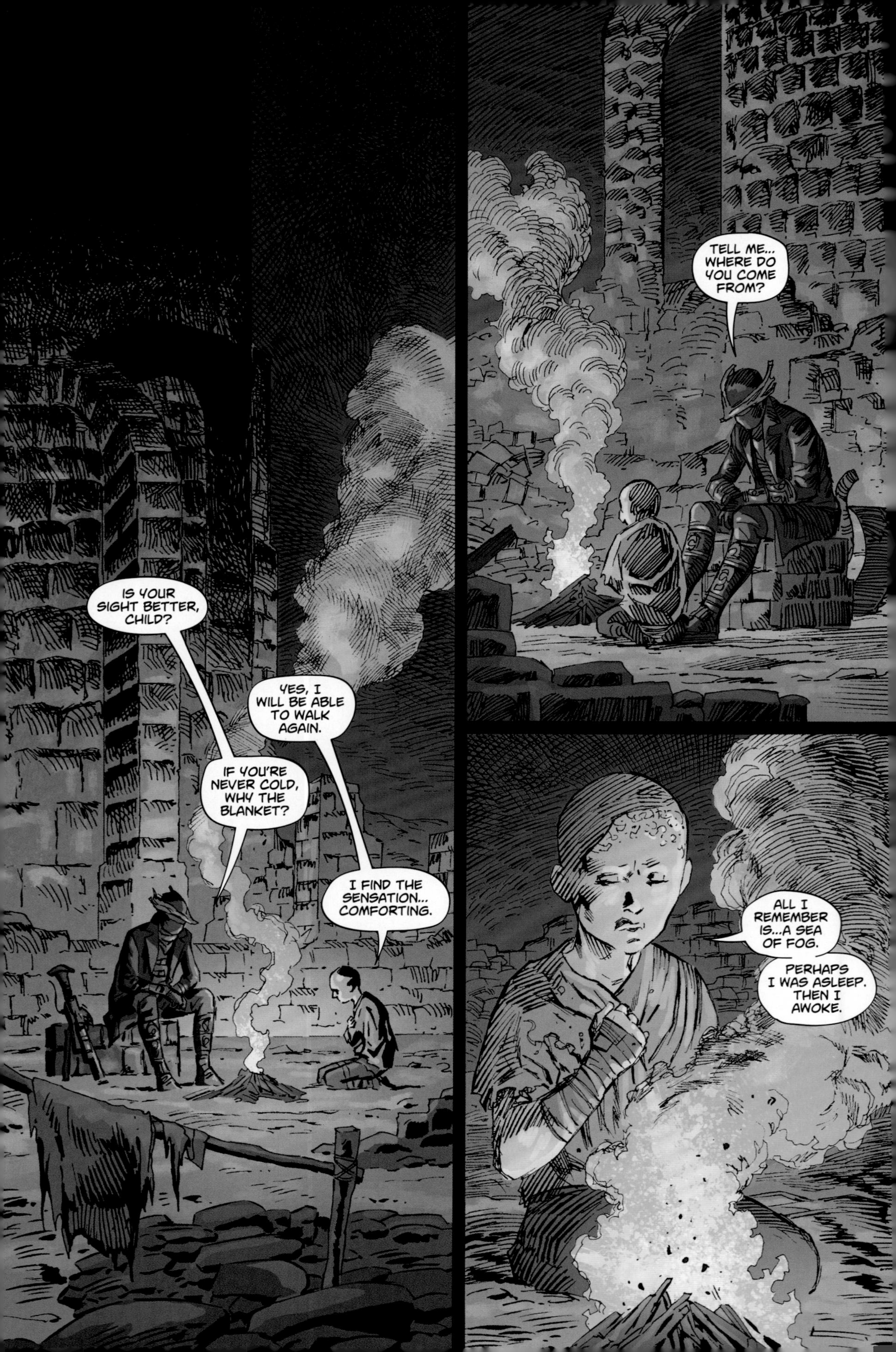
IS YOUR SIGHT BETTER, CHILD?
YES, I WILL BE ABLE TO WALK AGAIN.
IF YOU'RE NEVER COLD, WHY THE BLANKET?
I FIND THE SENSATION... COMFORTING.
TELL ME... WHERE DO YOU COME FROM?
ALL I REMEMBER IS...A SEA OF FOG.
PERHAPS I WAS ASLEEP. THEN I AWOKE.

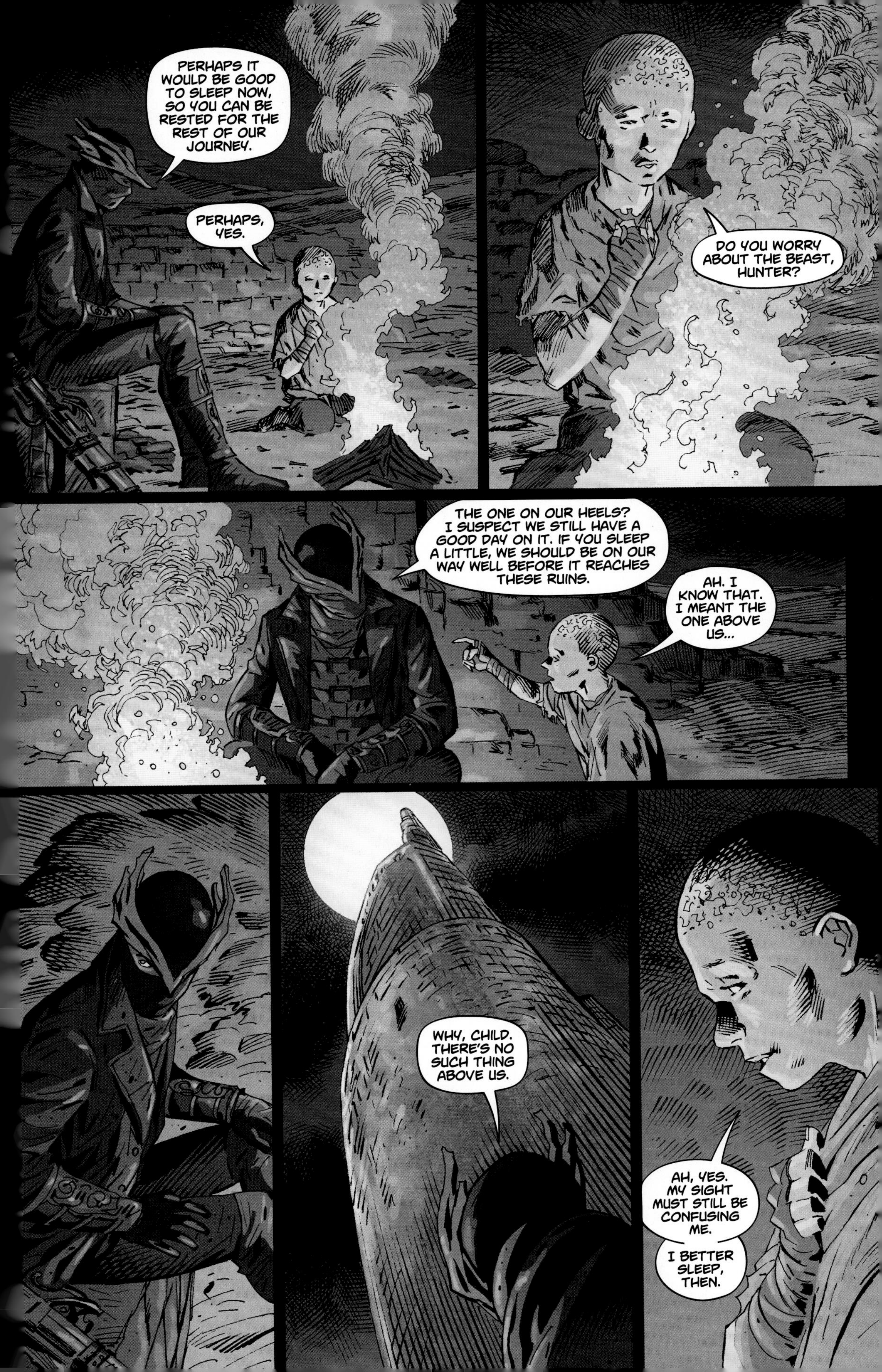
PERHAPS IT WOULD BE GOOD TO SLEEP NOW, SO YOU CAN BE RESTED FOR THE REST OF OUR JOURNEY.
PERHAPS, YES.
DO YOU WORRY ABOUT THE BEAST, HUNTER?
THE ONE ON OUR HEELS? I SUSPECT WE STILL HAVE A GOOD DAY ON IT. IF YOU SLEEP A LITTLE, WE SHOULD BE ON OUR WAY WELL BEFORE IT REACHES THESE RUINS.
AH. I KNOW THAT. I MEANT THE ONE ABOVE US...
WHY, CHILD. THERE'S NO SUCH THING ABOVE US.
AH, YES. MY SIGHT MUST STILL BE CONFUSING ME.
I BETTER SLEEP, THEN.

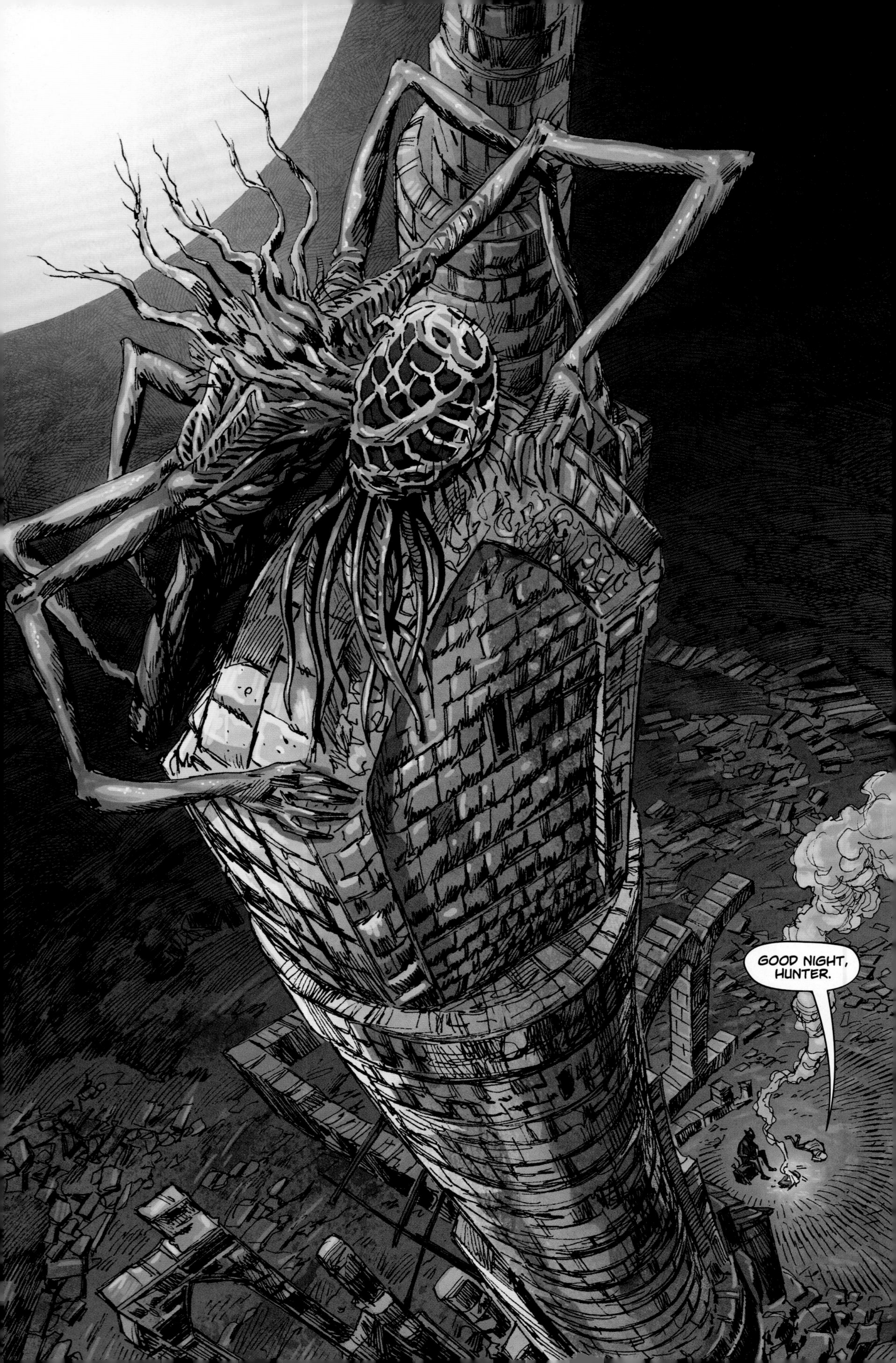
GOOD NIGHT, HUNTER.

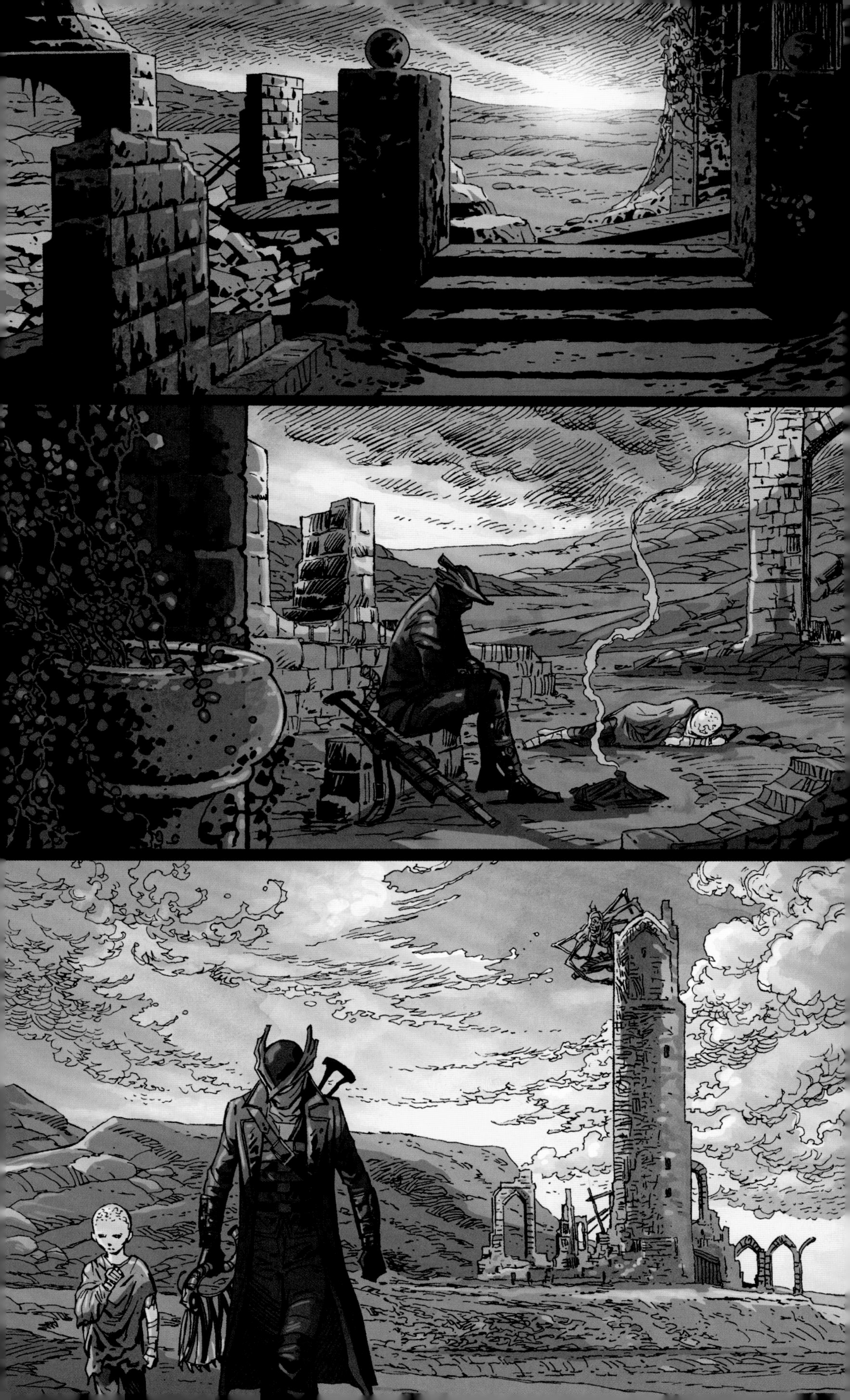

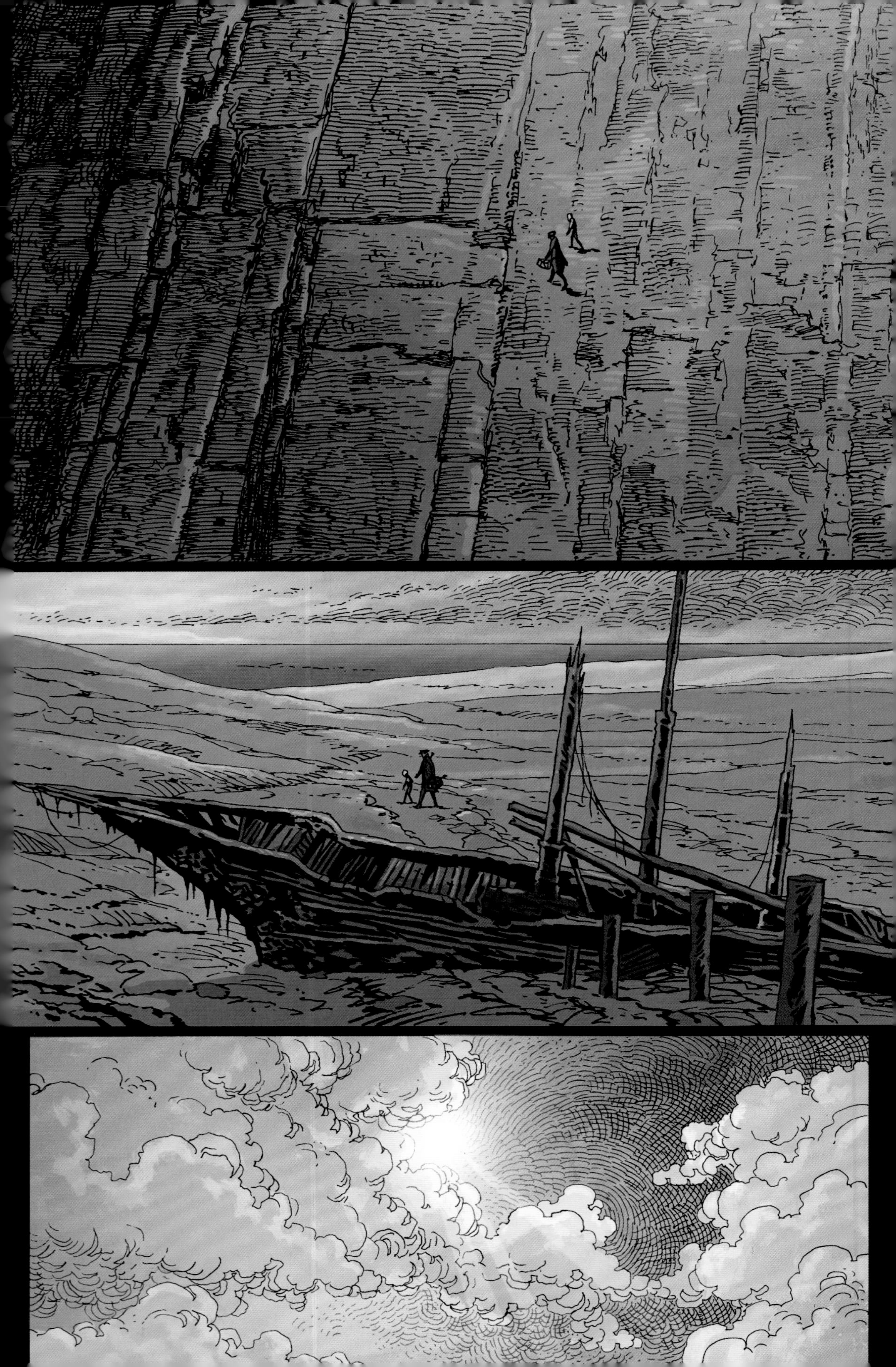

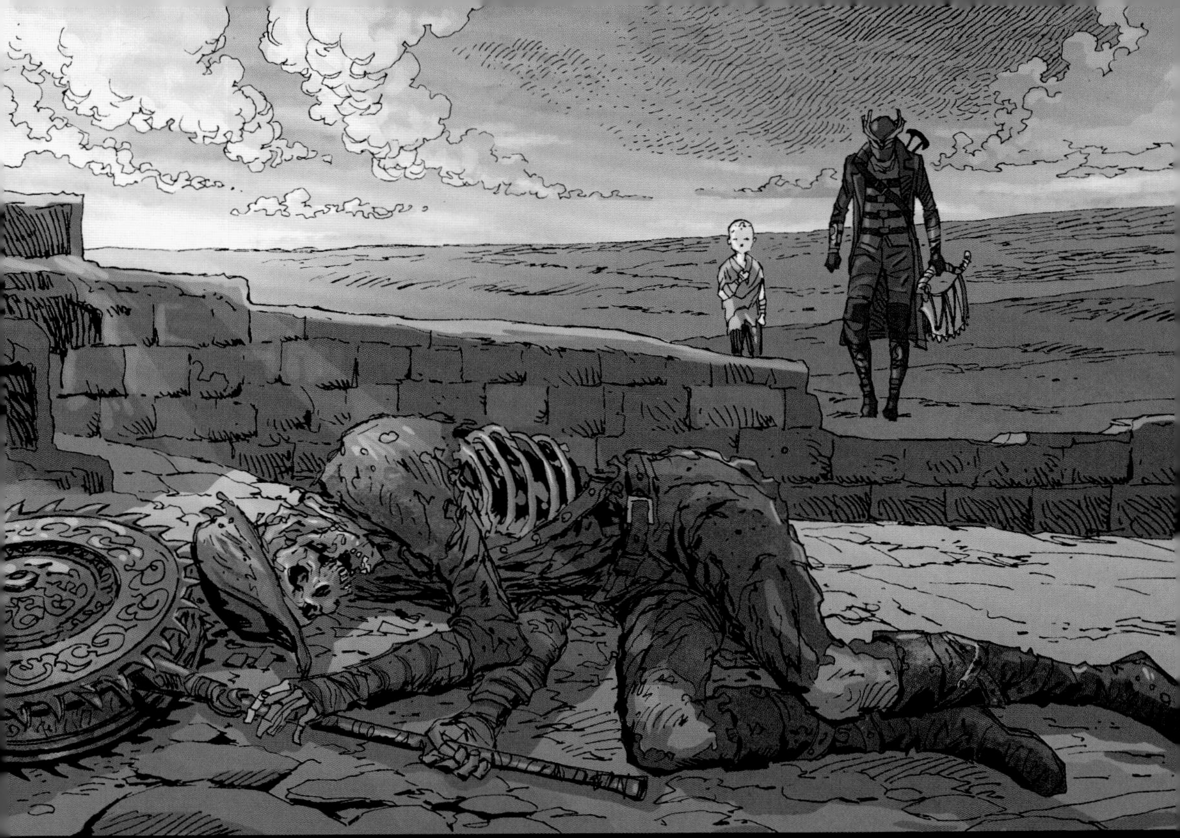

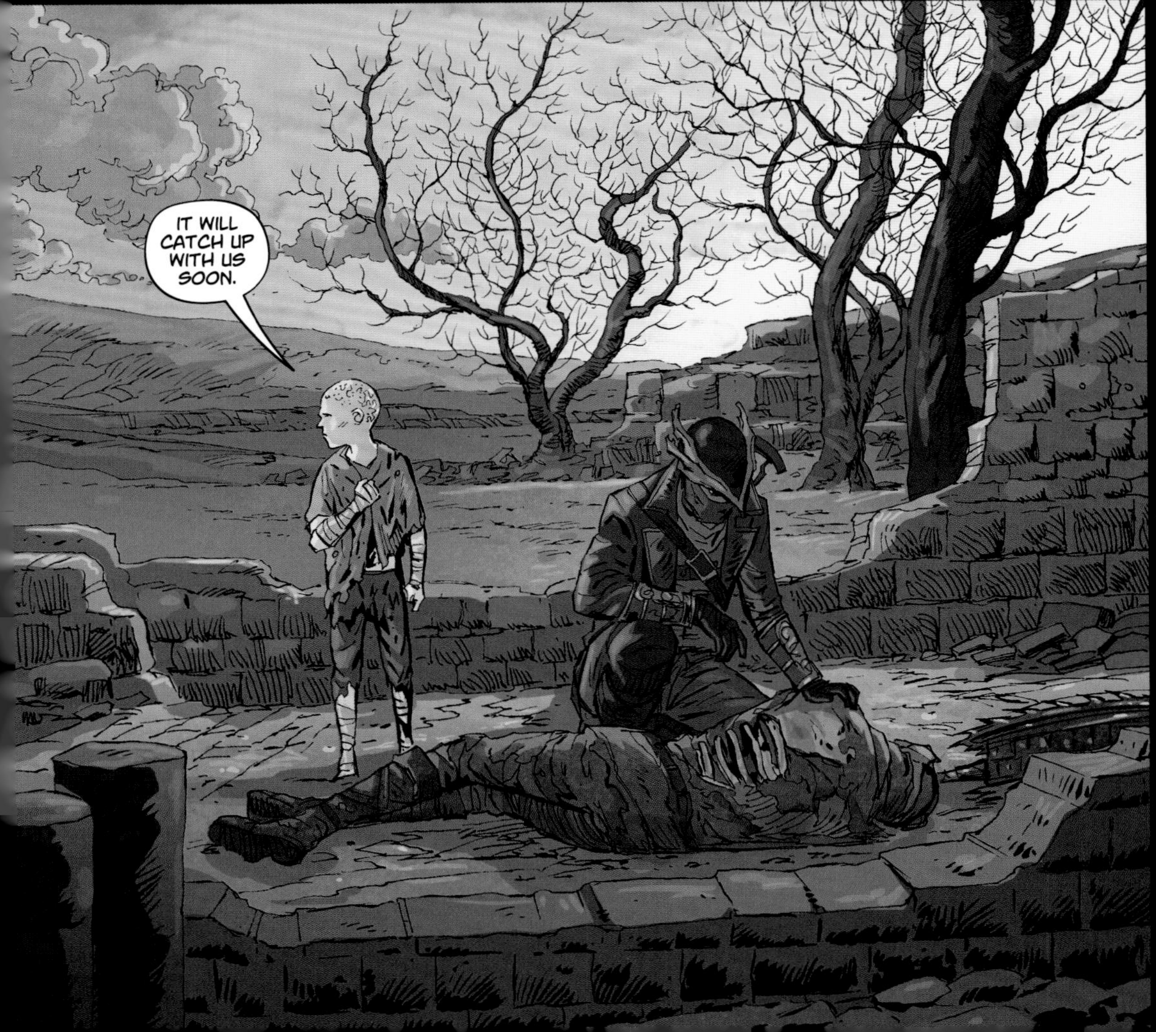
IT WILL CATCH UP WITH US SOON.

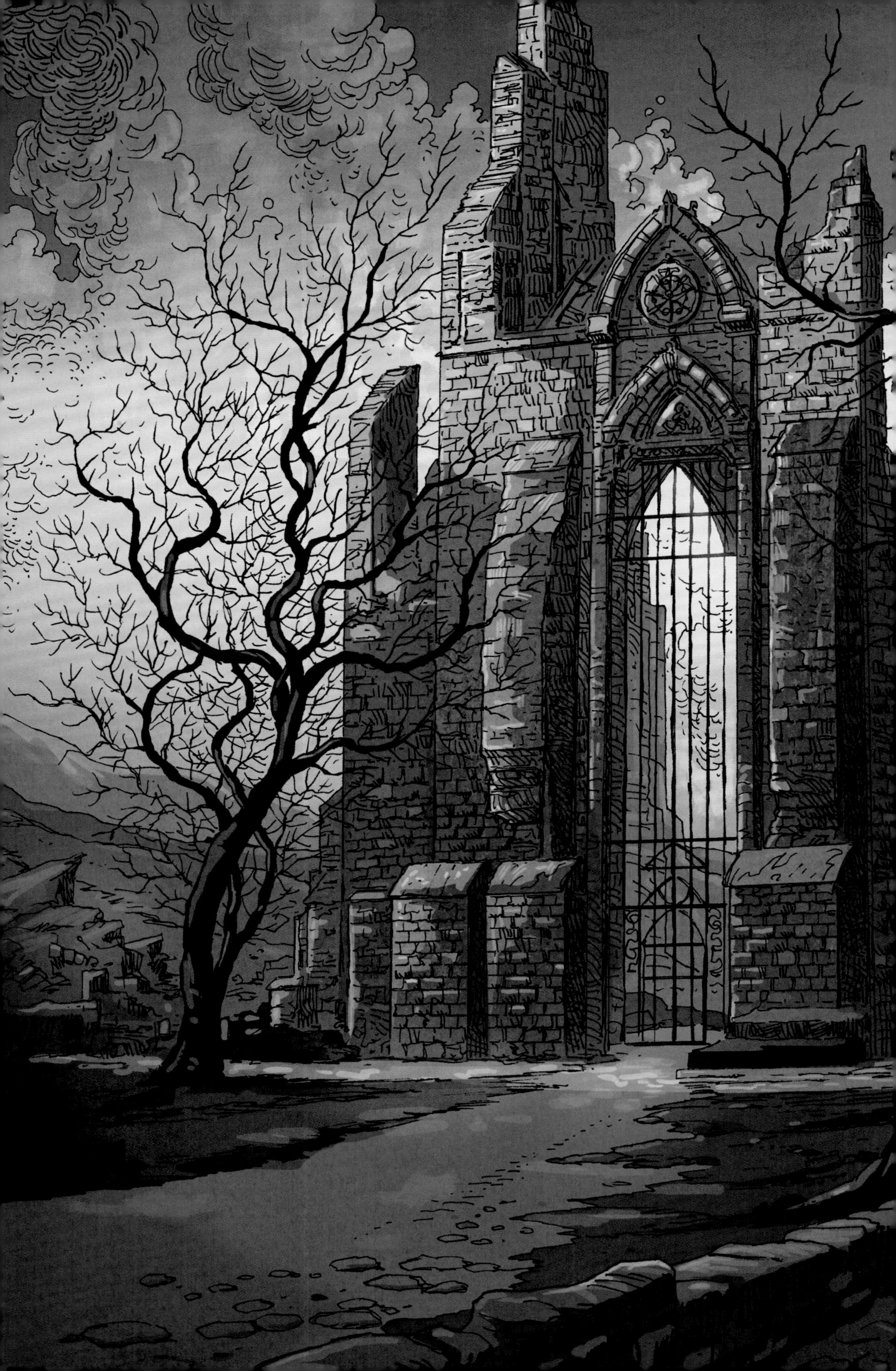

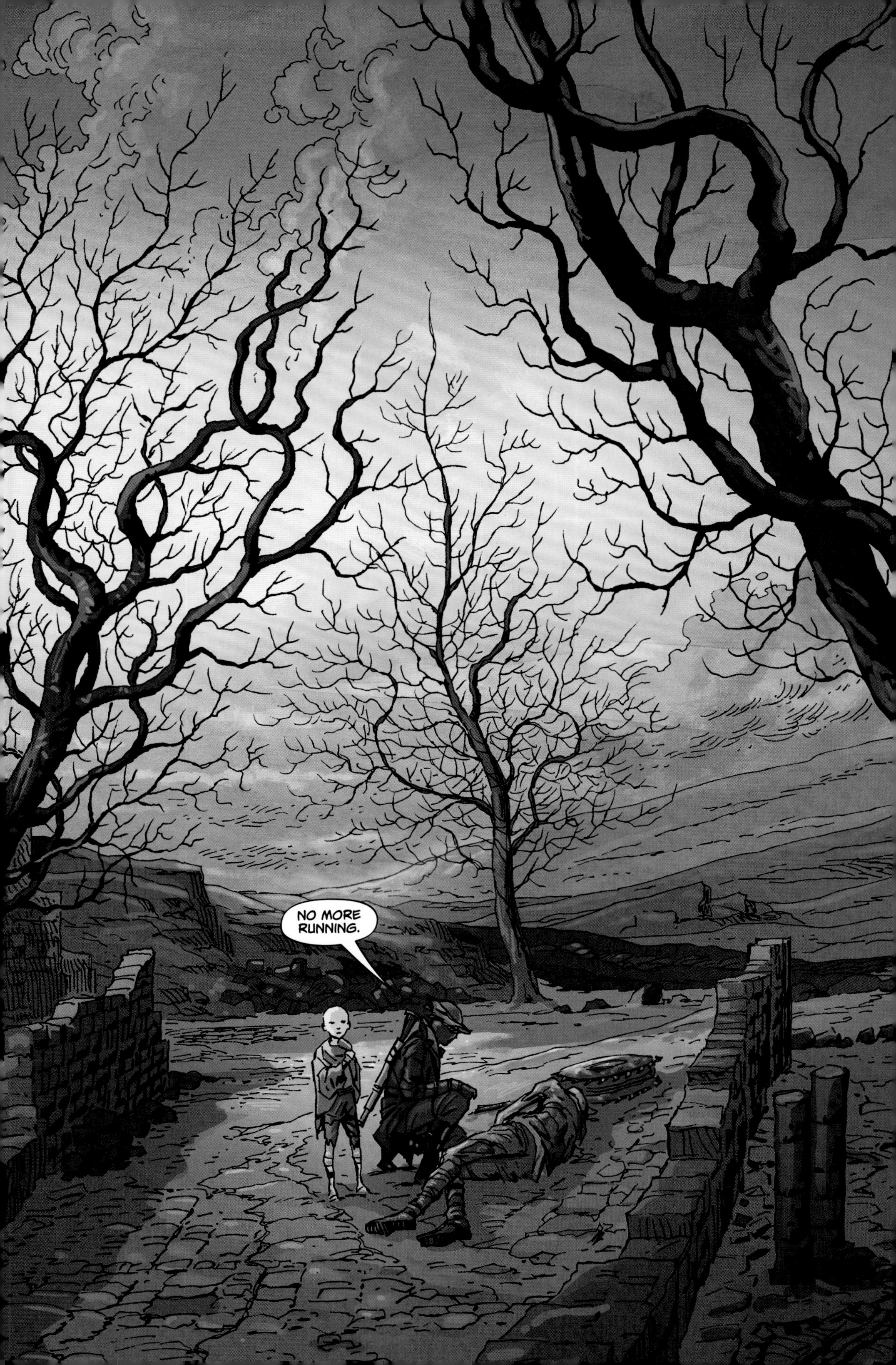
NO MORE RUNNING.

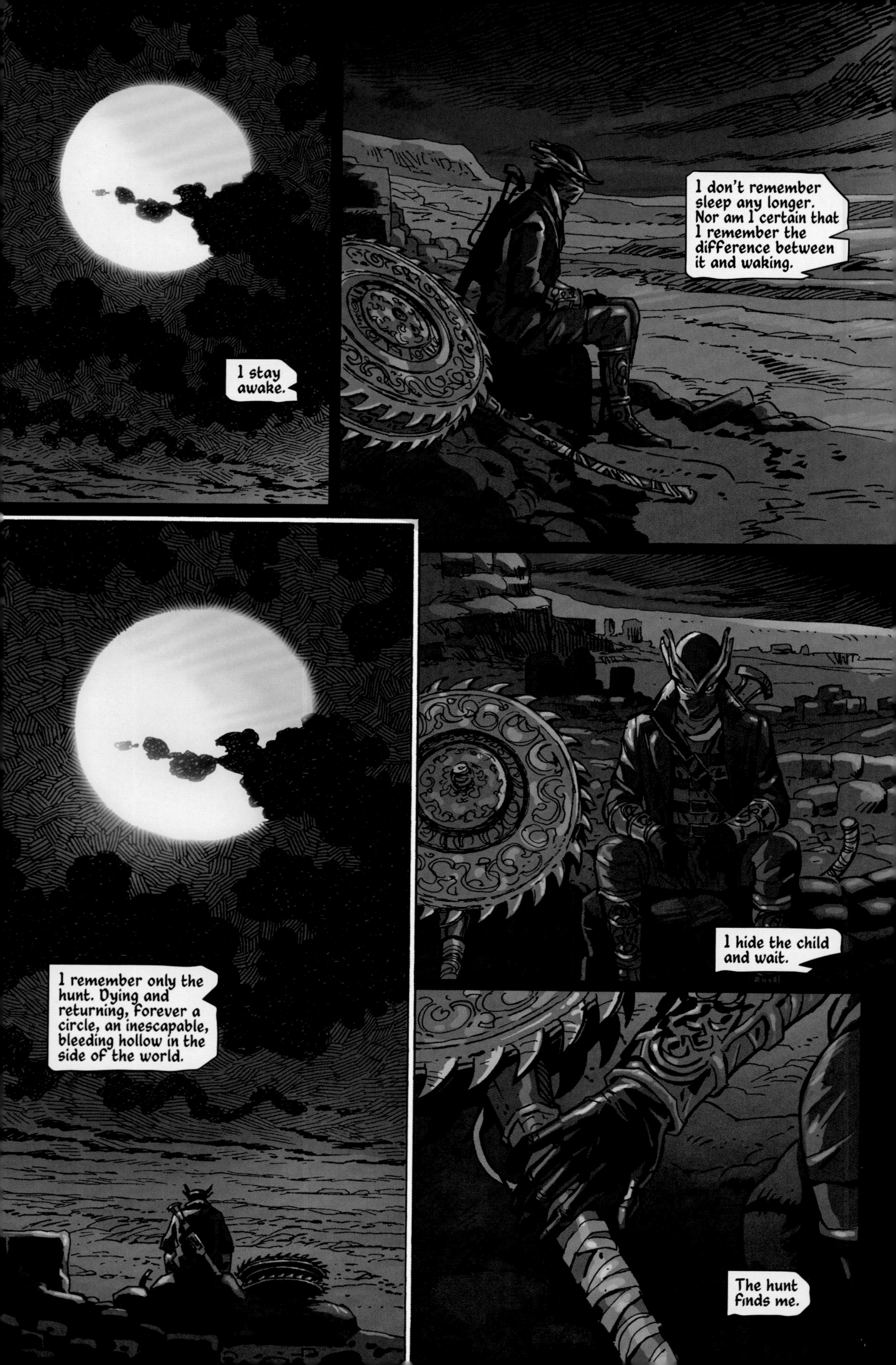
I stay awake.
I don't remember sleep any longer. Nor am I certain that I remember the difference between it and waking.
I remember only the hunt. Dying and returning, forever a circle, an inescapable, bleeding hollow in the side of the world.
I hide the child and wait.
The hunt finds me.

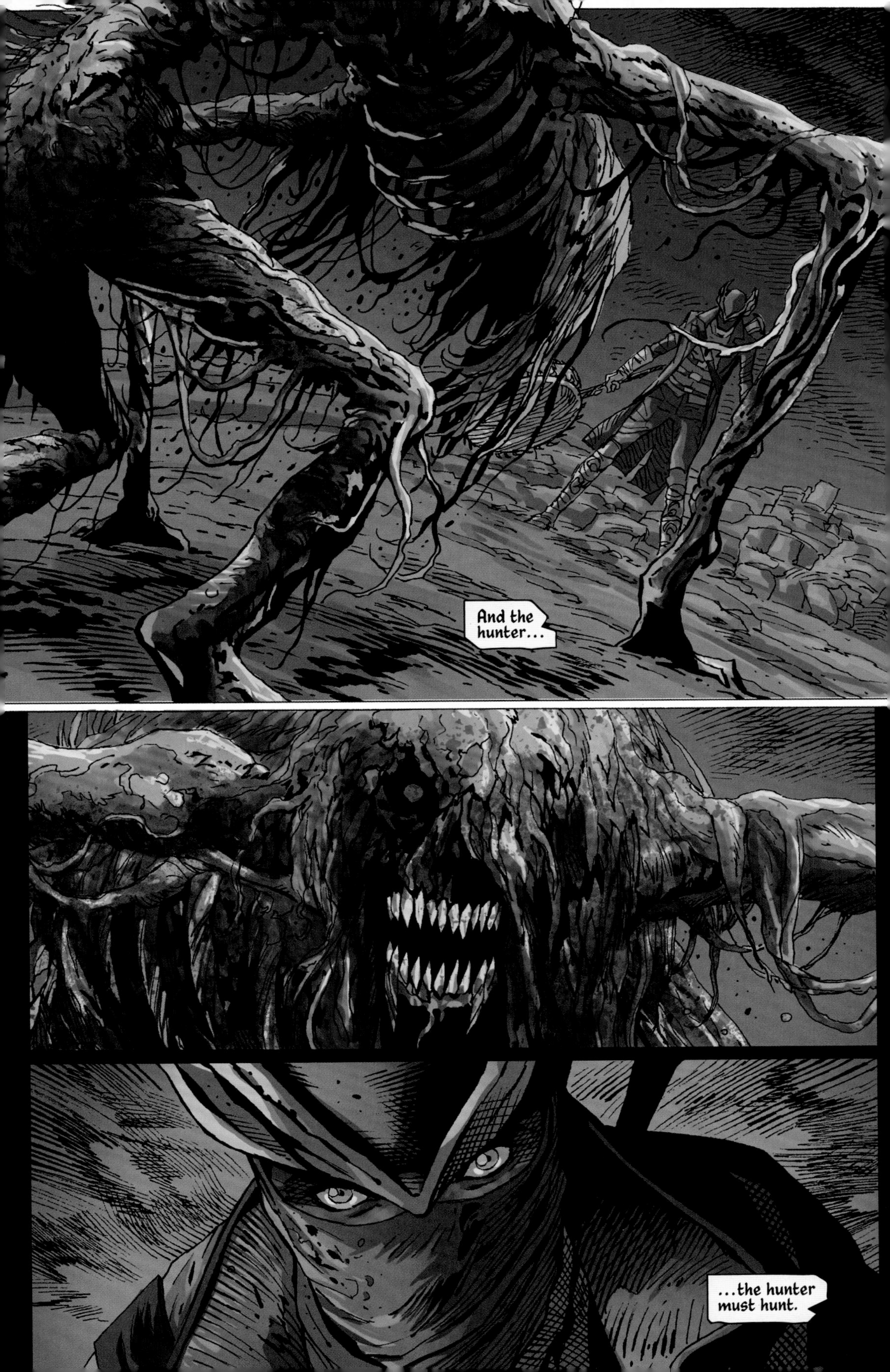
And the hunter...
...the hunter must hunt.

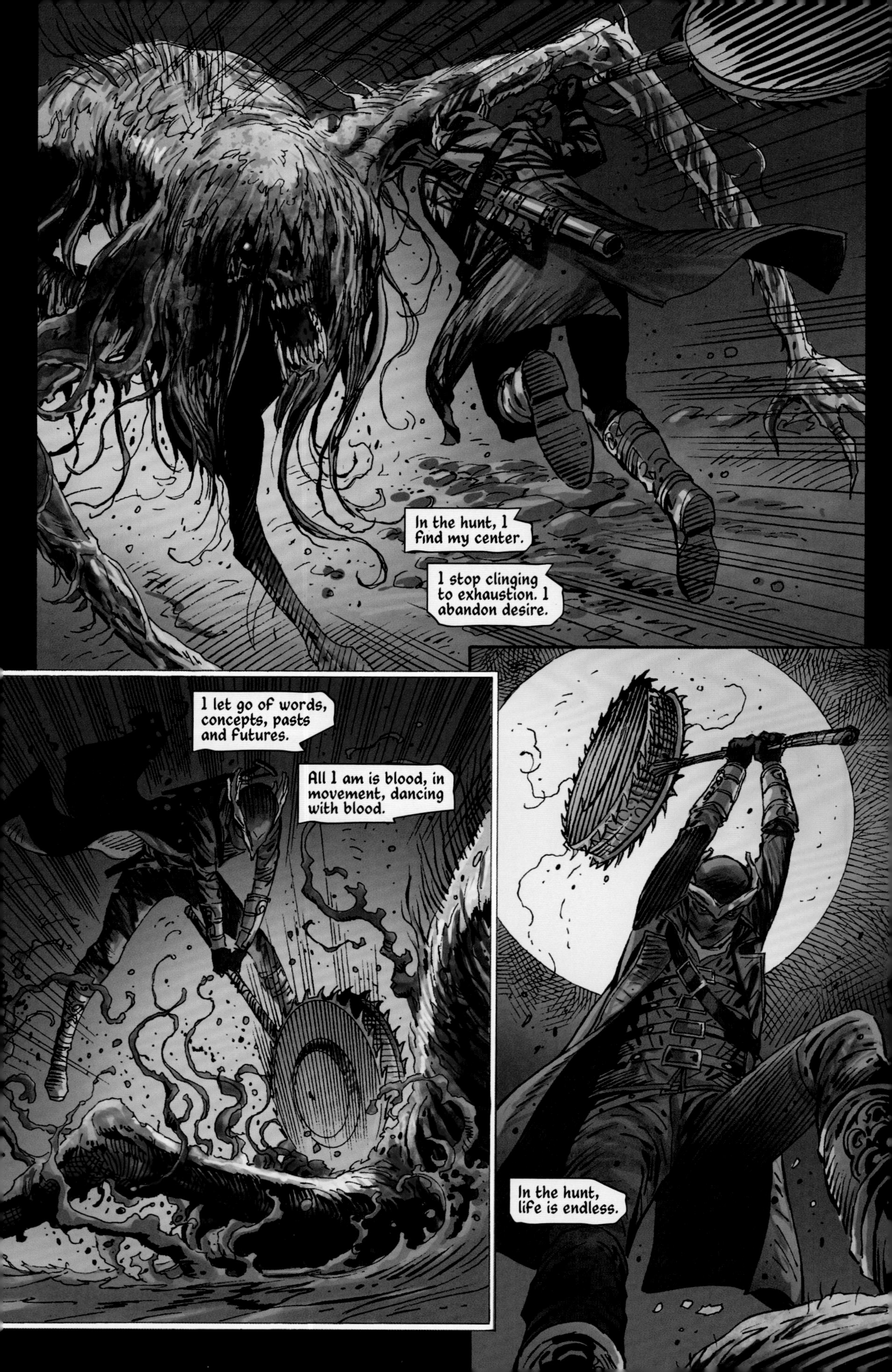
In the hunt, I find my center.
I stop clinging to exhaustion. I abandon desire.
I let go of words, concepts, pasts and futures.
All I am is blood, in movement, dancing with blood.
In the hunt, life is endless.

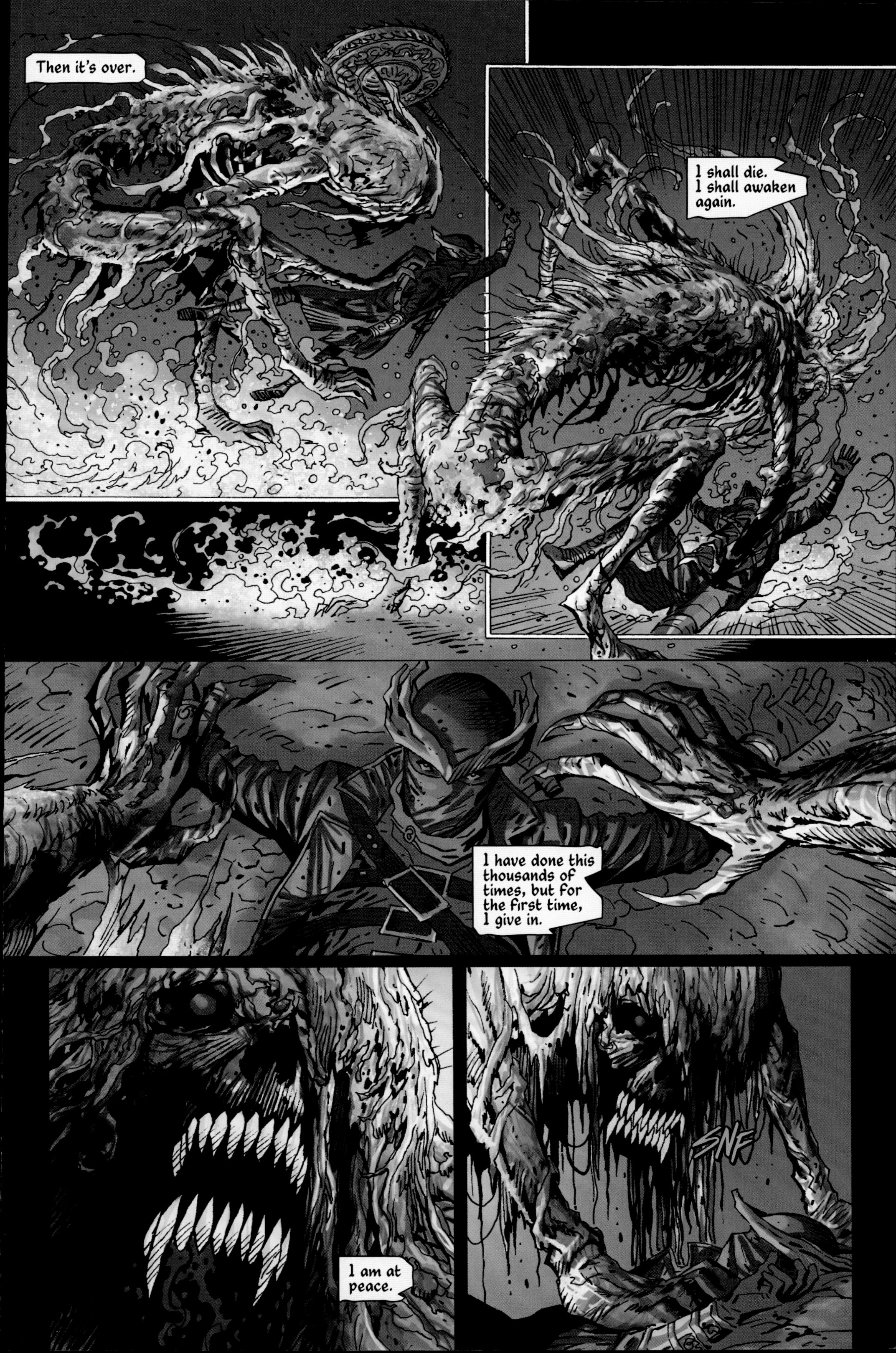
Then it's over.
I shall die. I shall awaken again.
I have done this thousands of times, but for the first time, I give in.
SNF
I am at peace.

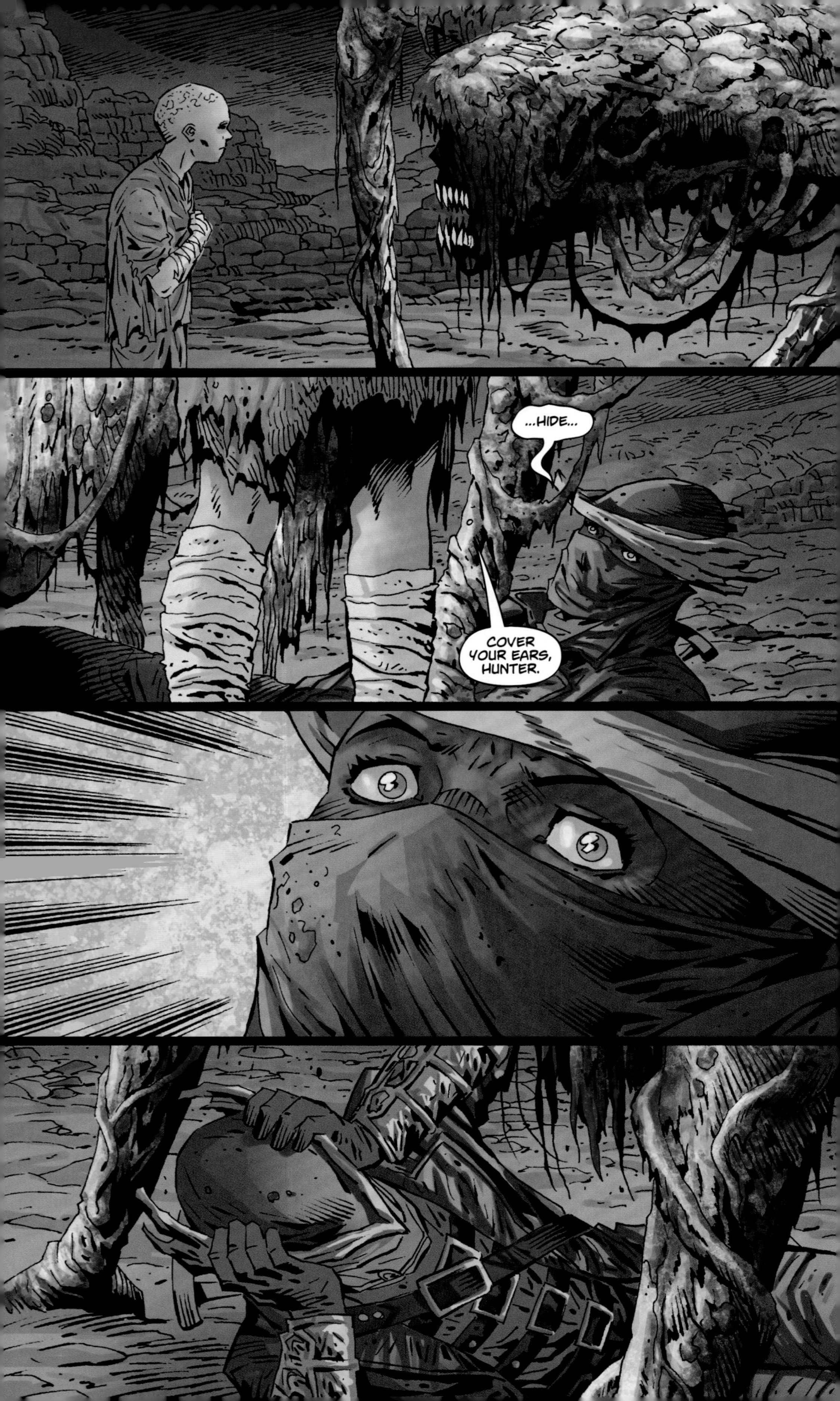
...HIDE...
COVER YOUR EARS, HUNTER.

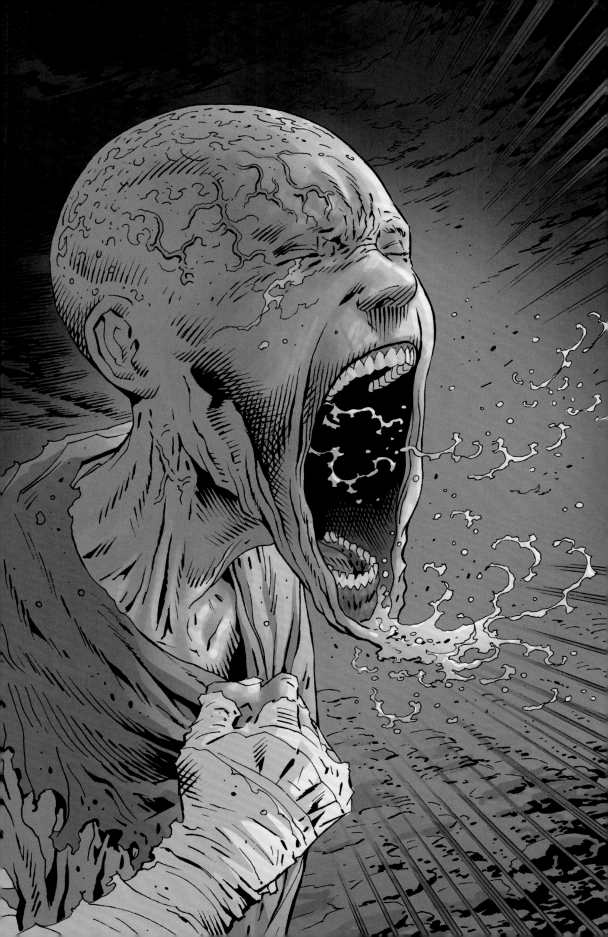

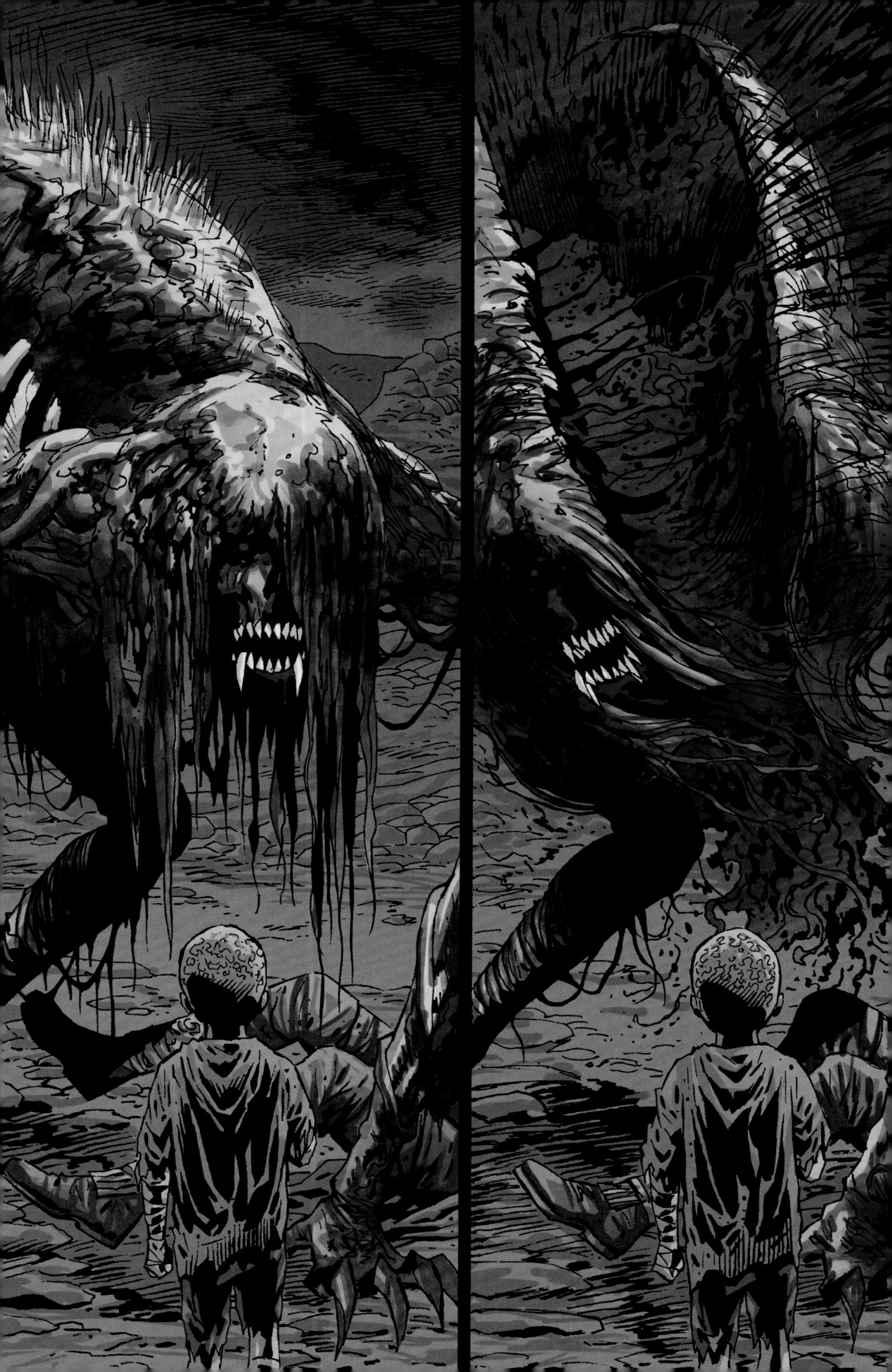

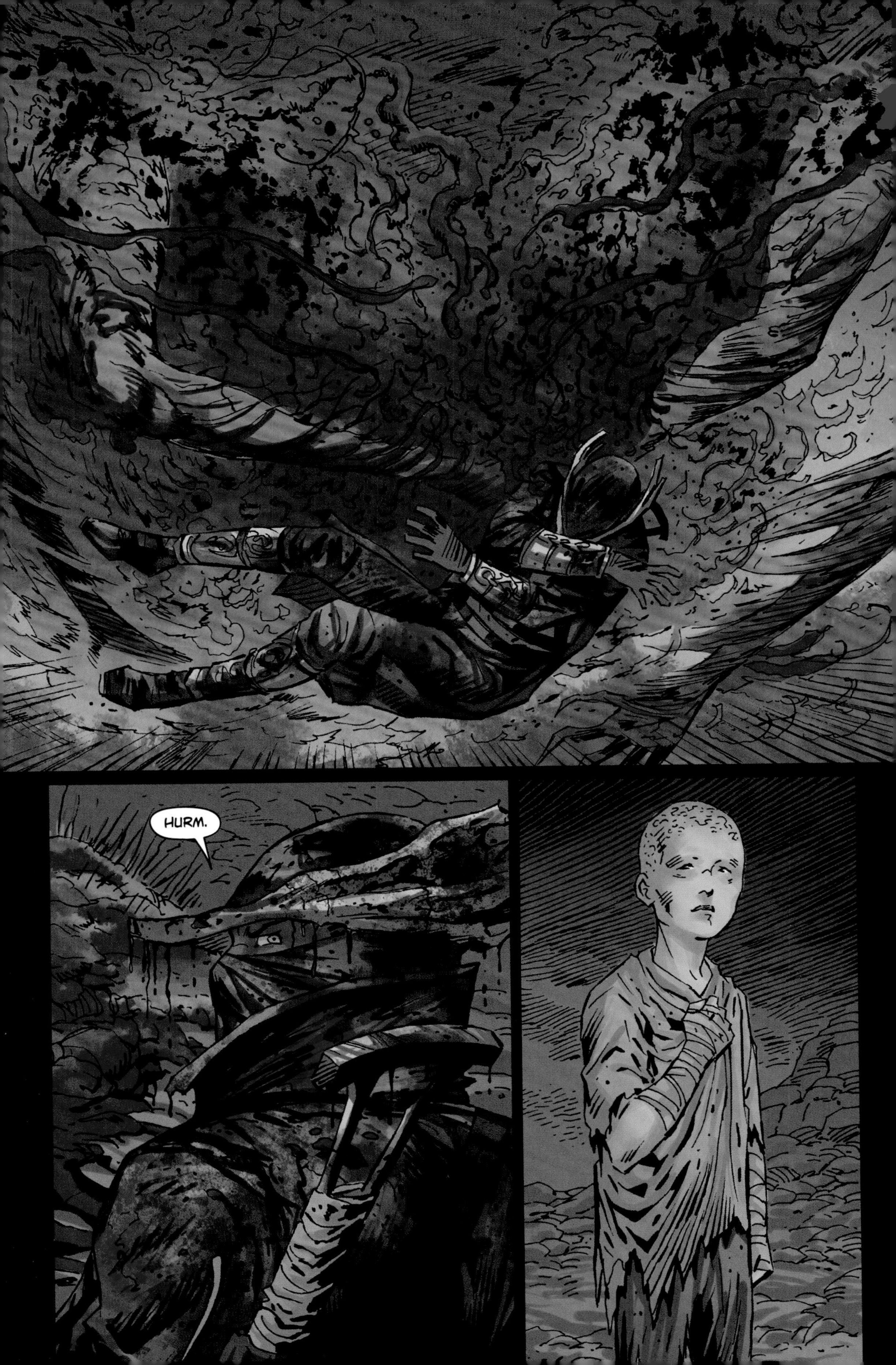
HURM.

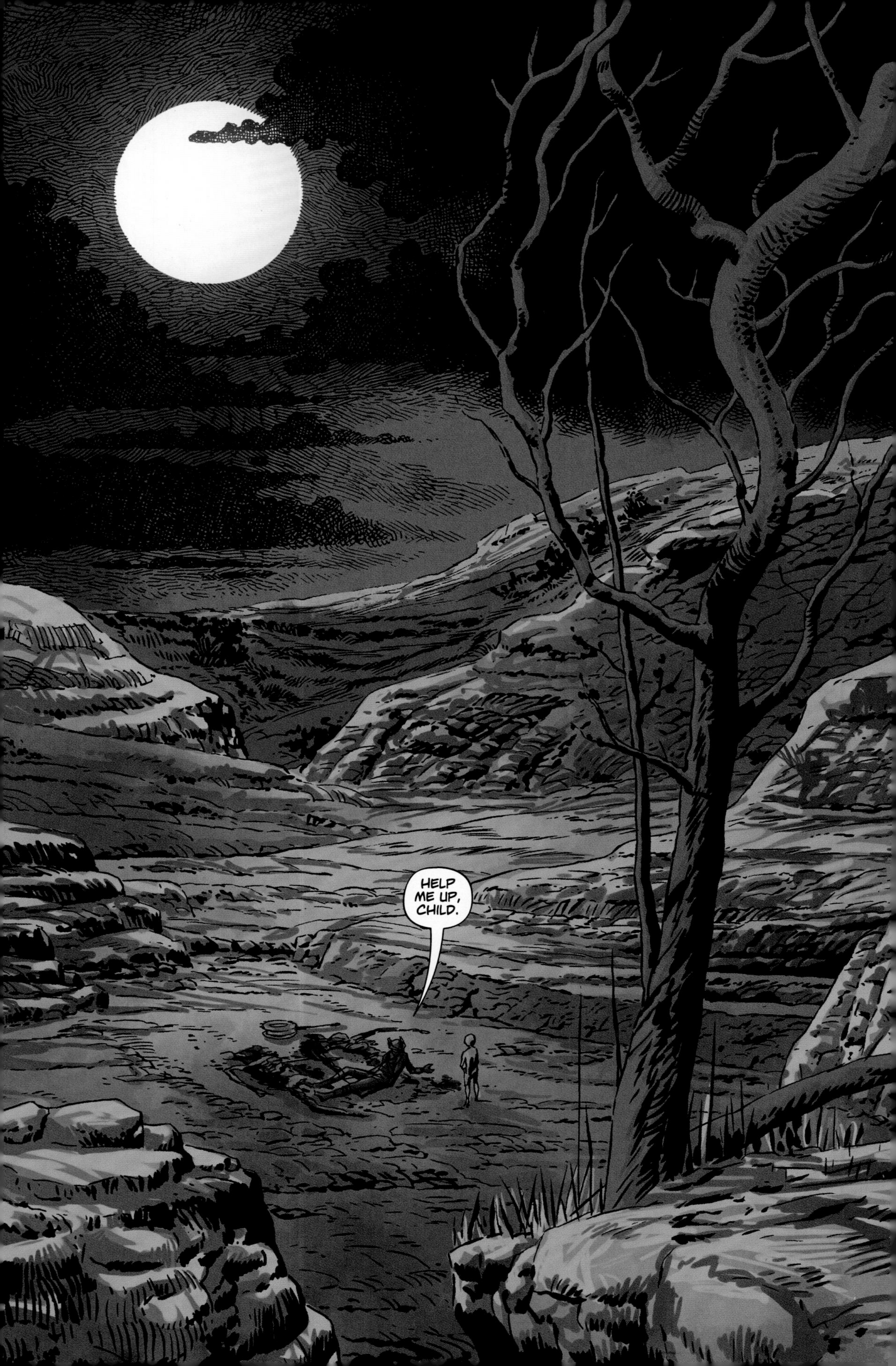
HELP ME UP, CHILD.

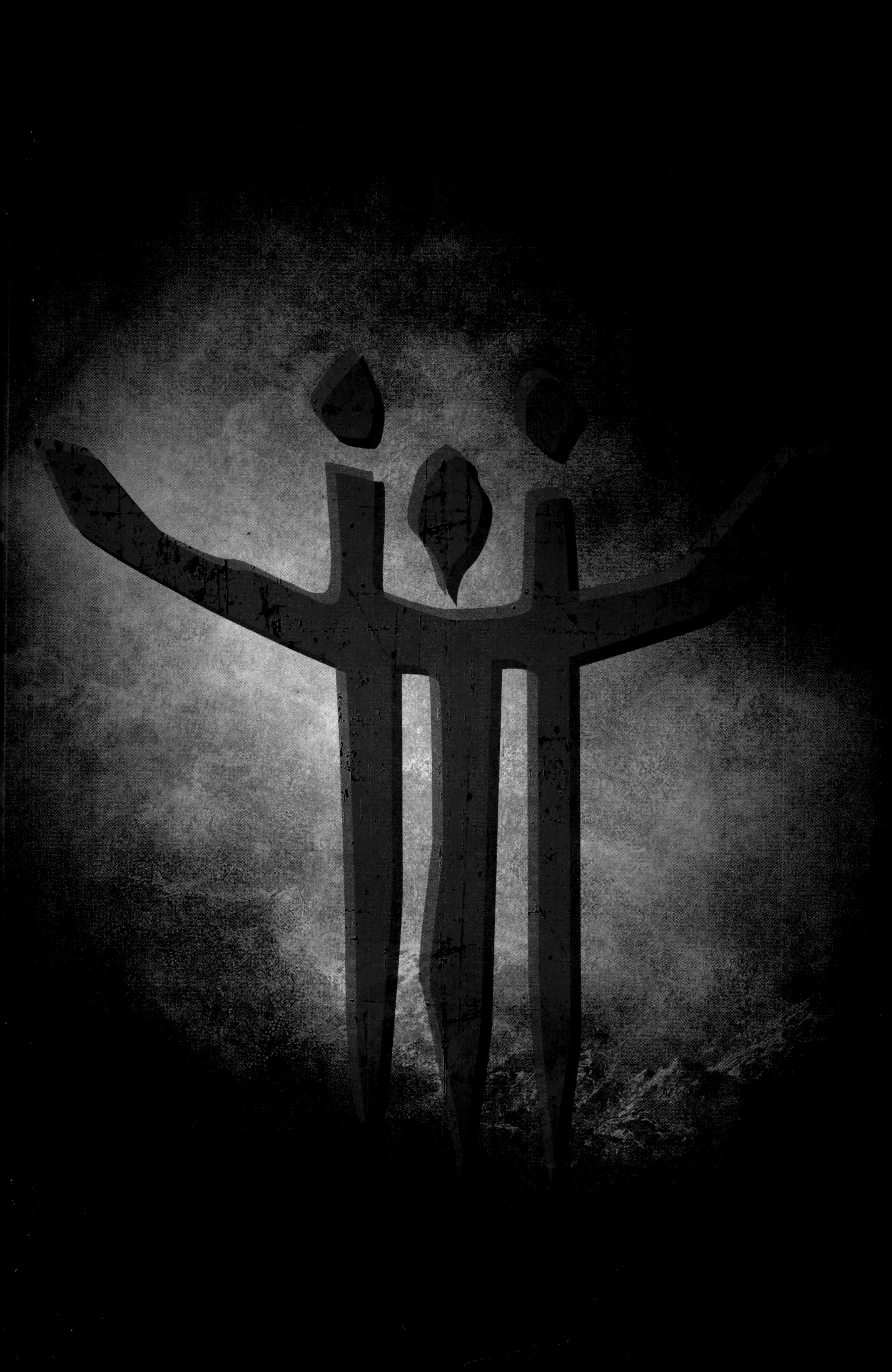

#4 COVER A
BY
VANESA DEL REY

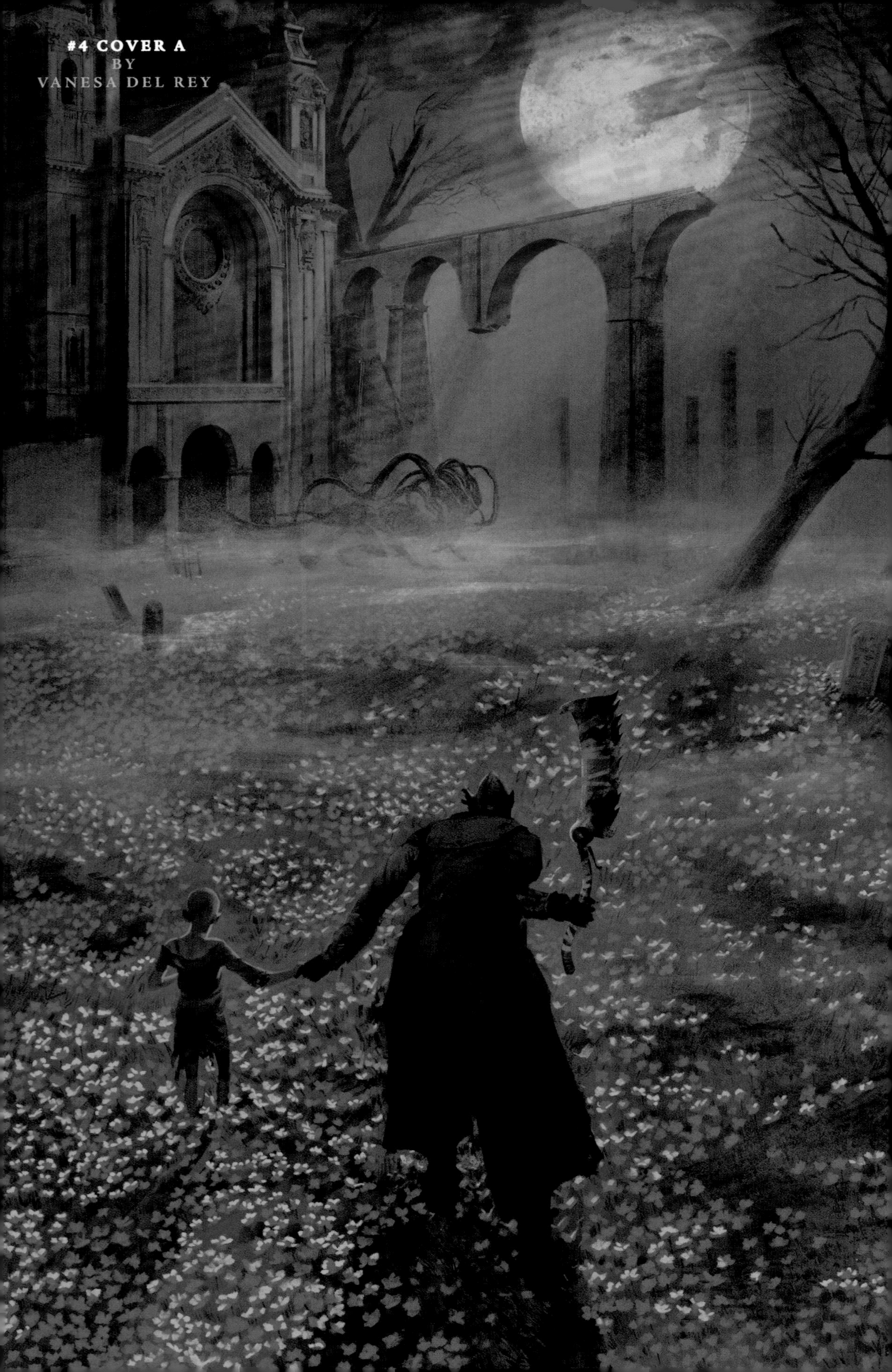

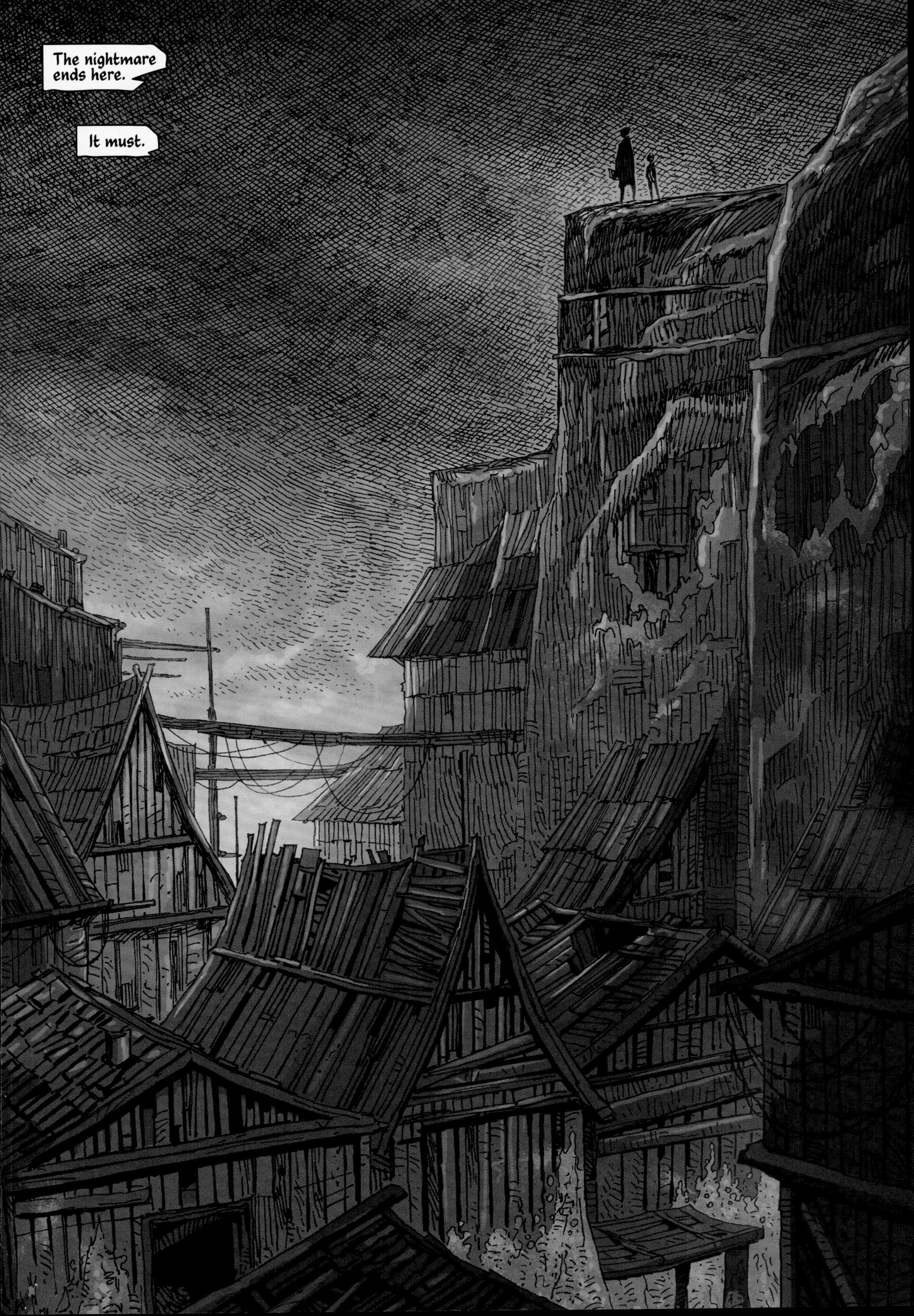
The nightmare ends here.
It must.

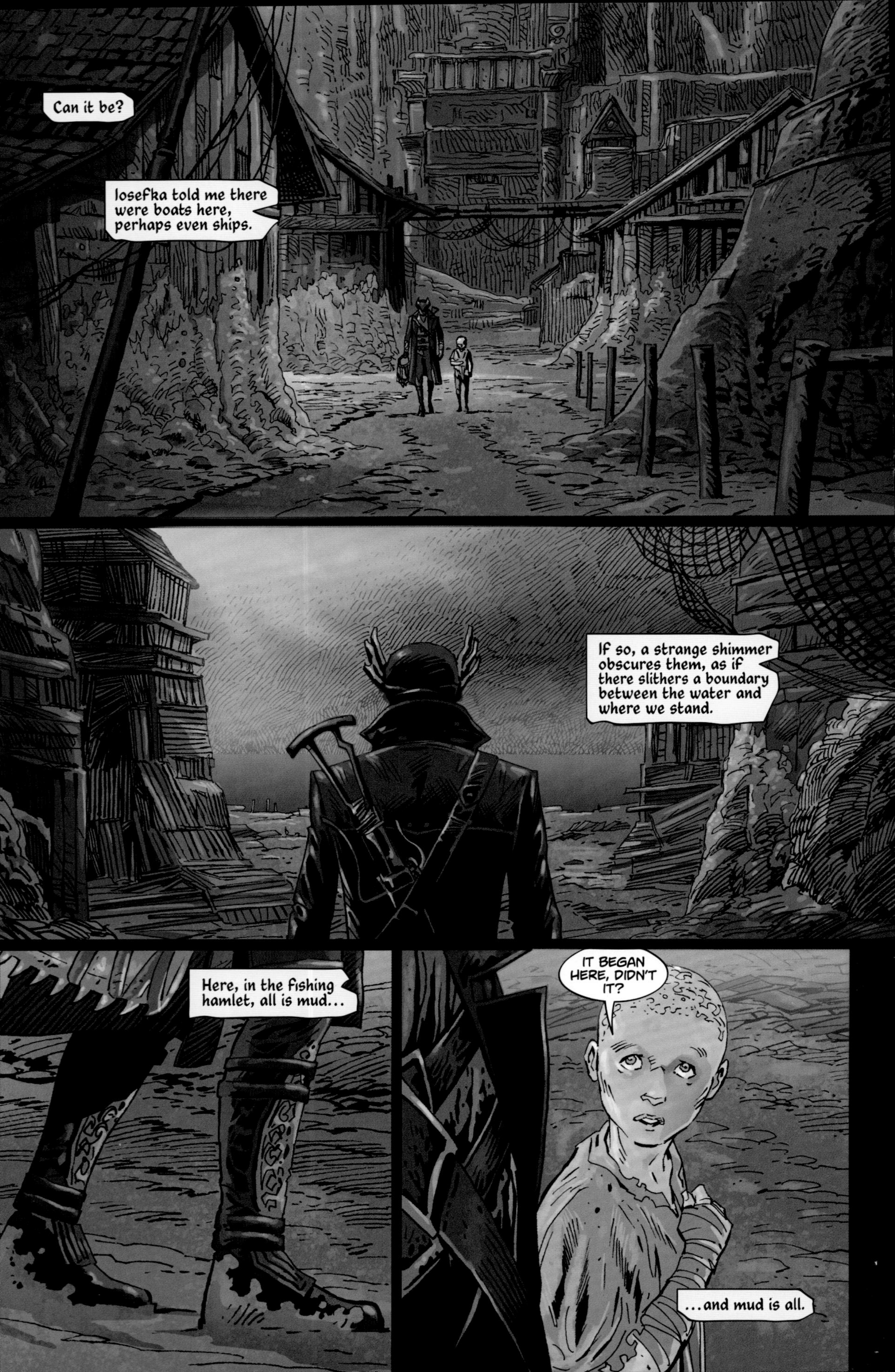
Can it be?
Iosefka told me there were boats here, perhaps even ships.
If so, a strange shimmer obscures them, as if there slithers a boundary between the water and where we stand.
Here, in the fishing hamlet, all is mud...
IT BEGAN HERE, DIDN'T IT?
...and mud is all.

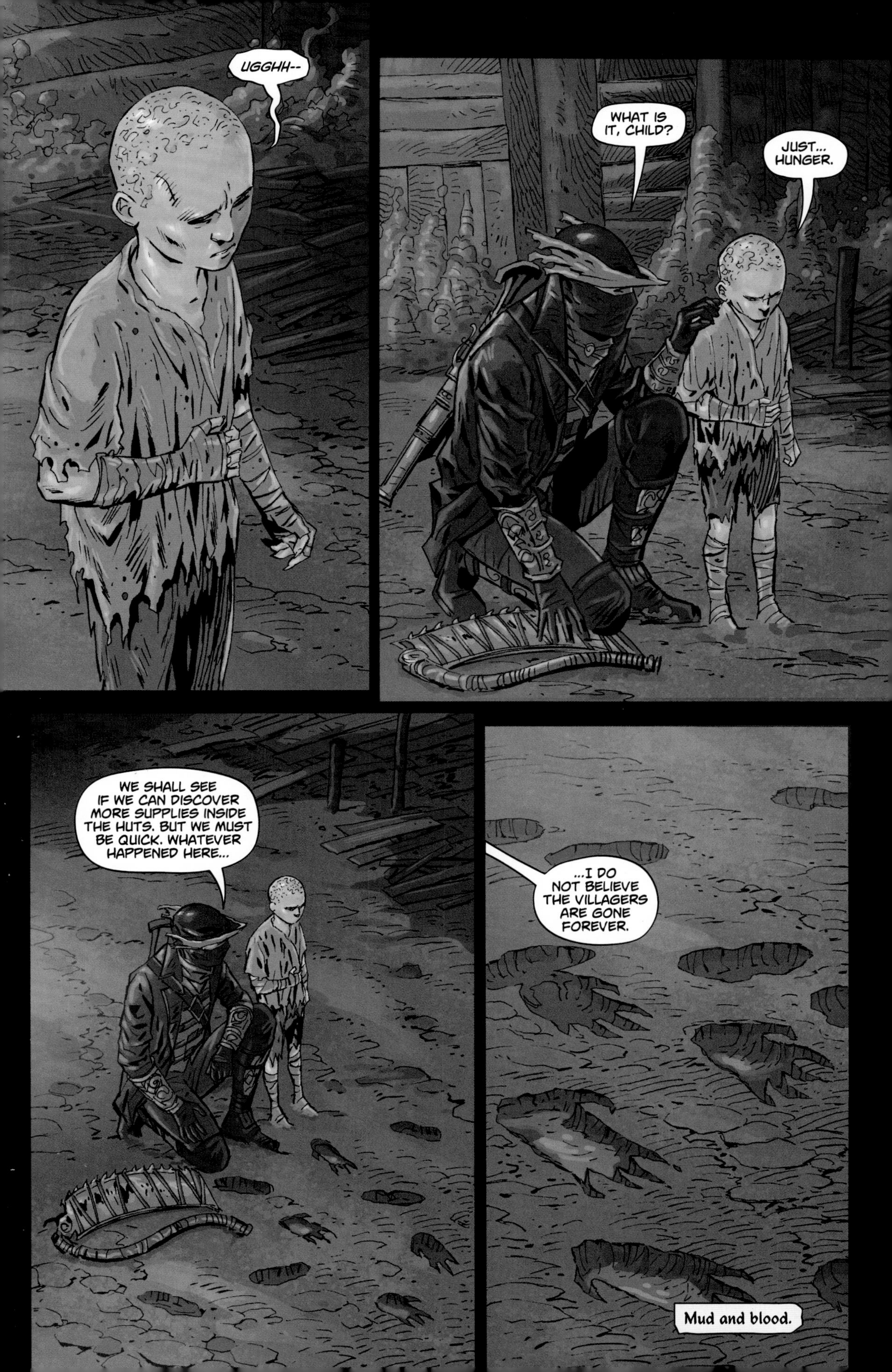
UGGHH--
WHAT IS IT, CHILD?
JUST... HUNGER.
WE SHALL SEE IF WE CAN DISCOVER MORE SUPPLIES INSIDE THE HUTS. BUT WE MUST BE QUICK. WHATEVER HAPPENED HERE...
...I DO NOT BELIEVE THE VILLAGERS ARE GONE FOREVER.
Mud and blood.

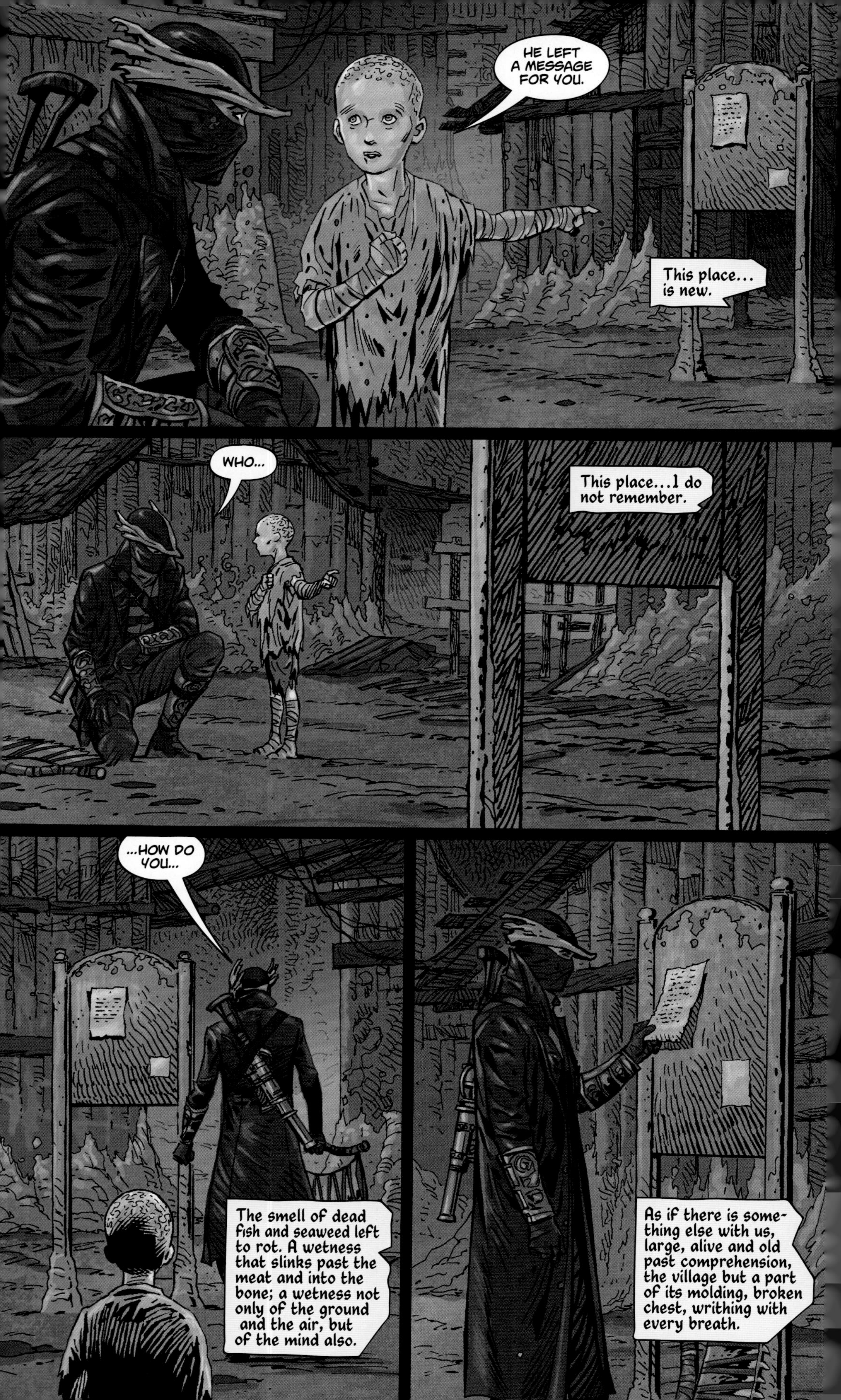

HE LEFT A MESSAGE FOR YOU.
This place... is new.
WHO...
This place...I do not remember.
...HOW DO YOU...
The smell of dead fish and seaweed left to rot. A wetness that slinks past the meat and into the bone; a wetness not only of the ground and the air, but of the mind also.
As if there is something else with us, large, alive and old past comprehension, the village but a part of its molding, broken chest, writhing with every breath.

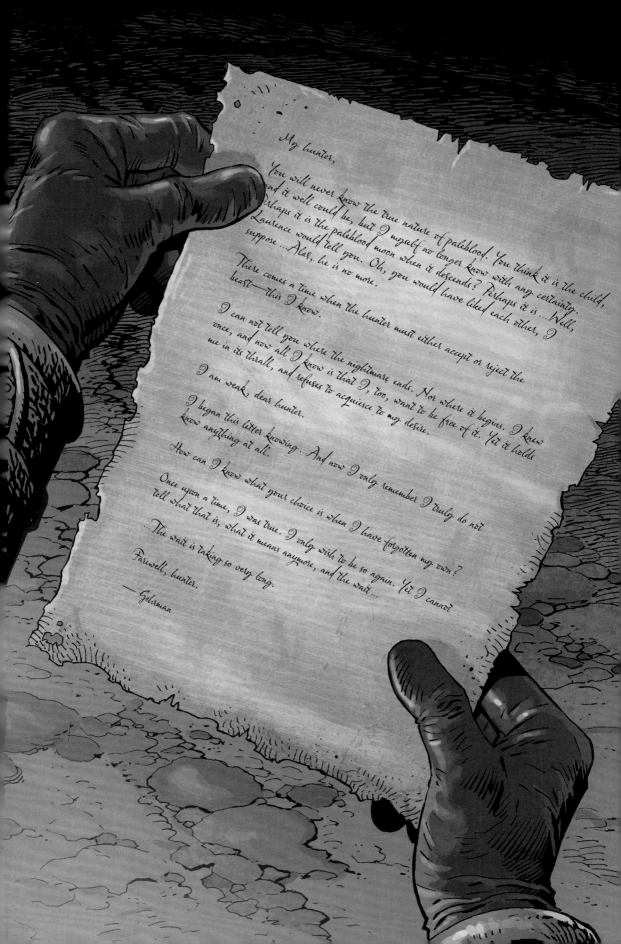

My hunter,

You will never know the true nature of paleblood. You think it is the child,
and it well could be, but I myself no longer know with any certainty.
Perhaps it is the paleblood moon when it descends? Perhaps it is ... Well,
Laurence would tell you. Oh, you would have liked each other, I
suppose ... Alas, he is no more.

There comes a time when the hunter must either accept or reject the
beast—this I know.

I can not tell you where the nightmare ends. Nor where it begins. I knew
once, and now all I know is that I, too, want to be free of it. Yet it holds
me in its thrall, and refuses to acquiesce to my desire.

I am weak, dear hunter.

I began this letter knowing ... And now I only remember I truly do not
know anything at all.

How can I know what your choice is when I have forgotten my own?

Once upon a time, I was true. I only wish to be so again. Yet I cannot
tell what that is, what it means anymore, and the wait ...

... The wait is taking so very long.

Farewell, hunter.

— Gehrman

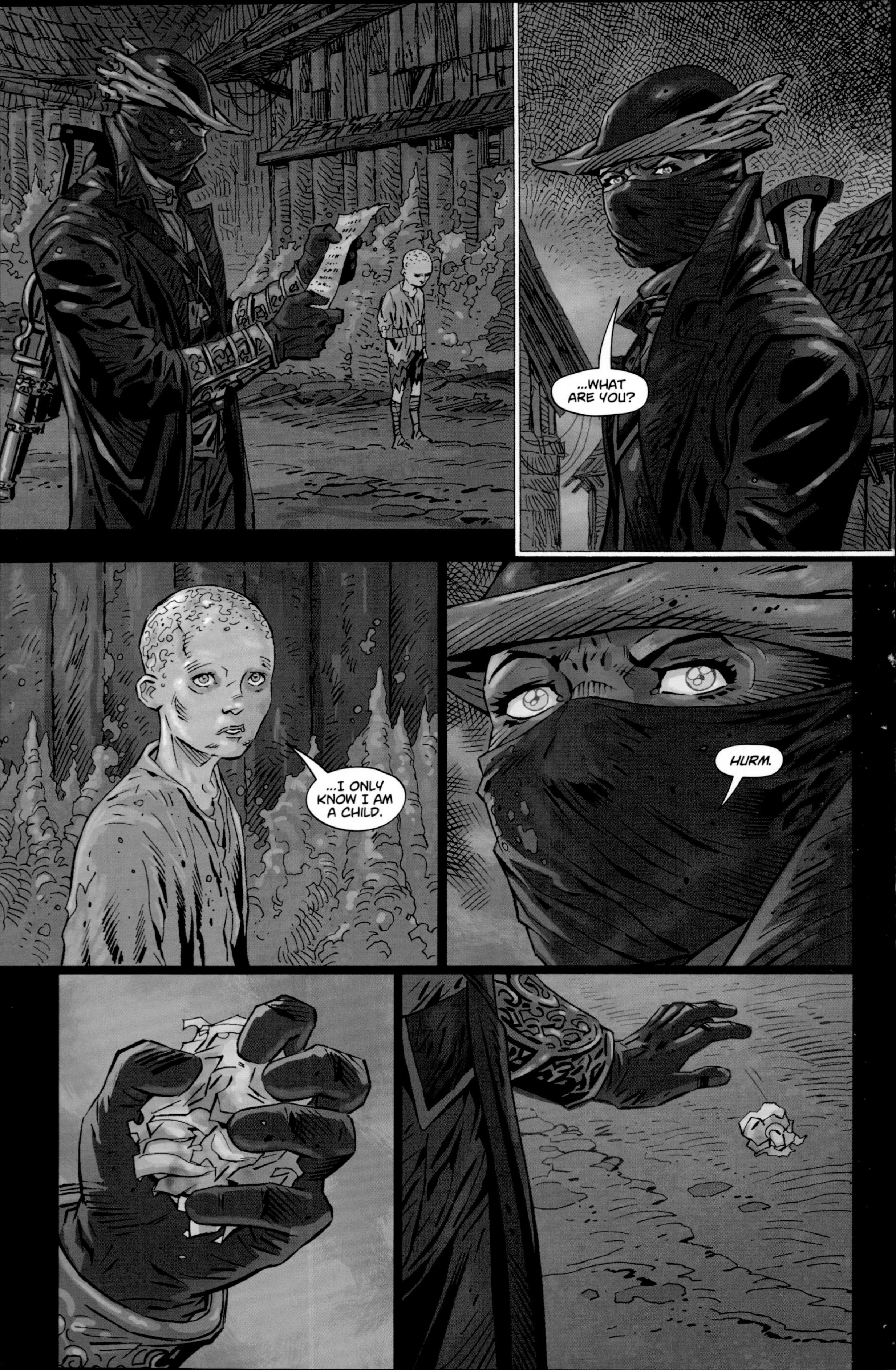
...WHAT ARE YOU?
...I ONLY KNOW I AM A CHILD.
HURM.

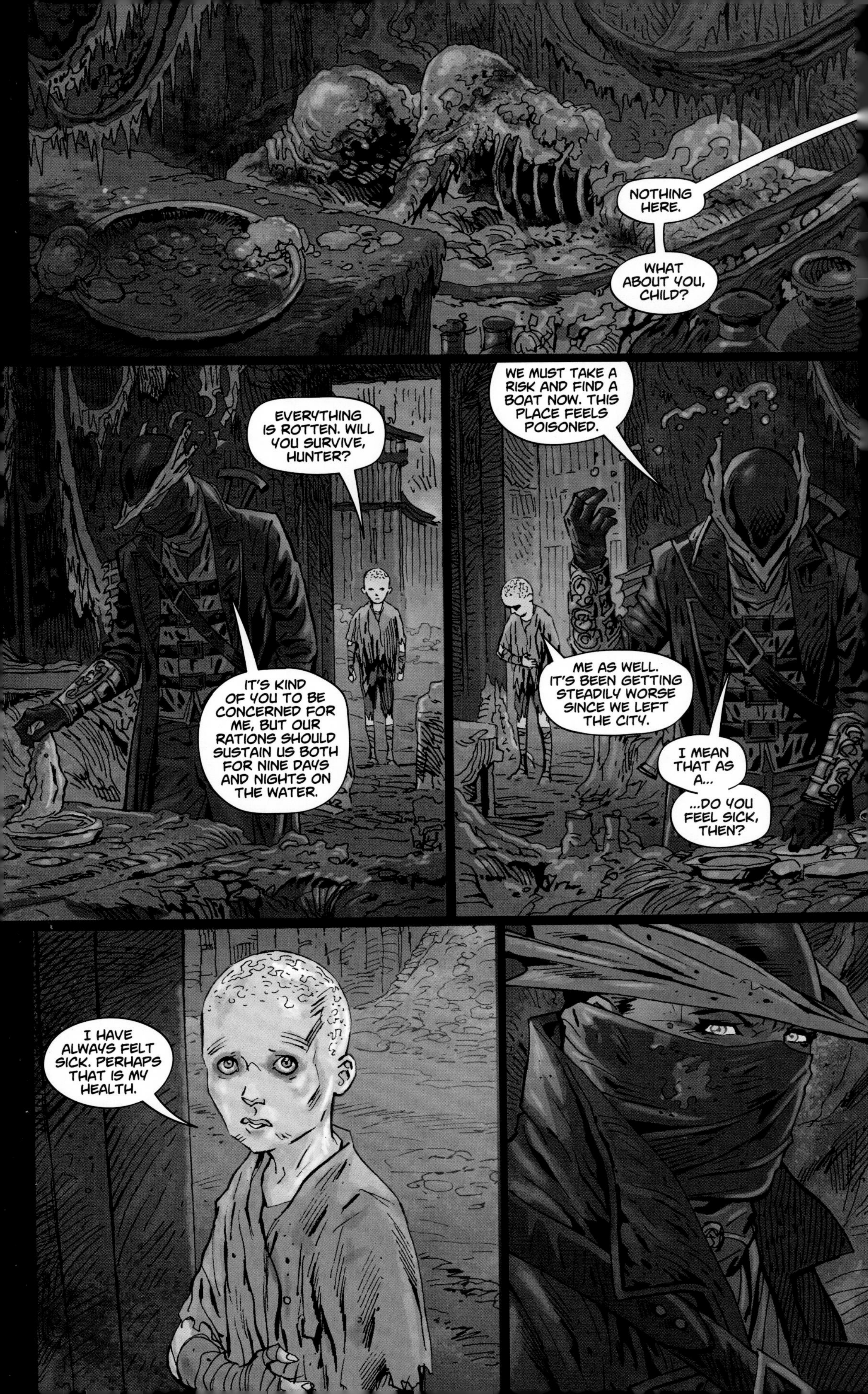
NOTHING HERE.
WHAT ABOUT YOU, CHILD?
EVERYTHING IS ROTTEN. WILL YOU SURVIVE, HUNTER?
IT'S KIND OF YOU TO BE CONCERNED FOR ME, BUT OUR RATIONS SHOULD SUSTAIN US BOTH FOR NINE DAYS AND NIGHTS ON THE WATER.
WE MUST TAKE A RISK AND FIND A BOAT NOW. THIS PLACE FEELS POISONED.
ME AS WELL. IT'S BEEN GETTING STEADILY WORSE SINCE WE LEFT THE CITY.
I MEAN THAT AS A...
...DO YOU FEEL SICK, THEN?
I HAVE ALWAYS FELT SICK. PERHAPS THAT IS MY HEALTH.

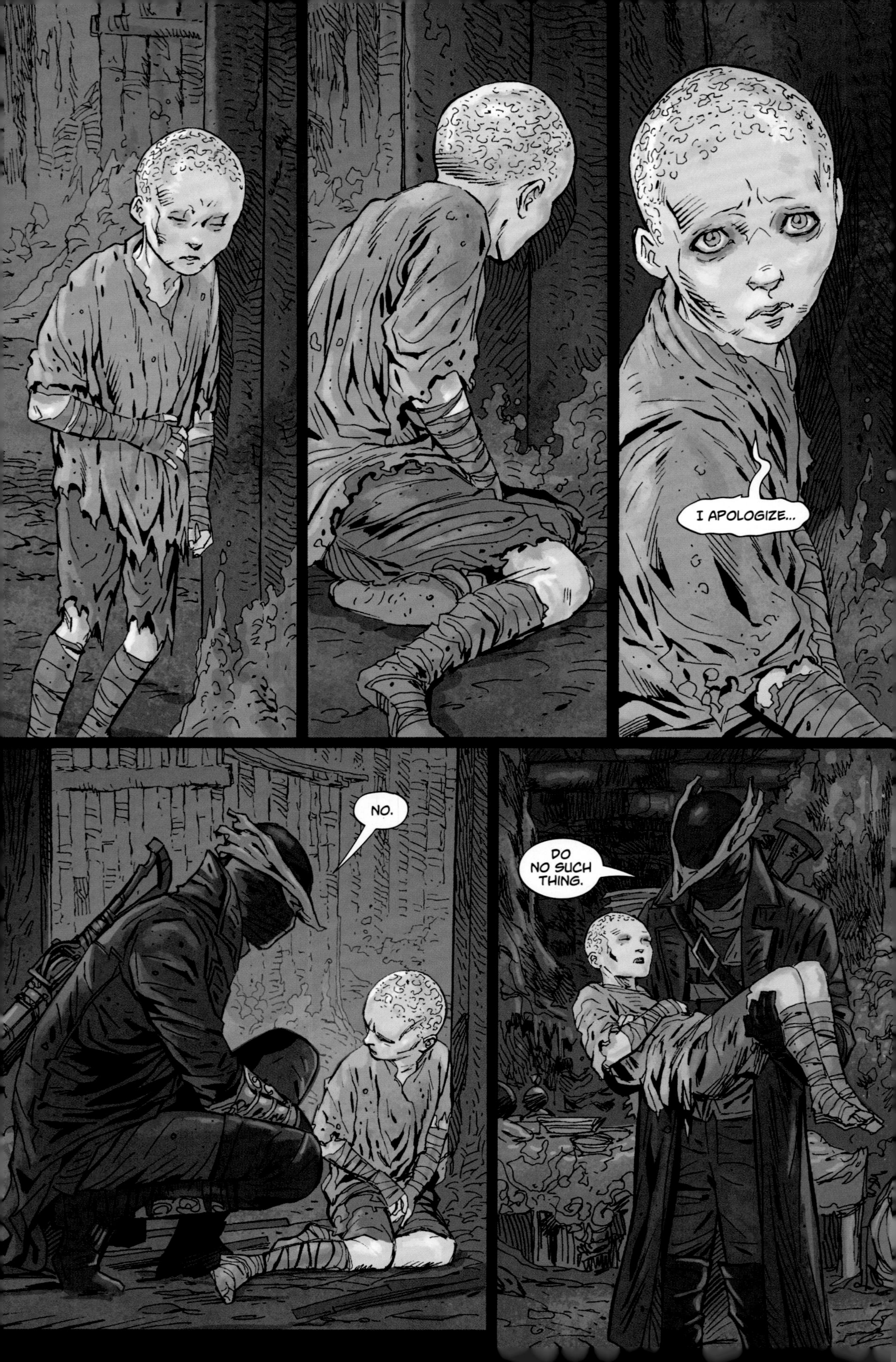
I APOLOGIZE...
NO.
DO NO SUCH THING.

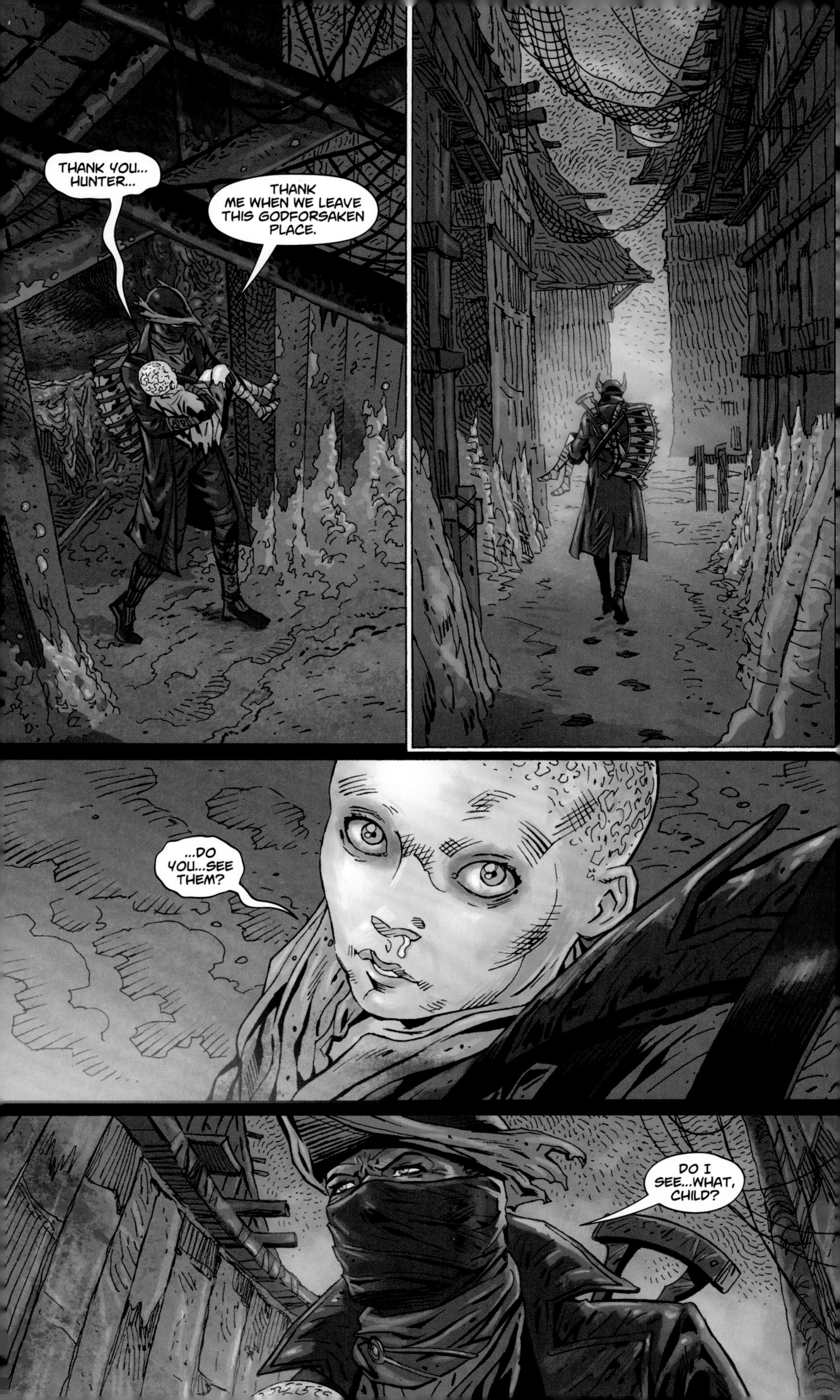
THANK YOU... HUNTER...
THANK ME WHEN WE LEAVE THIS GODFORSAKEN PLACE.
...DO YOU...SEE THEM?
DO I SEE...WHAT, CHILD?

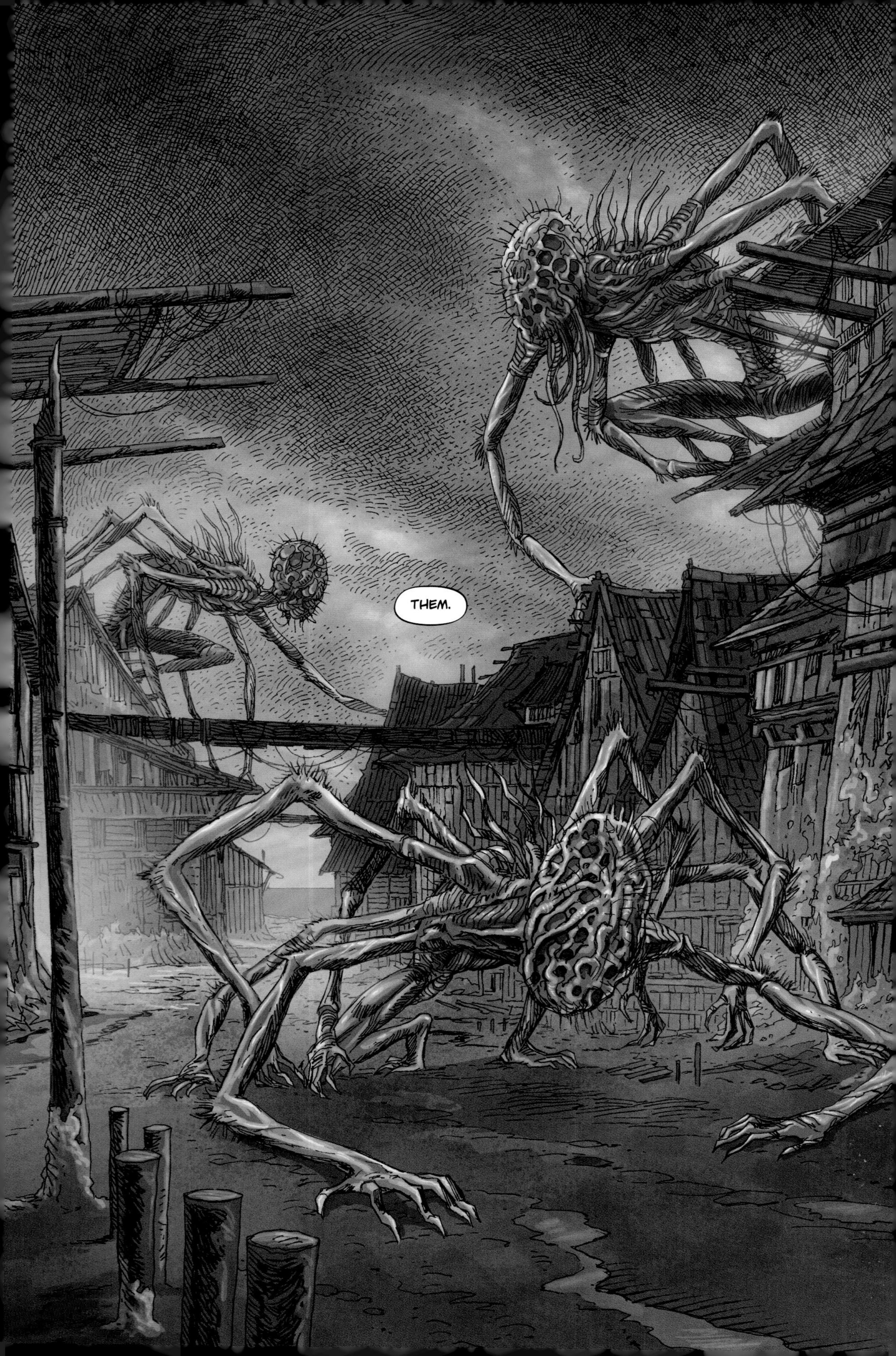
THEM.

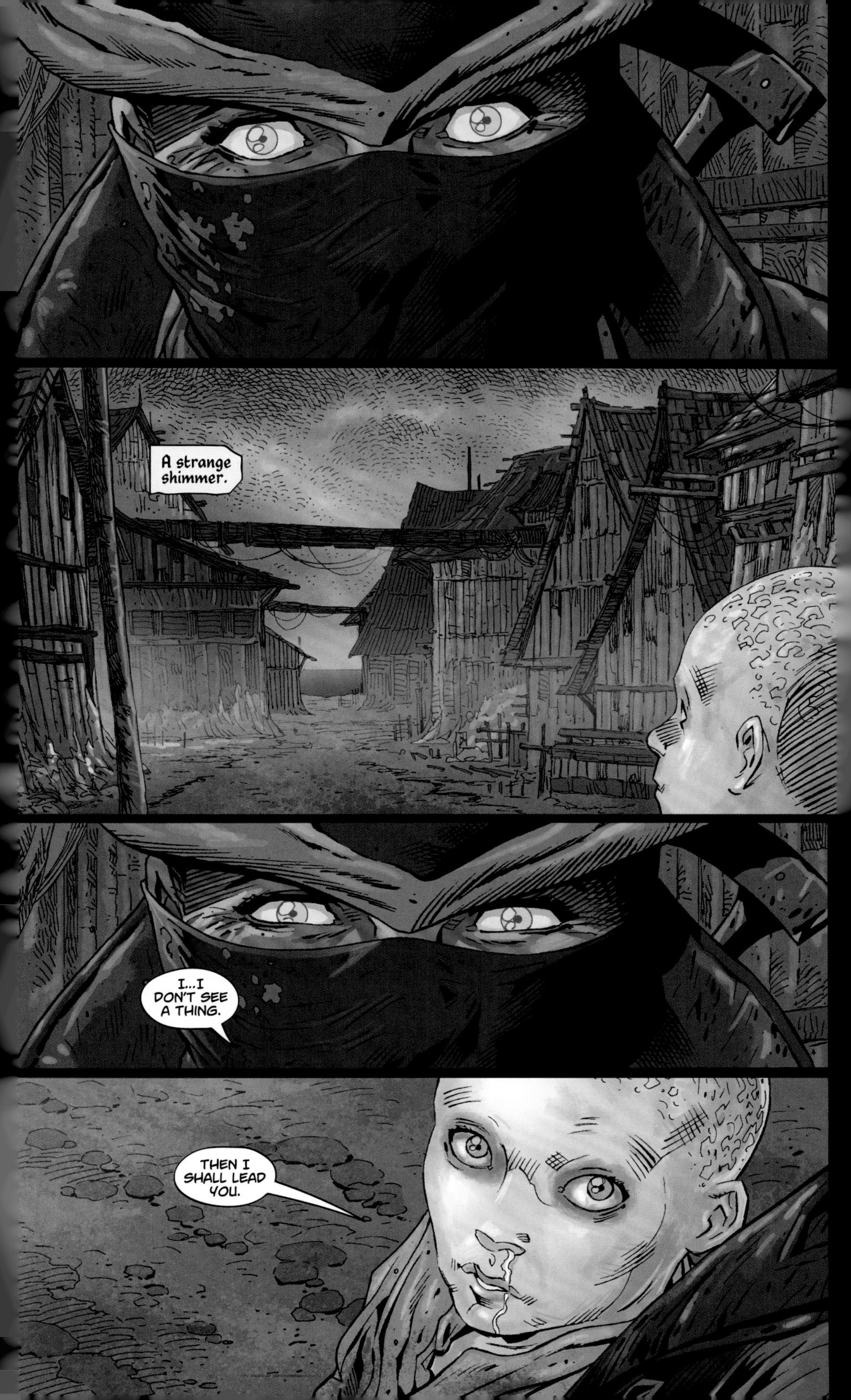
A strange shimmer.
I...I DON'T SEE A THING.
THEN I SHALL LEAD YOU.

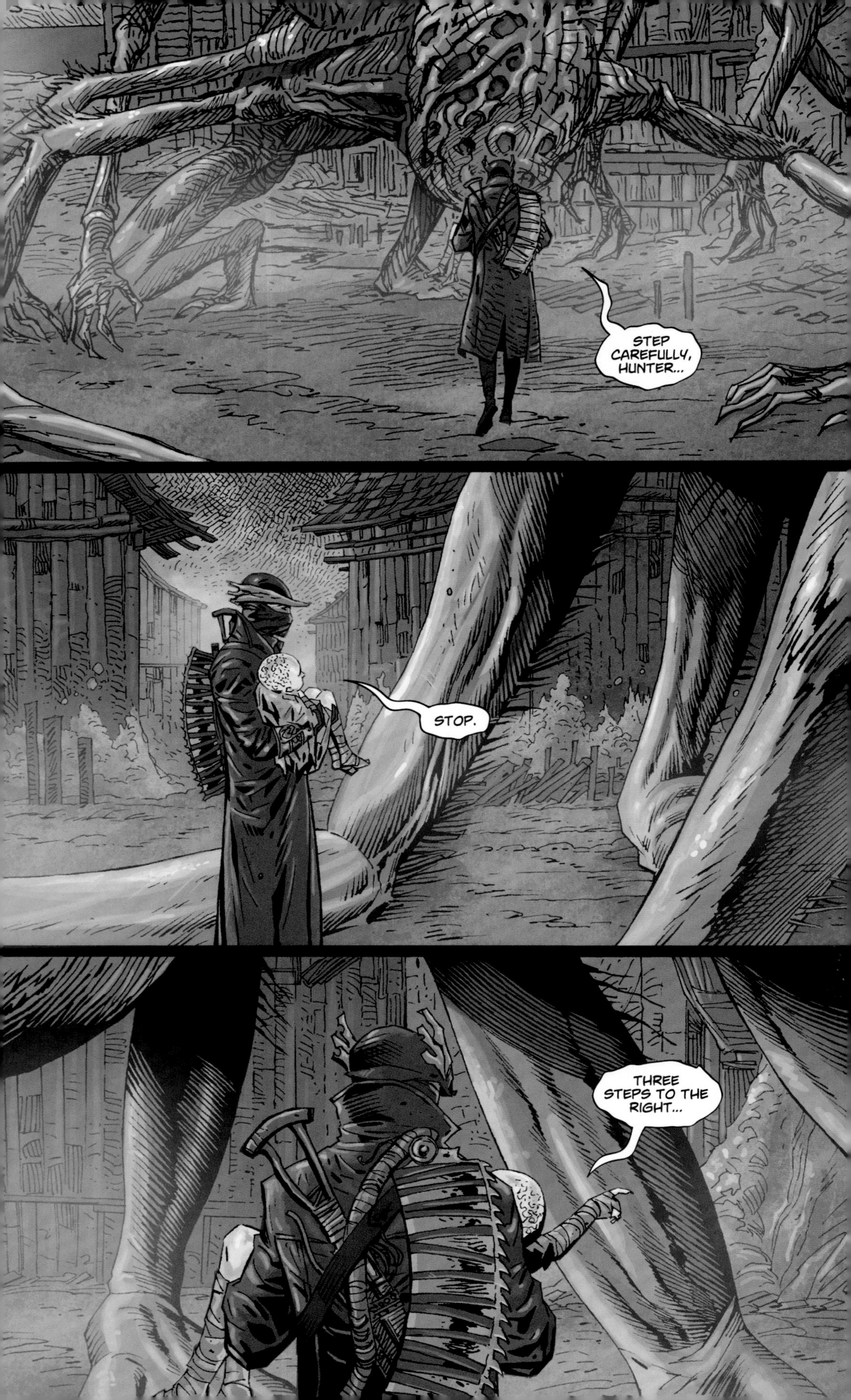
STEP CAREFULLY, HUNTER...
STOP.
THREE STEPS TO THE RIGHT...

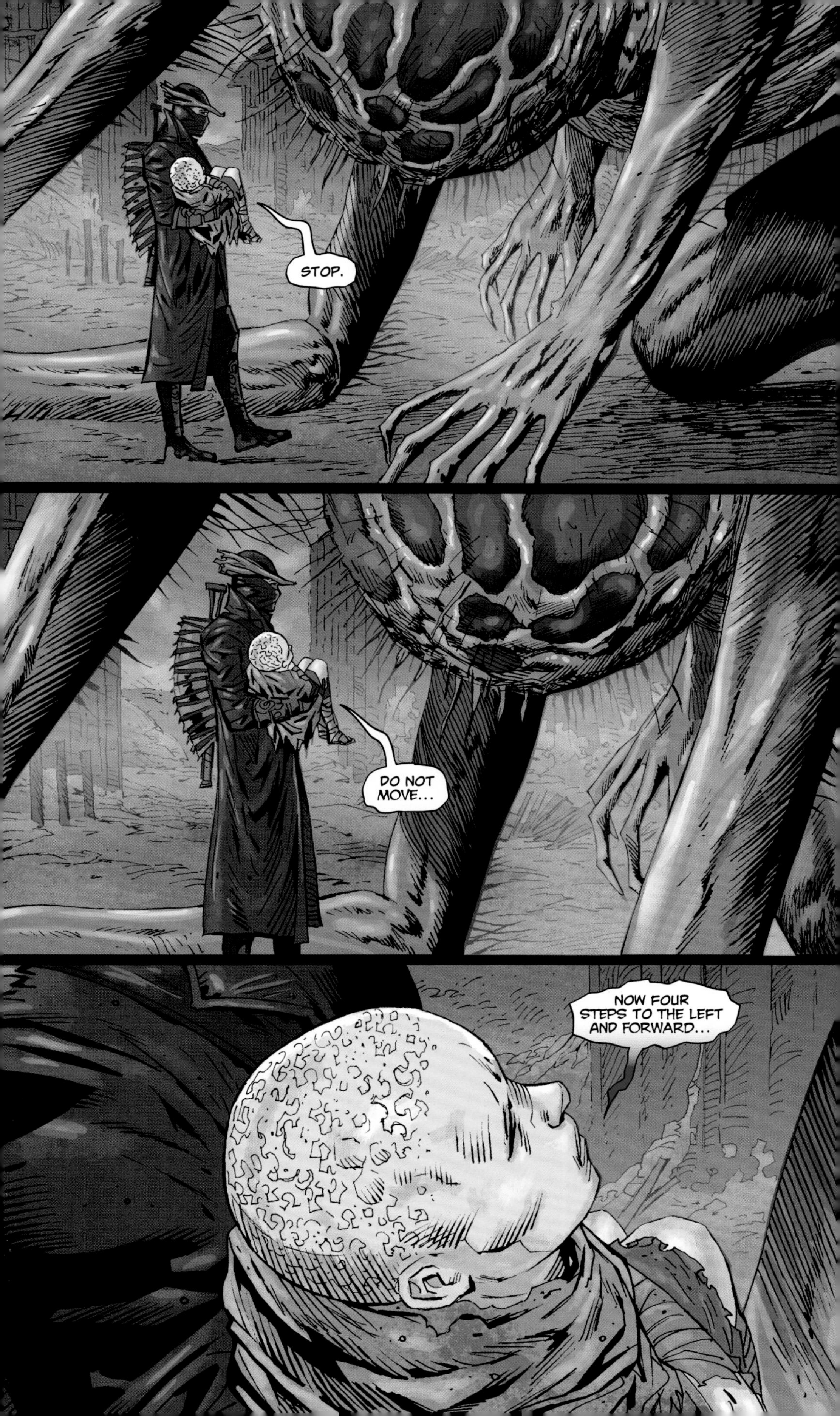
STOP.
DO NOT MOVE...
NOW FOUR STEPS TO THE LEFT AND FORWARD...

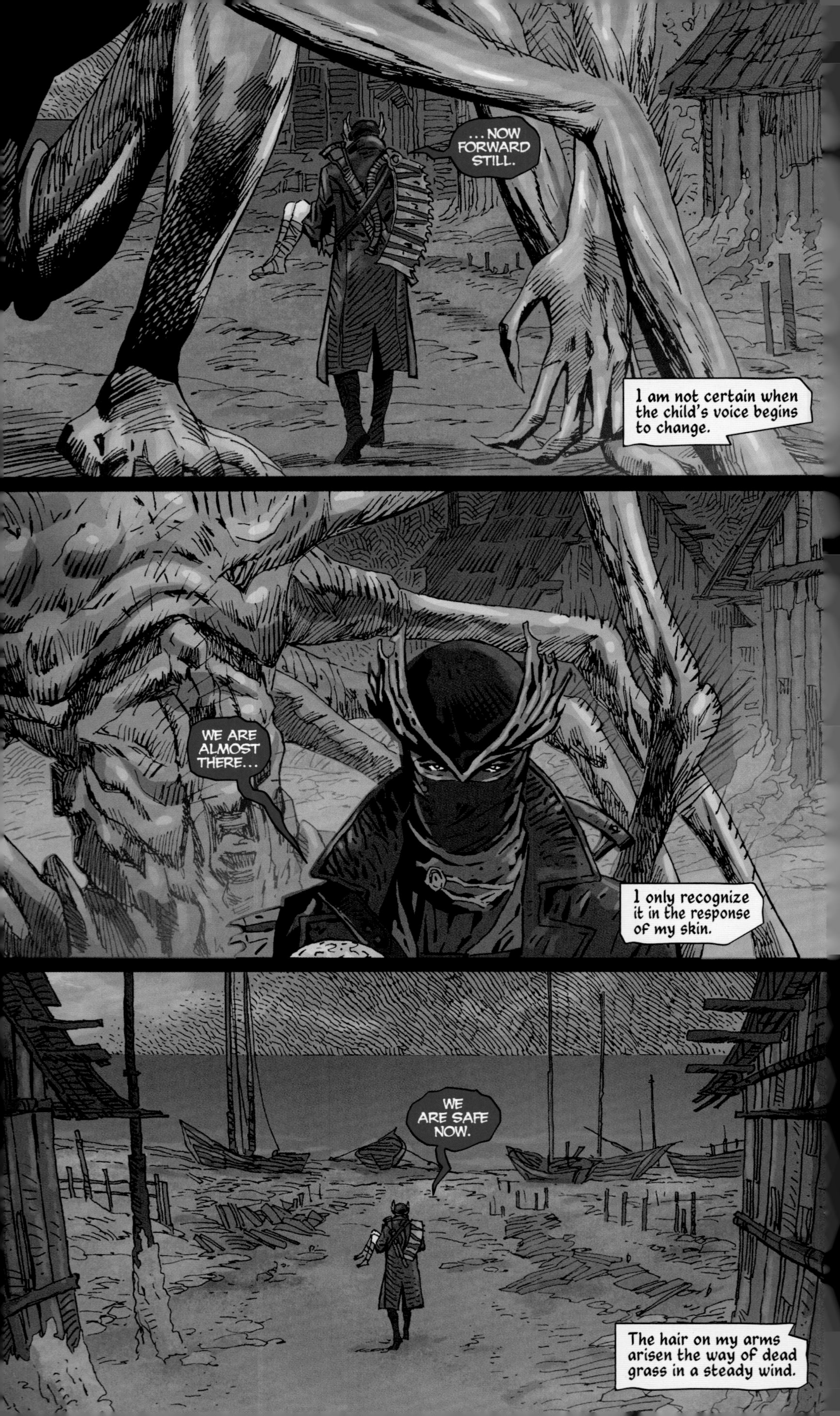
...NOW FORWARD STILL.
I am not certain when the child's voice begins to change.
WE ARE ALMOST THERE...
I only recognize it in the response of my skin.
WE ARE SAFE NOW.
The hair on my arms arisen the way of dead grass in a steady wind.

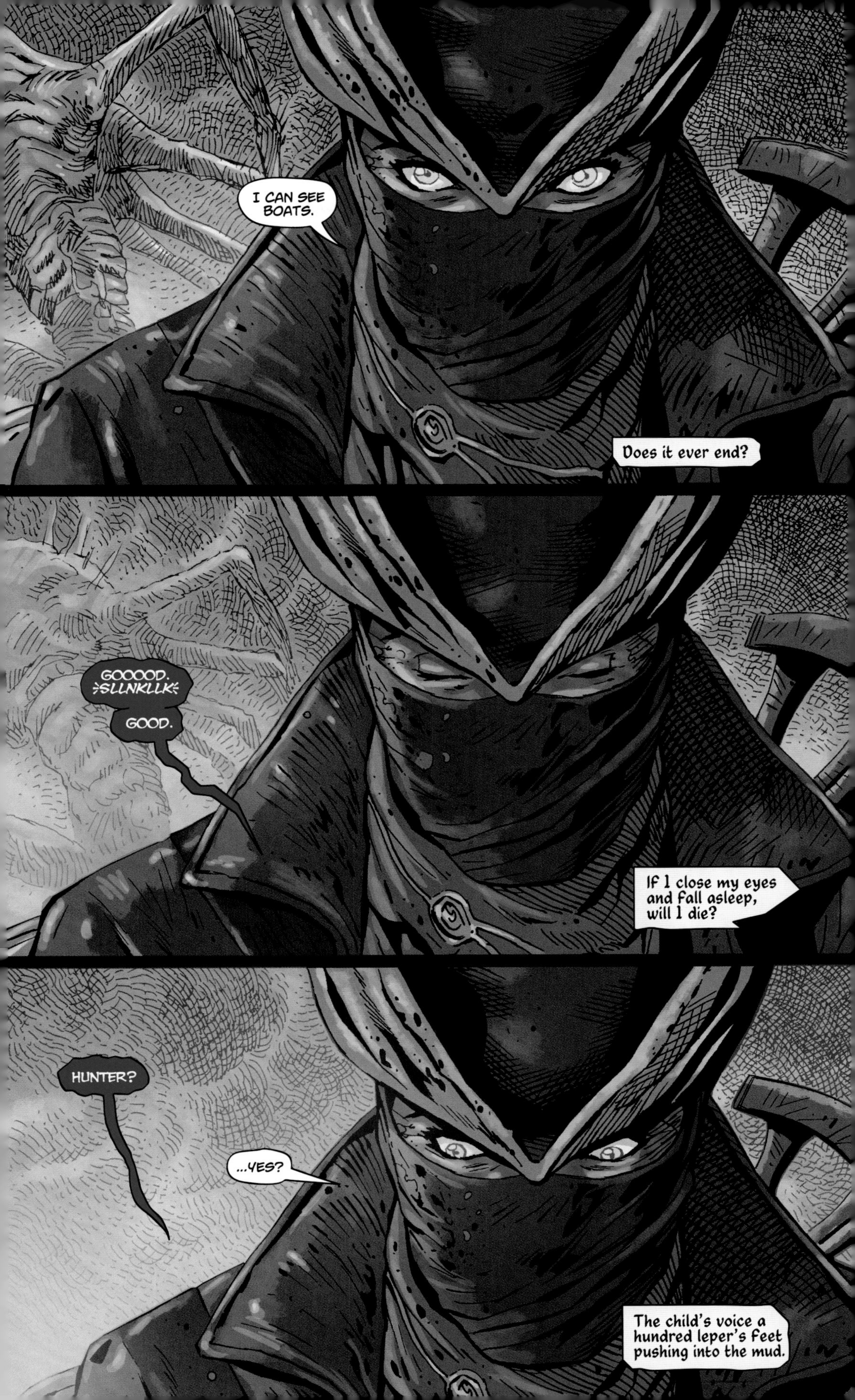
I CAN SEE BOATS.
Does it ever end?
GOOOOD. SLLNKLLK
GOOD.
If I close my eyes and fall asleep, will I die?
HUNTER?
...YES?
The child's voice a hundred leper's feet pushing into the mud.

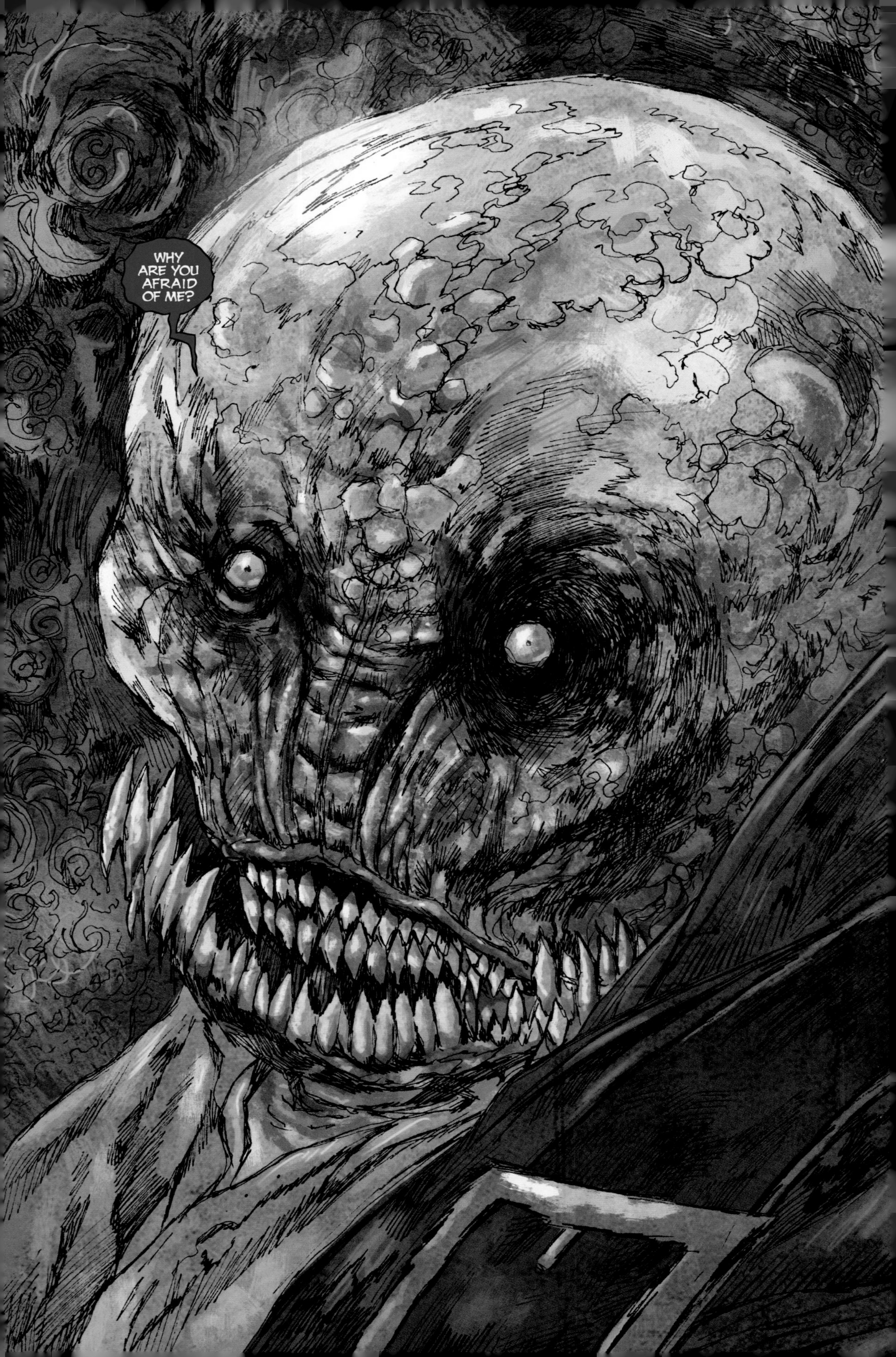
WHY ARE YOU AFRAID OF ME?

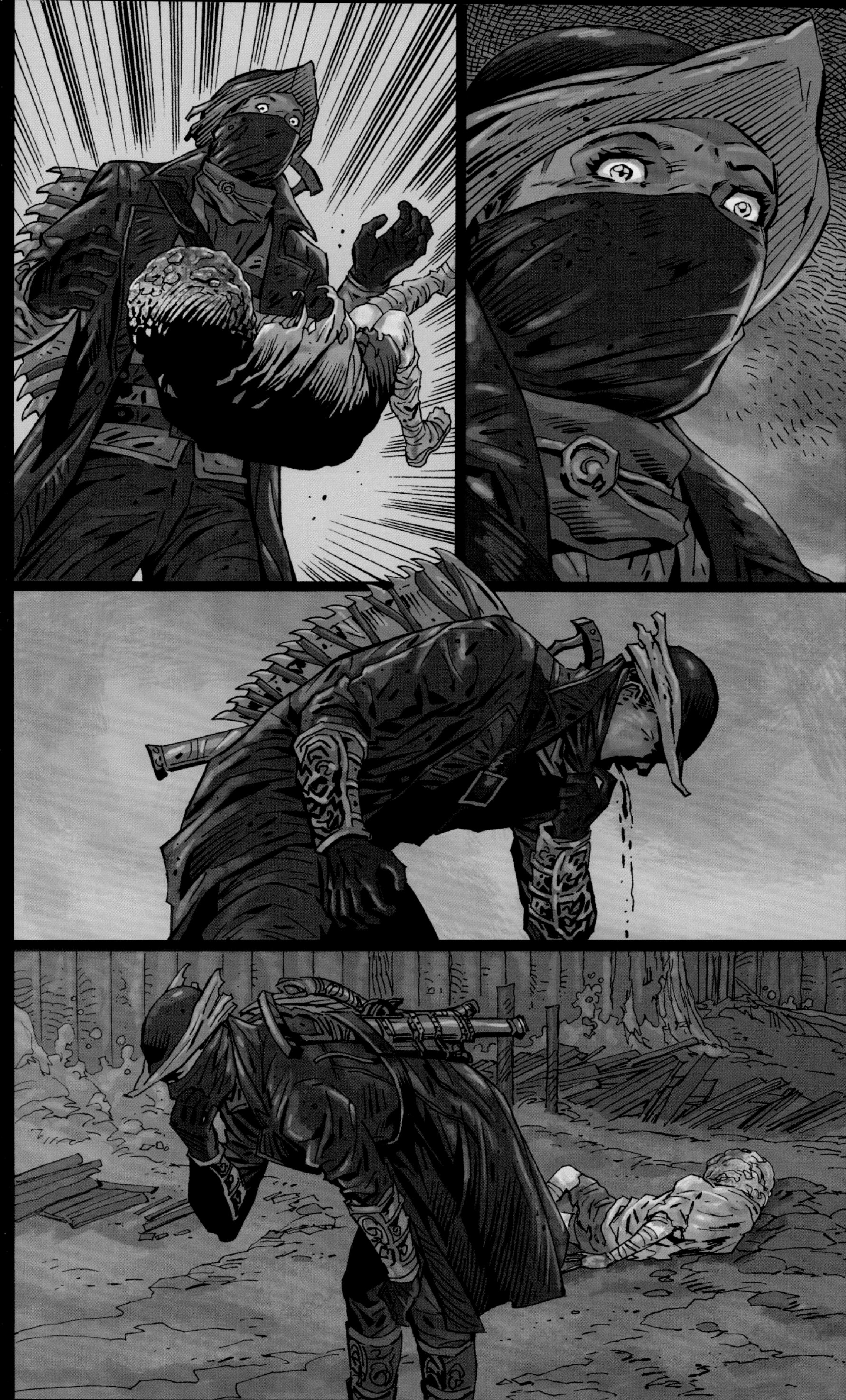

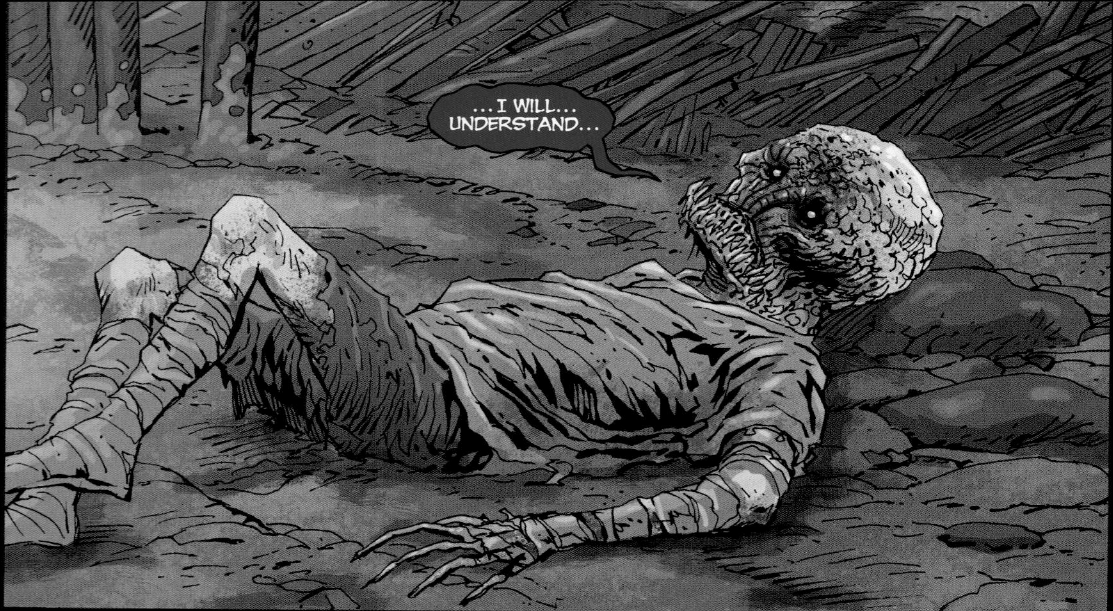
...I WILL... UNDERSTAND...

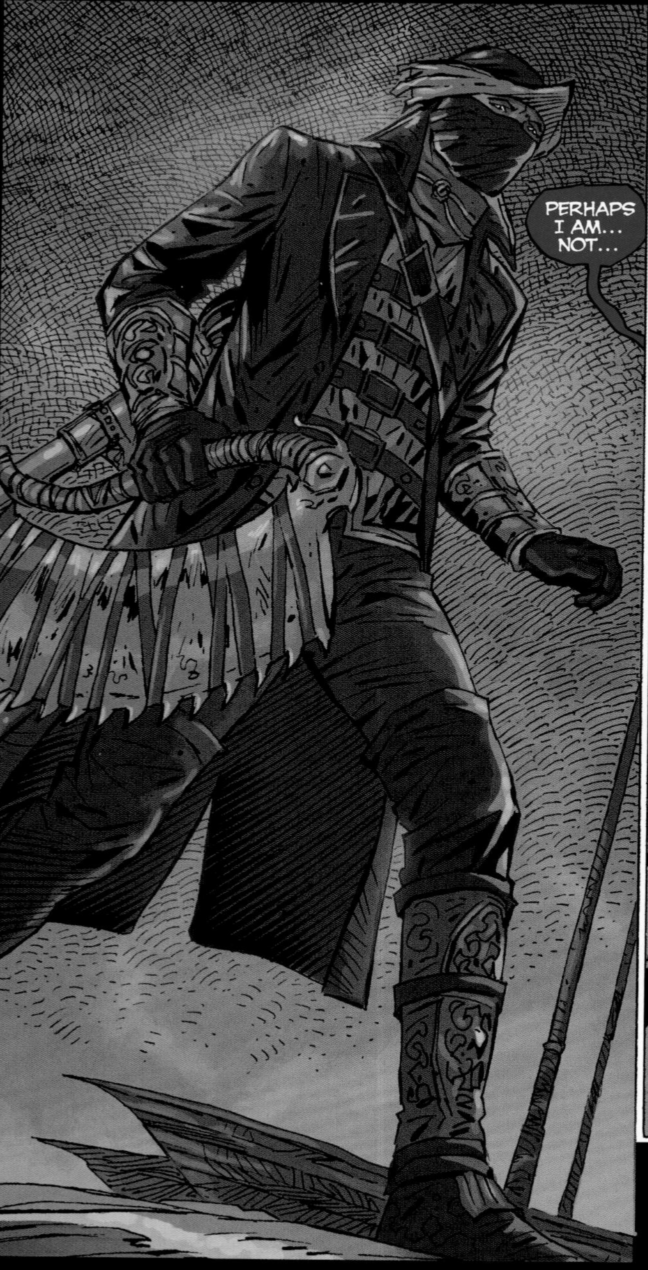
PERHAPS I AM... NOT...

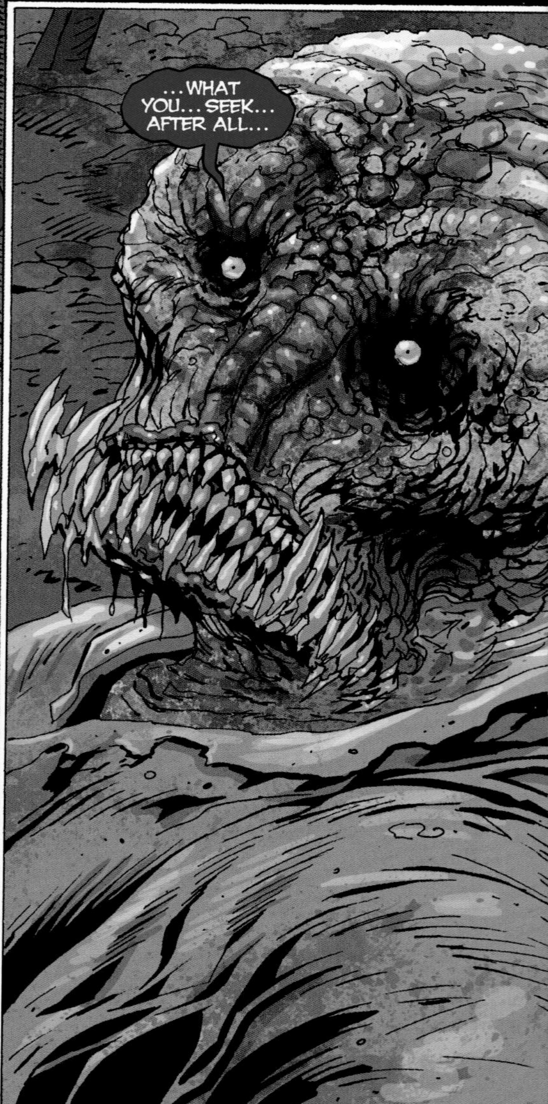
...WHAT YOU... SEEK... AFTER ALL...

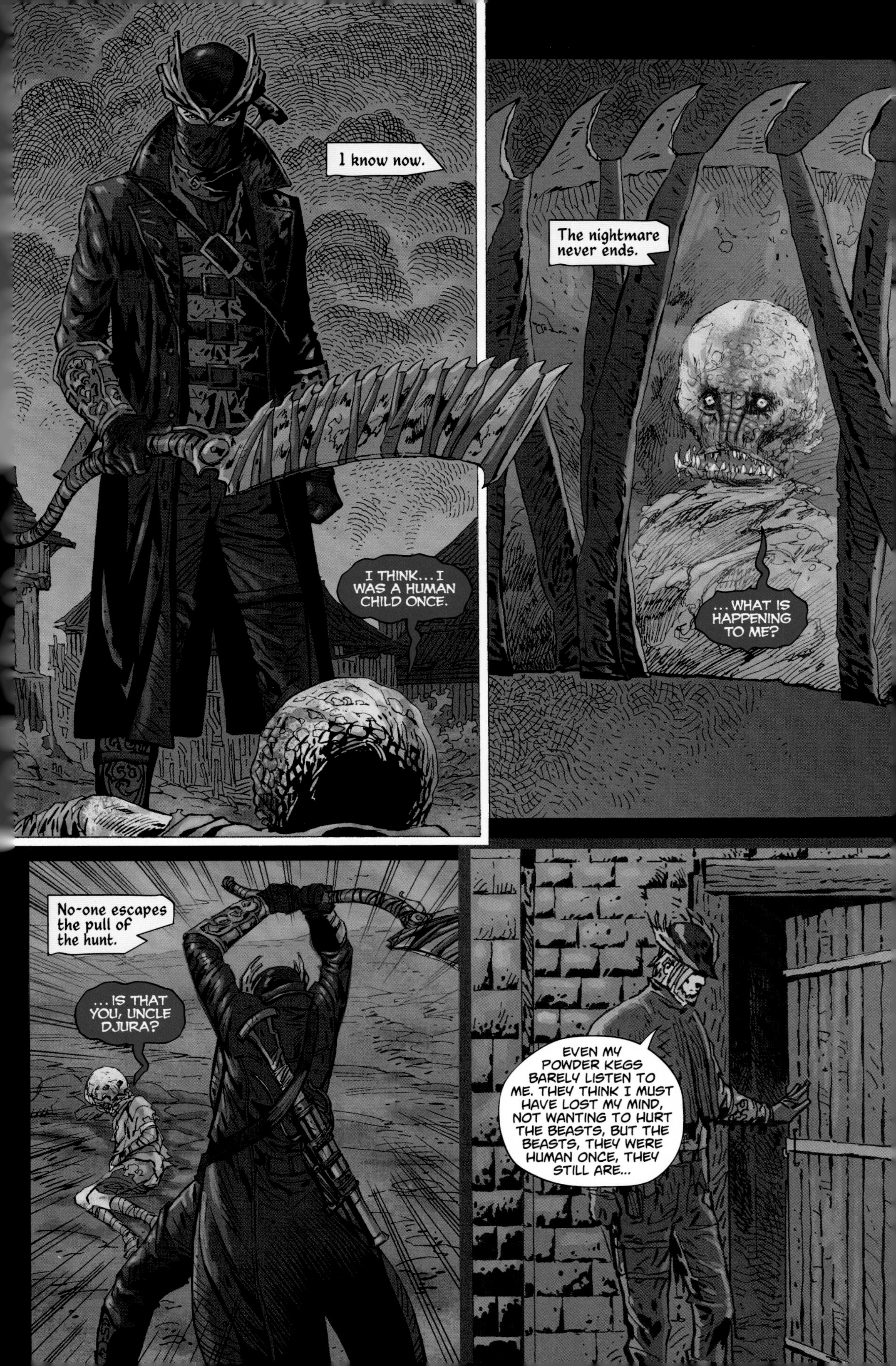
I know now.
I THINK... I WAS A HUMAN CHILD ONCE.
The nightmare never ends.
...WHAT IS HAPPENING TO ME?
No-one escapes the pull of the hunt.
...IS THAT YOU, UNCLE DJURA?
EVEN MY POWDER KEGS BARELY LISTEN TO ME. THEY THINK I MUST HAVE LOST MY MIND, NOT WANTING TO HURT THE BEASTS, BUT THE BEASTS, THEY WERE HUMAN ONCE, THEY STILL ARE...

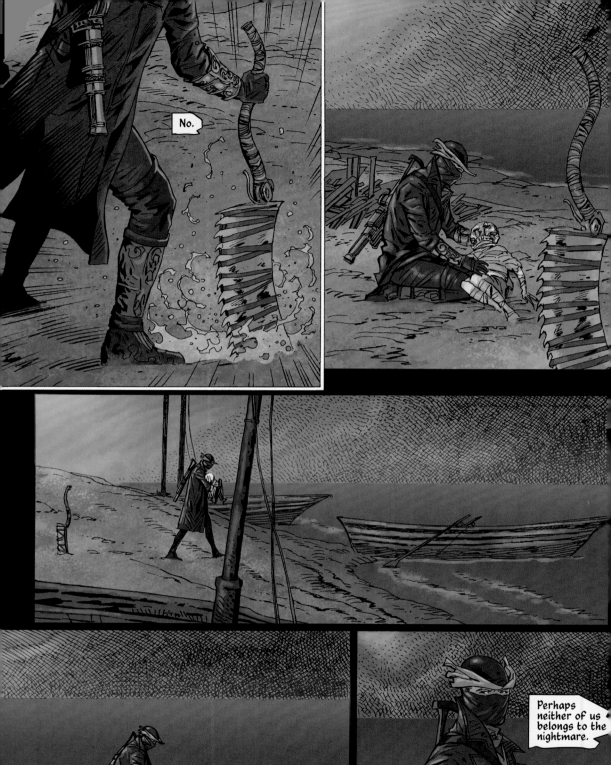

No.

Perhaps neither of us belongs to the nightmare.

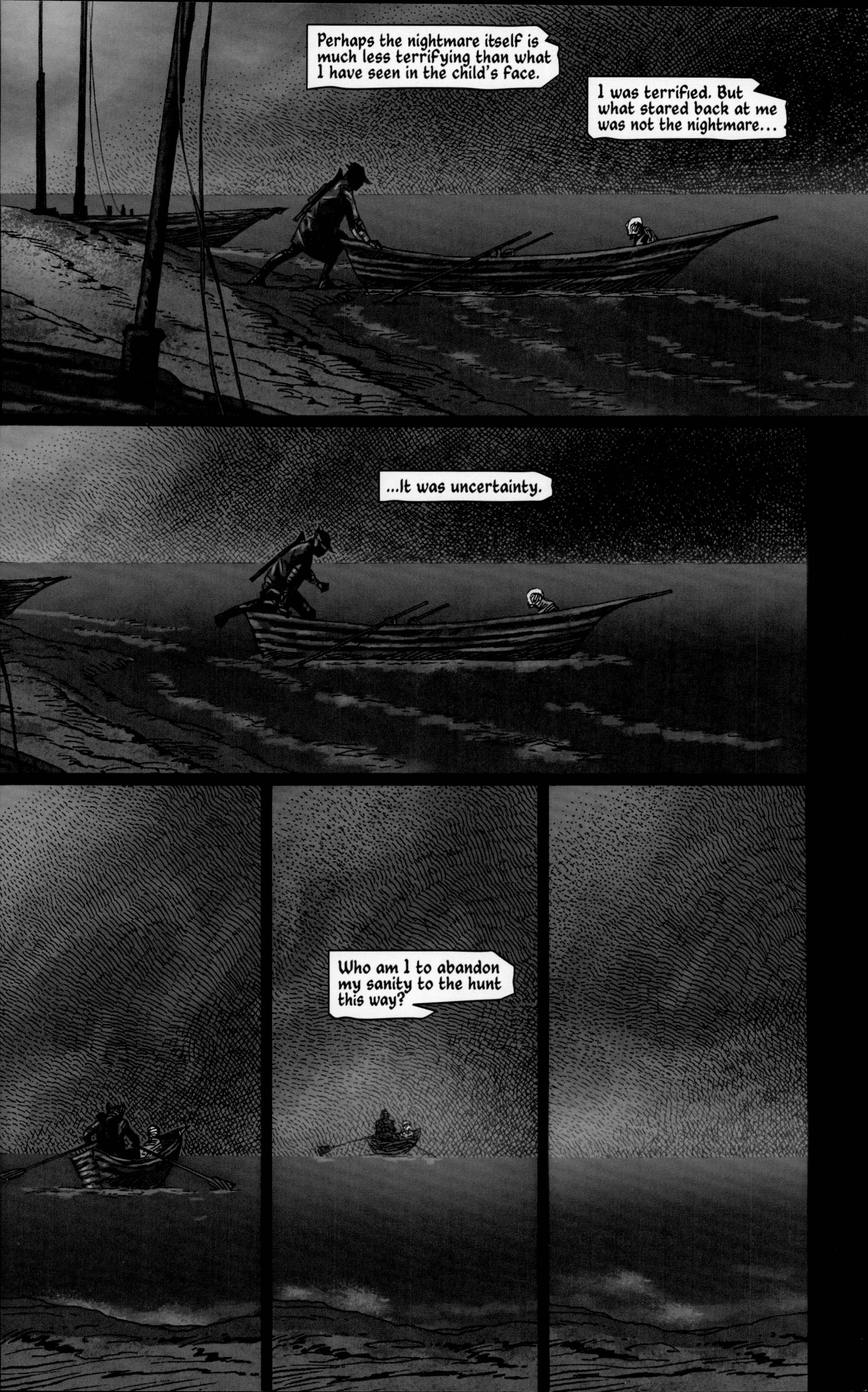

Perhaps the nightmare itself is much less terrifying than what I have seen in the child's face.
I was terrified. But what stared back at me was not the nightmare...
...It was uncertainty.
Who am I to abandon my sanity to the hunt this way?

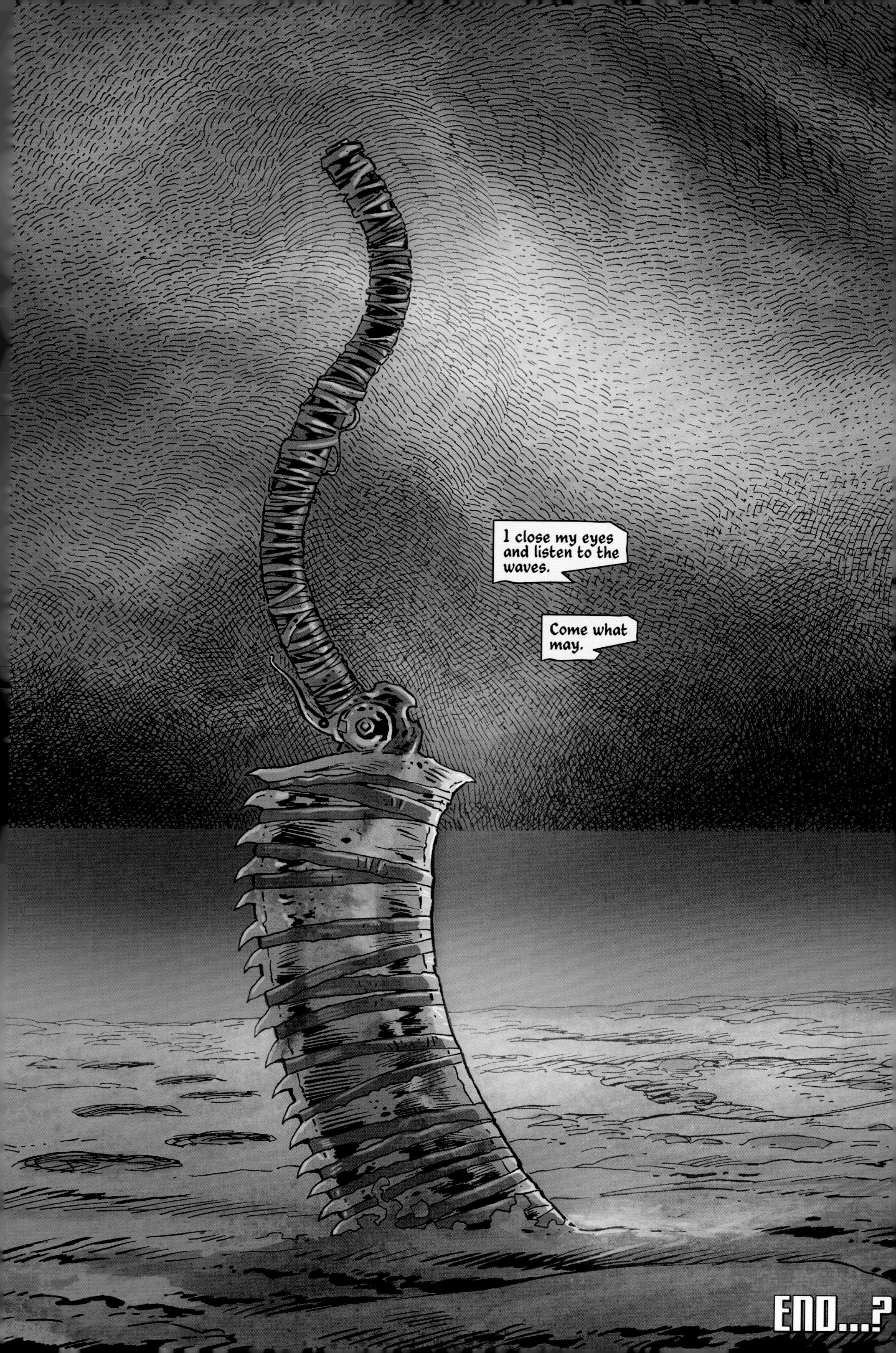
I close my eyes and listen to the waves.
Come what may.
END...?

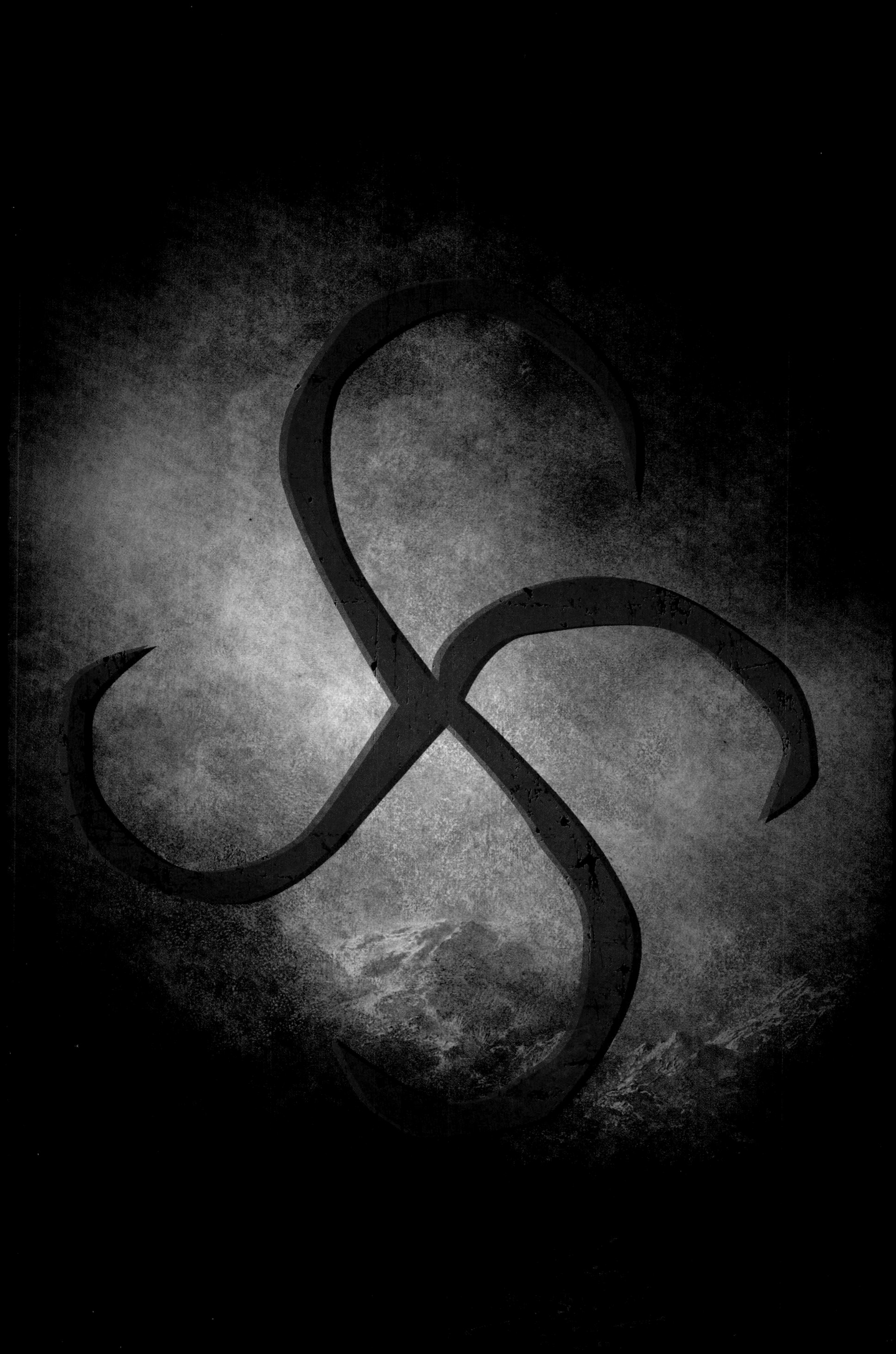

Bloodborne
COVER GALLERY

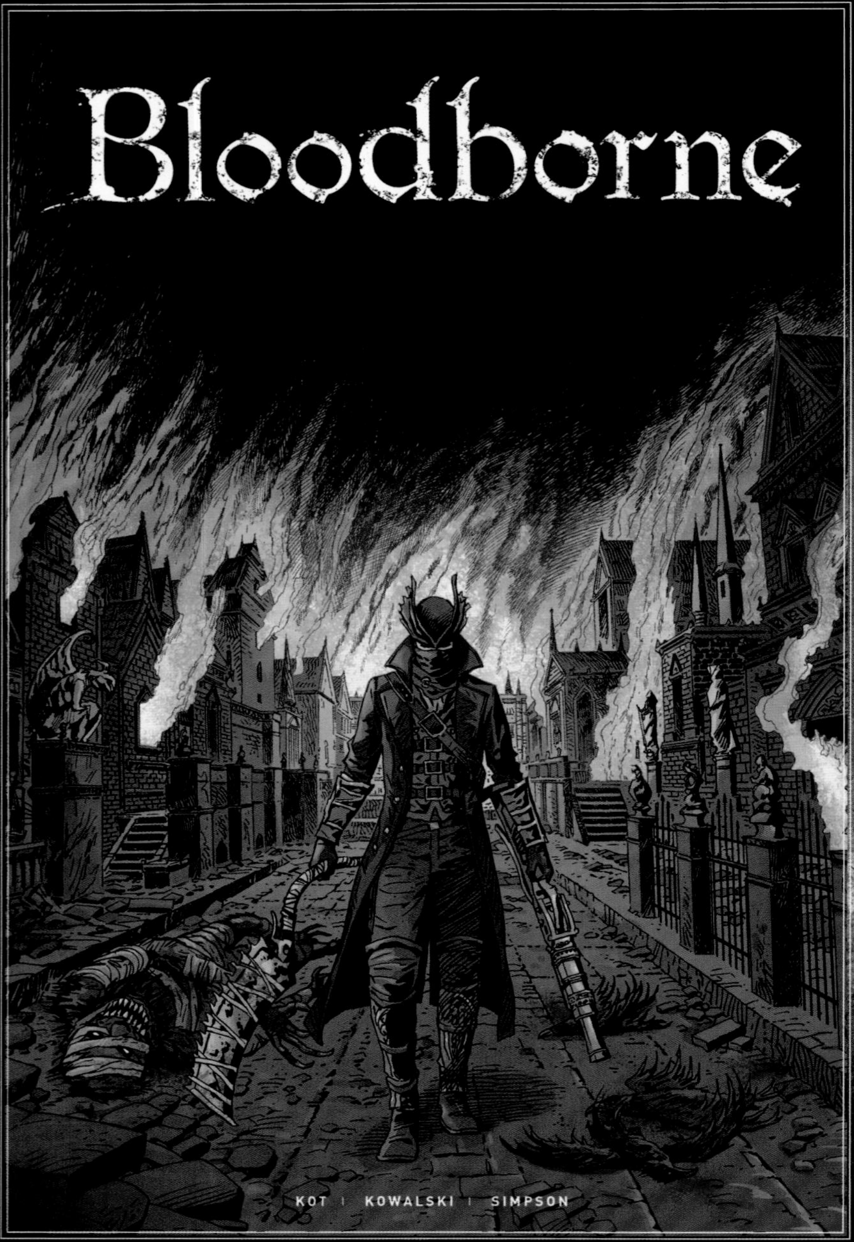
Bloodborne
KOT | KOWALSKI | SIMPSON

#1 COVER C
PIOTR KOWALSKI
& BRAD SIMPSON

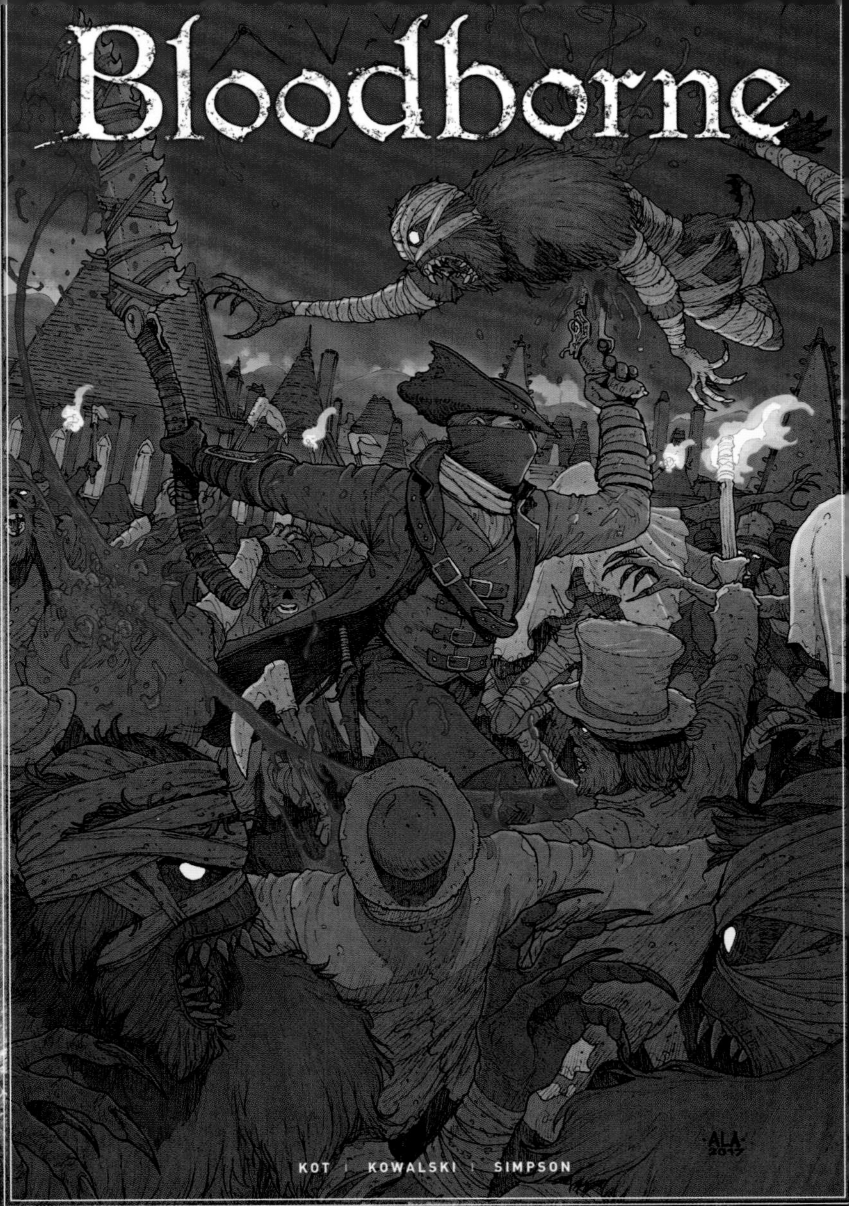
Bloodborne
KOT | KOWALSKI | SIMPSON
ALA 2017

ISSUE #1 COVER D
ANDRE LIMA ARAUJO
& CHIS O'HALLORAN

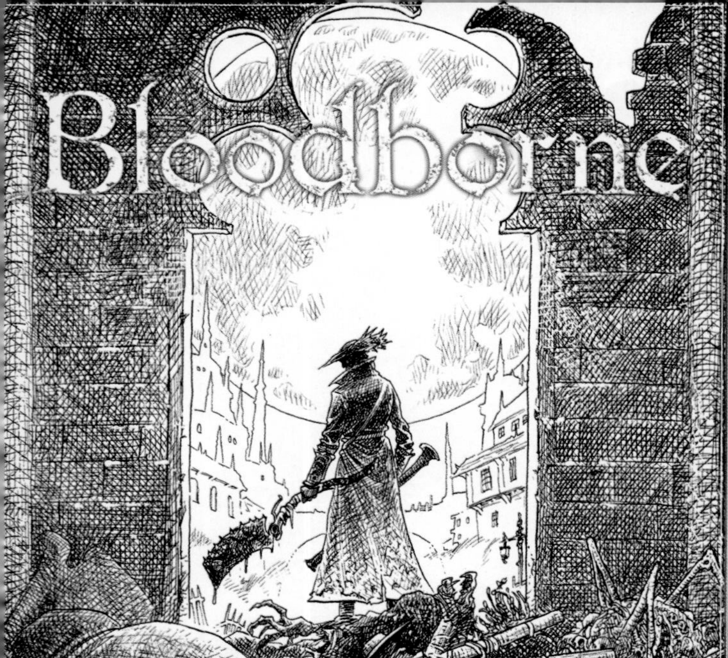
Bloodborne
KOT
KOWALSKI
SIMPSON
AFTER DORÉ

ISSUE #1
REPRINT COVER A
JEFF STOKELY

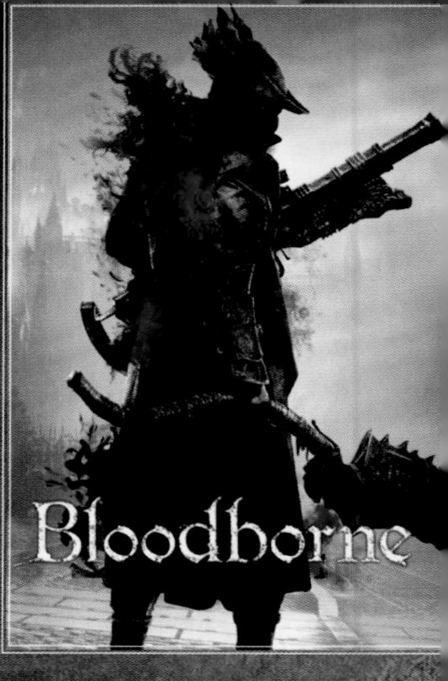
Bloodborne

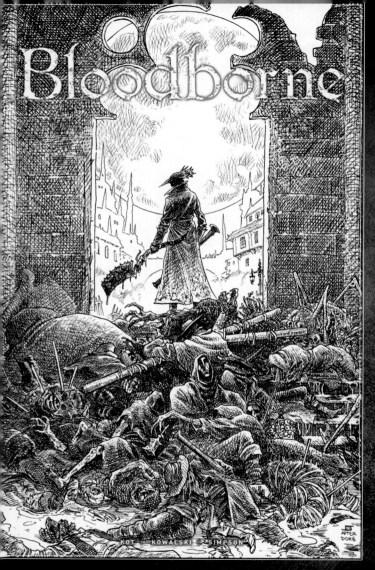

#1 FP/JETPACK VARIANT
GAME COVER

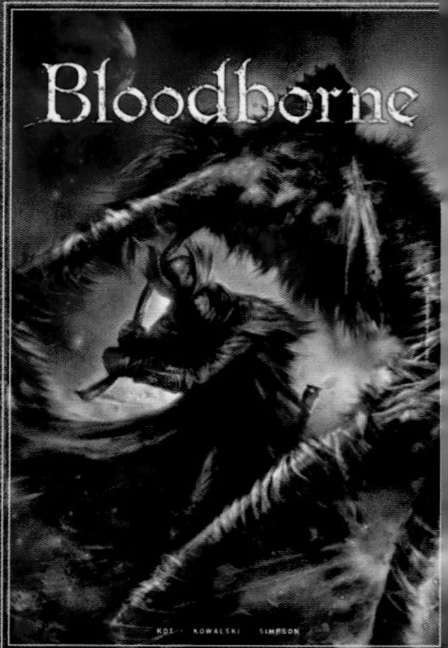
Bloodborne
KOT
KOWALSKI
SIMPSON

ISSUE #1
BORDERLANDS VARIANT
NICK PERCIVAL

GAME COVERS

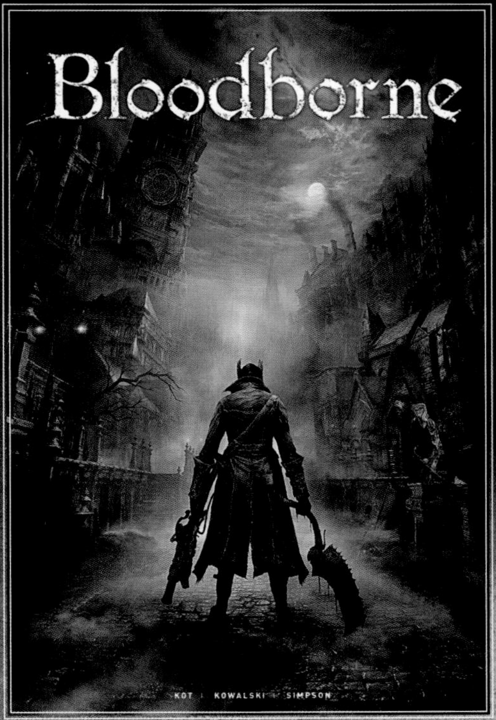
Bloodborne
KOT | KOWALSKI | SIMPSON

ISSUE #1

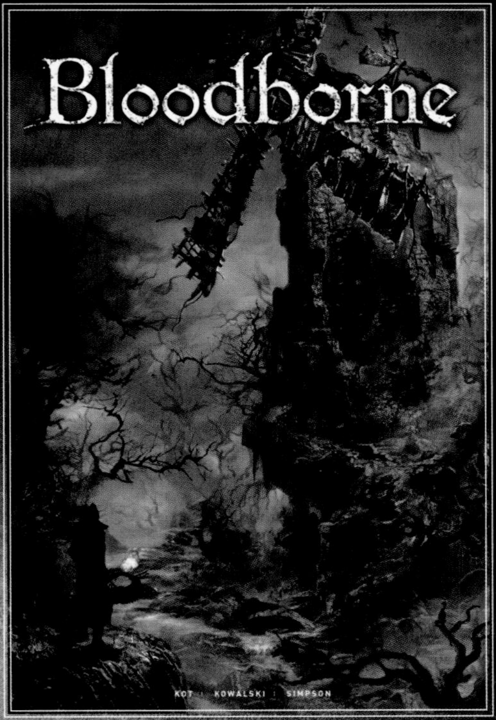
Bloodborne
KOT | KOWALSKI | SIMPSON

ISSUE #2

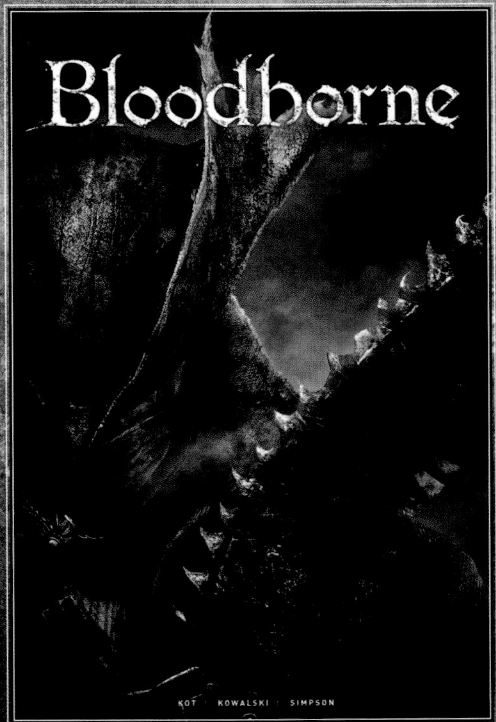
Bloodborne
KOT | KOWALSKI | SIMPSON

ISSUE #3

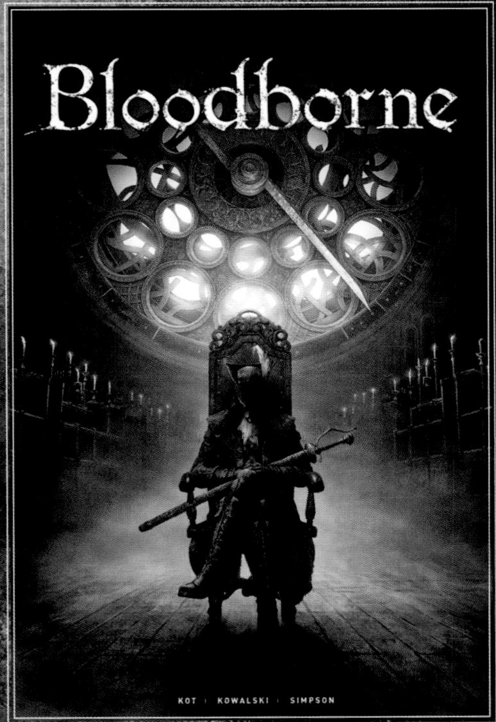
Bloodborne
KOT | KOWALSKI | SIMPSON

ISSUE #4

ART PROCESS

Here's a quick glimpse into the artistic process required to bring the horrors and gnarled beauty of *Bloodborne* to the page.

Okay, Piotr...consider this chapter one long take, in film terms. I want this to feel like we never leave the protagonists -- even though we cut a few times because the time changes, we never go to anyone else but the Hunter and the Child. We stay with them throughout the issue.

Of equal importance to this are Friedrich's paintings. Brad, Piotr, this note is for you both -- let's please replicate the openness, melancholy and solemn beauty of decay Friedrich repeatedly shows. I'll include specific painting references throughout the script -- please use them for further inspiration in both drawing and coloring.

PAGE 12-13

Splash page.

This is a direct homage to this Caspar David Friedrich painting. Including colors.

The Hunter and the Child remain in their poses from the previous pag

That's all.

SCRIPT BY ALES KOT

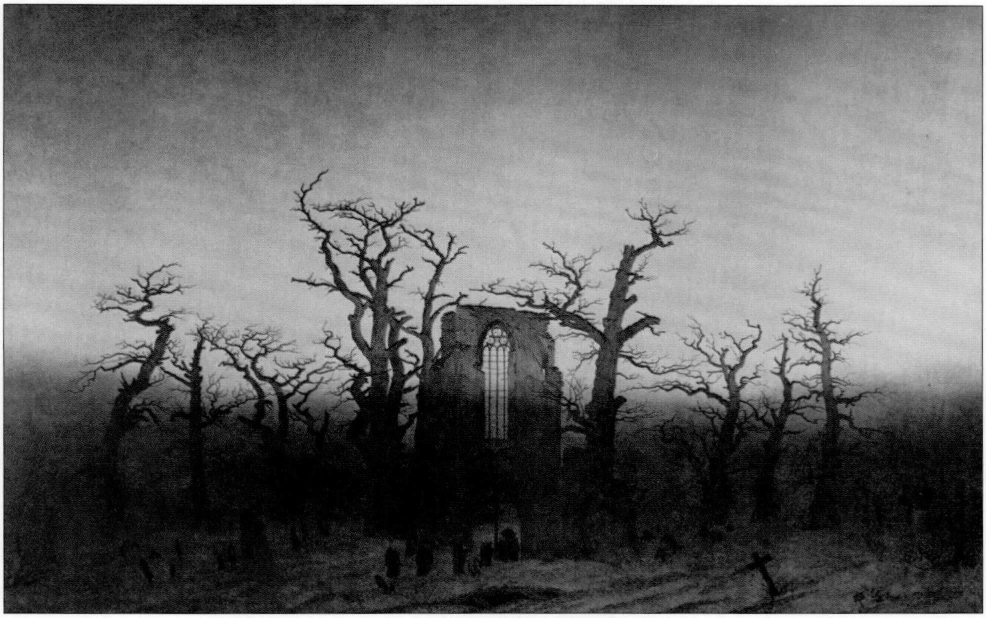

'THE ABBEY IN THE OAKWOOD' BY CASPAR DAVID FRIEDRICH

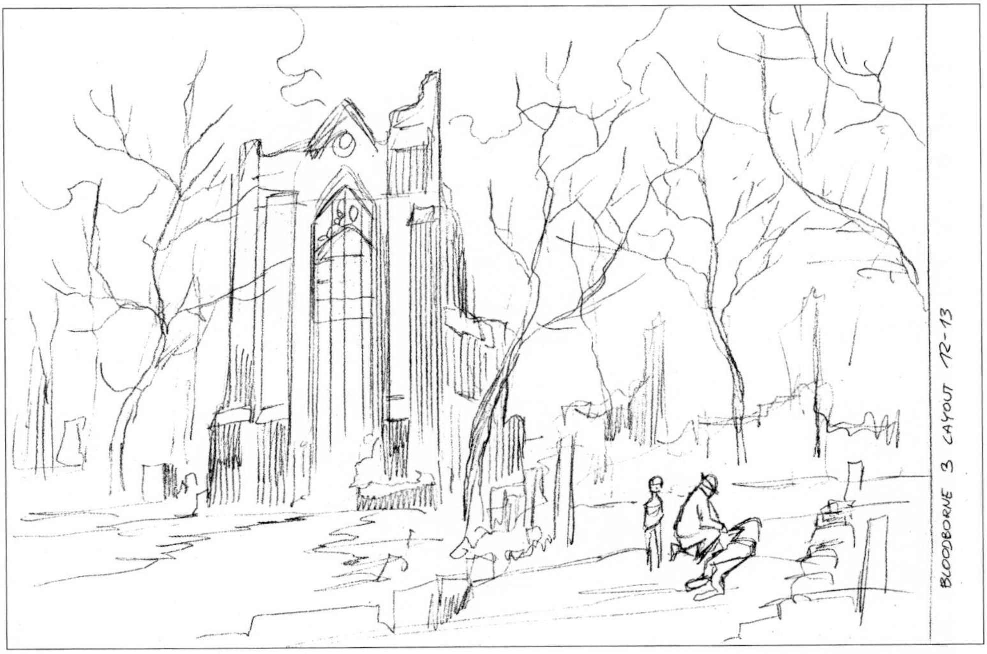
BLOODBORNE 3 LAYOUT 12-13

THUMBNAILS BY PIOTR KOWALSKI

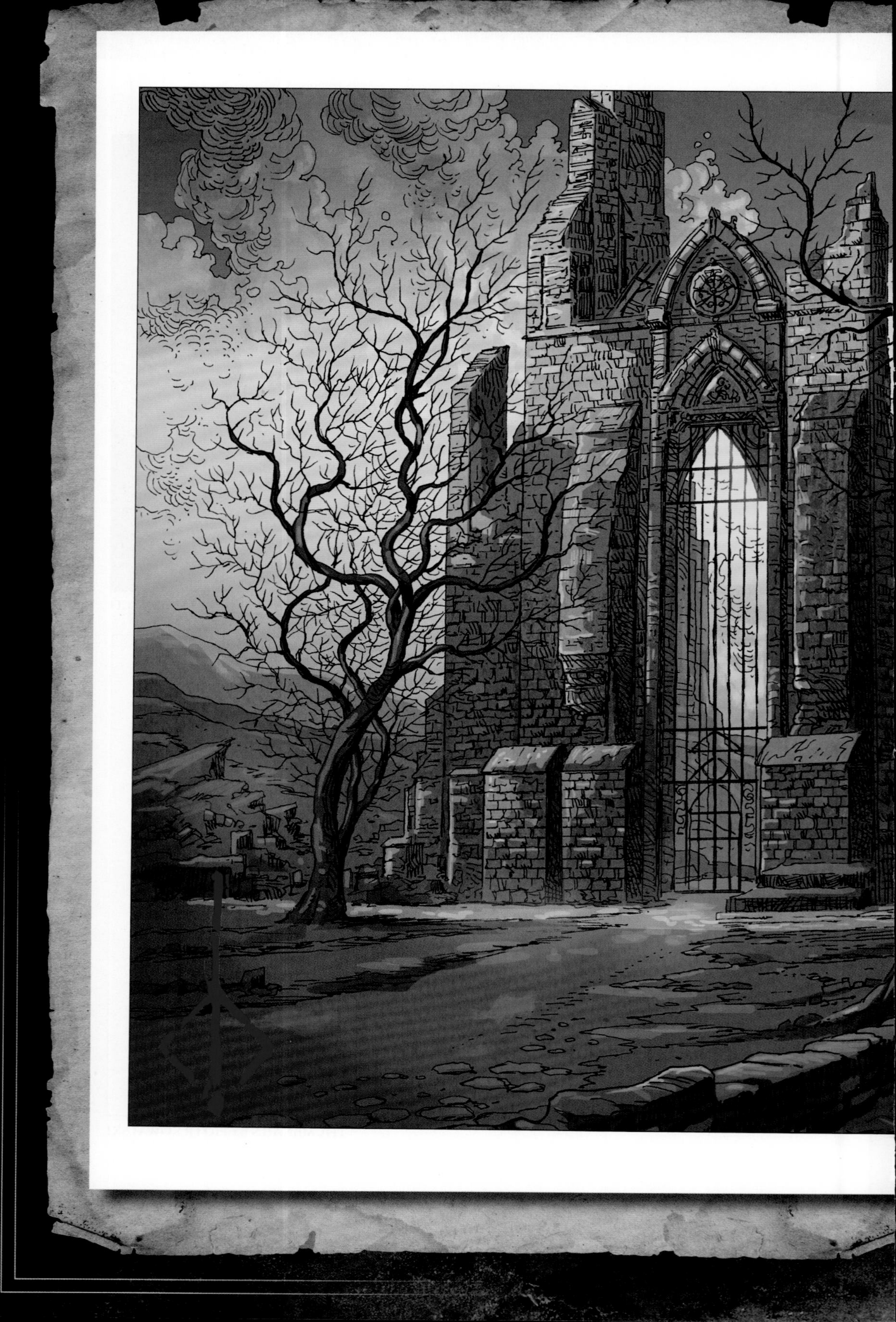

INKS BY PIOTR KOWALSKI

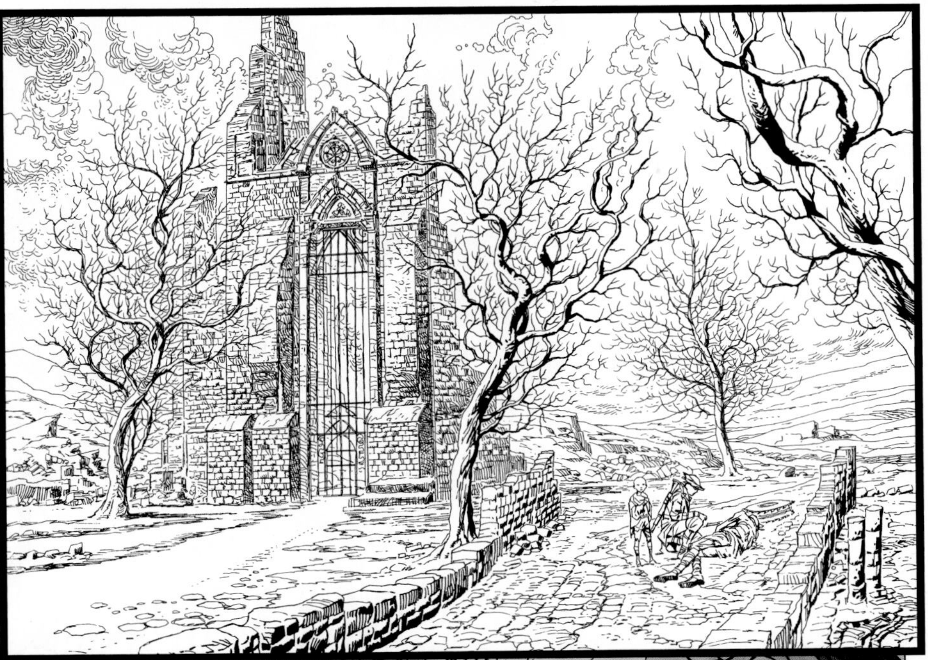

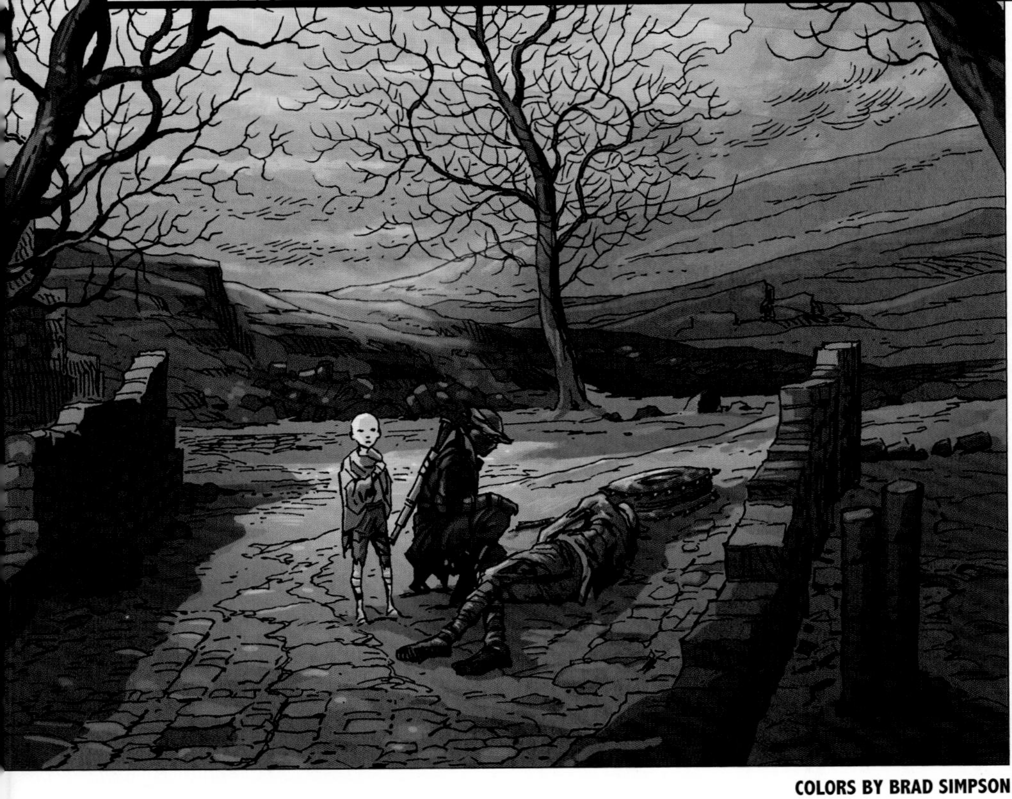

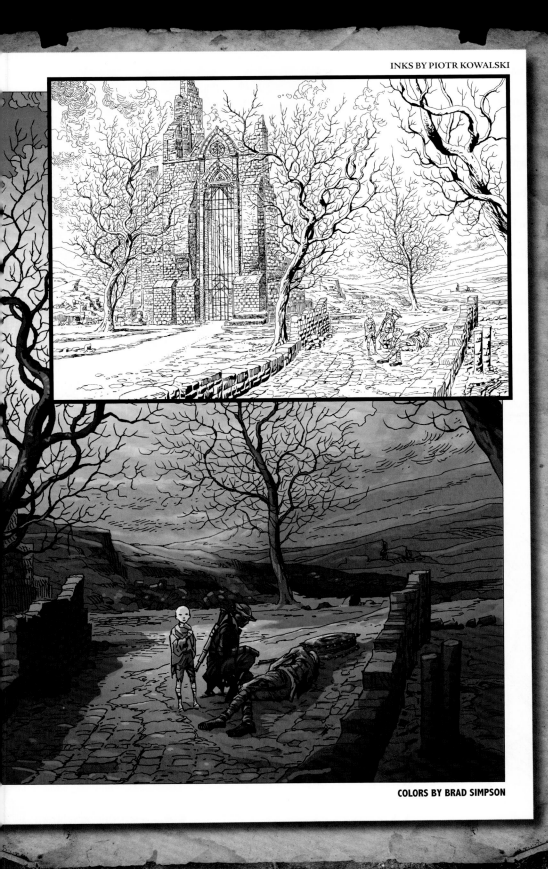

COLORS BY BRAD SIMPSON

AGE 14

plash page.

he Hunter faces the
lood-Starved Beast.

n between them, most of the
athedral, and the chaos.

More beasts pouring in.

We are behind the Hunter.

The Blood-Starved Beast stars at
us from the door, now fully visible.

The fire spreads, illuminating it--

THE HUNTER (CAPTION): ...YOU.

THE HUNTER (CAPTION):
...AGAIN?

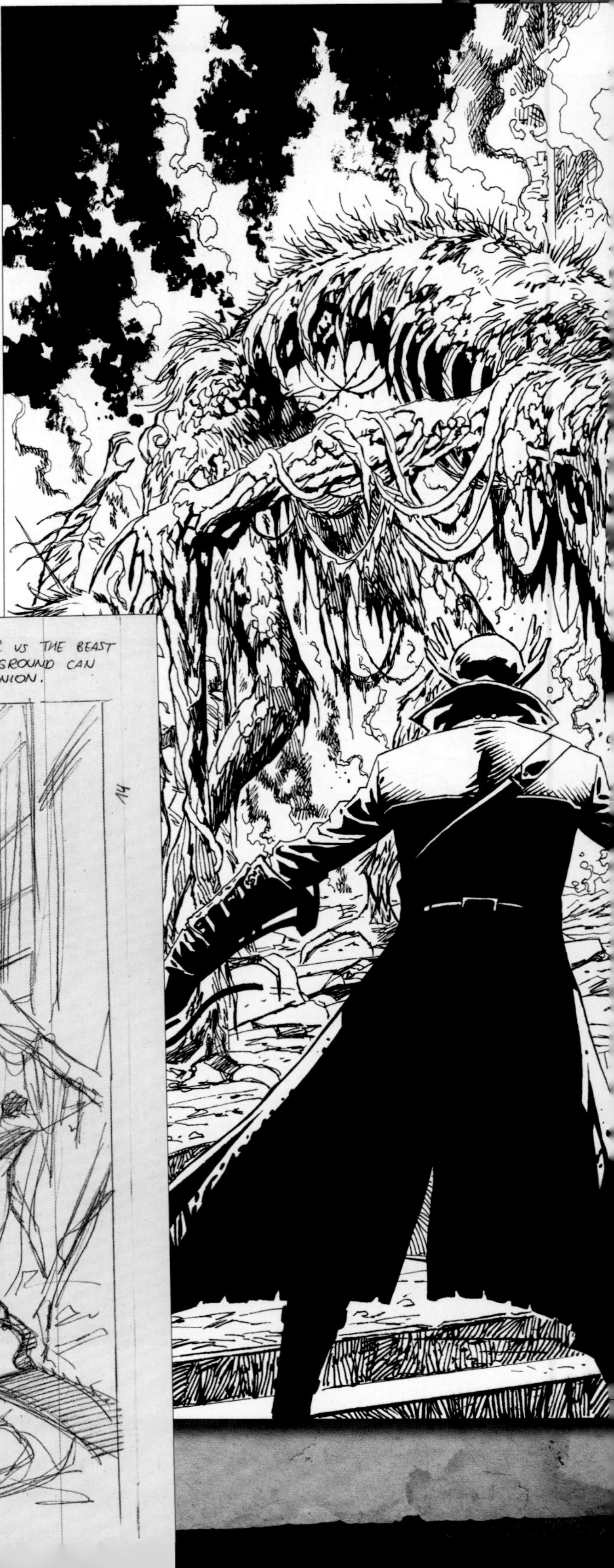

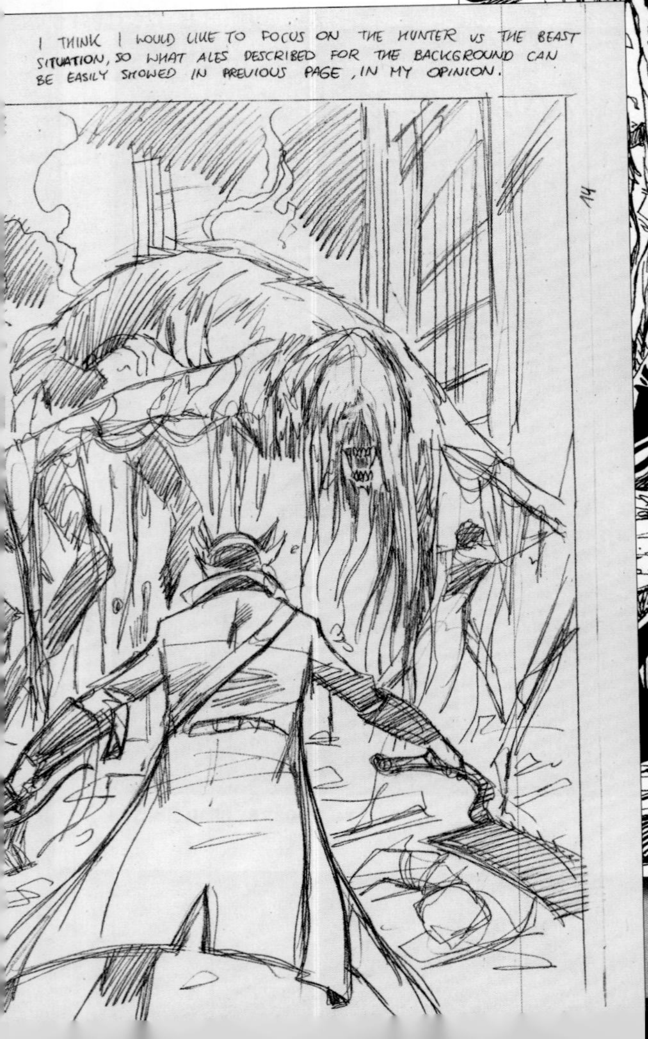
I THINK I WOULD LIKE TO FOCUS ON THE HUNTER VS THE BEAST SITUATION, SO WHAT ALES DESCRIBED FOR THE BACKGROUND CAN BE EASILY SHOWED IN PREVIOUS PAGE, IN MY OPINION.
14

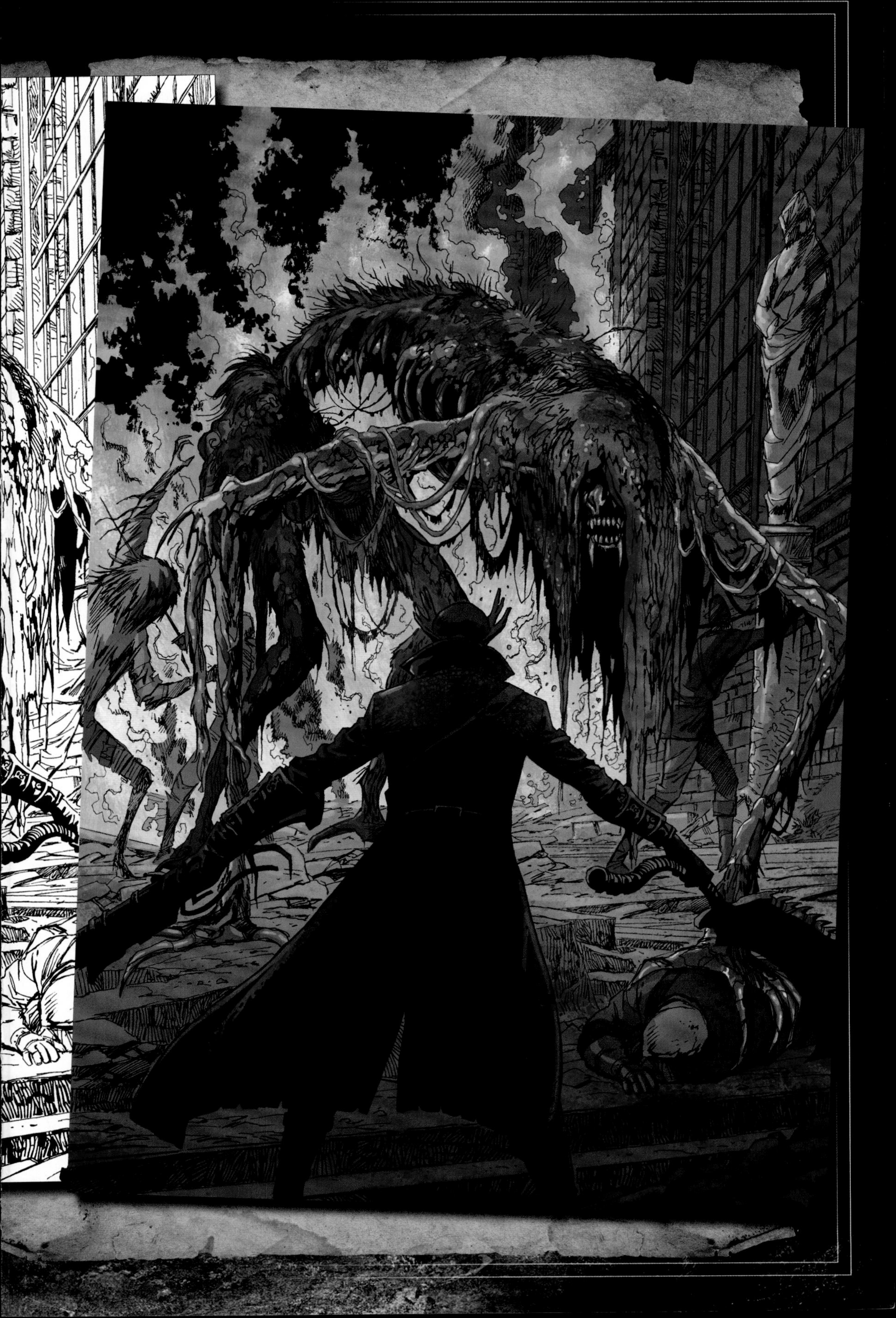

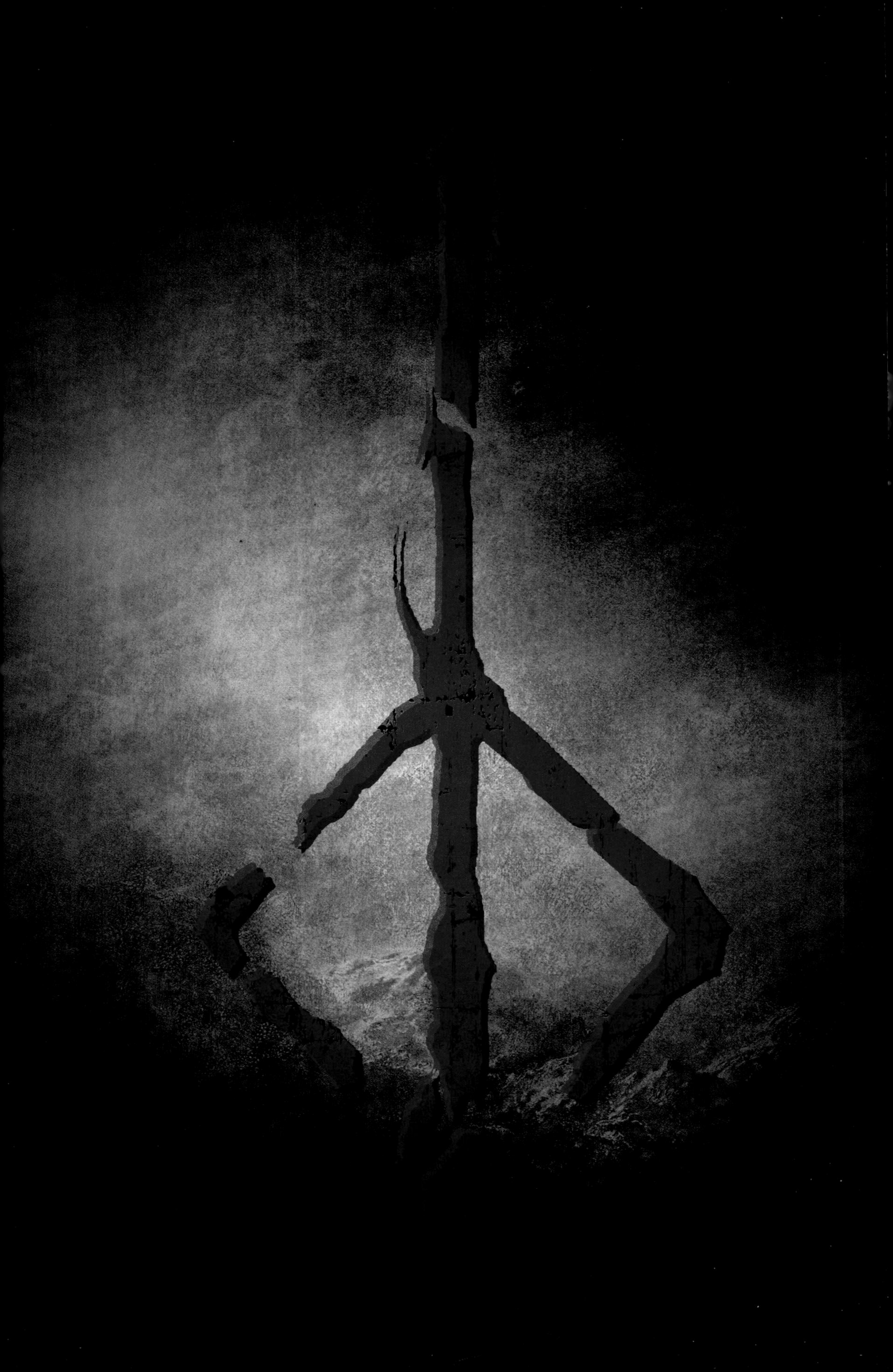

CREATOR BIOS

ALEŠ KOT

ALEŠ KOT is a writer, director and producer with primary focus on film, comics, television and video games. He's responsible for politically-charged Image titles such as *Zero, Wolf, Material, Change, The Surface, Wild Children* and *Days of Hate*, comics which have received many accolades from media such as *Wired, The Guardian, The Hollywood Reporter, Entertainment Weekly*, and many others. He lives, unsurprisingly, mostly in Los Angeles.

PIOTR KOWALSKI

PIOTR KOWALSKI is a Polish comic book artist. Breaking into the French and Belgian markets with *Gail*, Kowalski's recent foray into the US comics has seen him tackle some of the industry's most iconic characters. Since then, Kowalski's dark foreboding style has appeared in a range of titles including *Robocop, 30 Days of Night, Marvel Knights: Hulk, The Dark Tower, Terminal Hero, Sex, Dark Souls* and Titan's *Wolfenstein* series.

BRAD SIMPSON

BRAD SIMPSON is an American comic book colorist based in San Francisco. In addition to gracing the pages of many Marvel Comics titles such as *Deadpool, Vengeance,* and *The Amazing Spider-Man*, Simpson's stunning color choices have also proved invaluable in breathing life into such titles as *Godland, Sex, Sovereign, 30 Days of Night* and *The Witcher*.

ADITYA BIDIKAR

ADITYA BIDIKAR is a comic book letterer and calligrapher. Best known for his hand-drawn approach, Bidikar has become one of the industry's most highly sought letterers, with his work appearing in titles such as *Grant Morrison's 18 Days, Grafity's Wall, Paradiso, Winnebago Graveyard, Kid Lobotomy, Motor Crush* and *Drifter*.

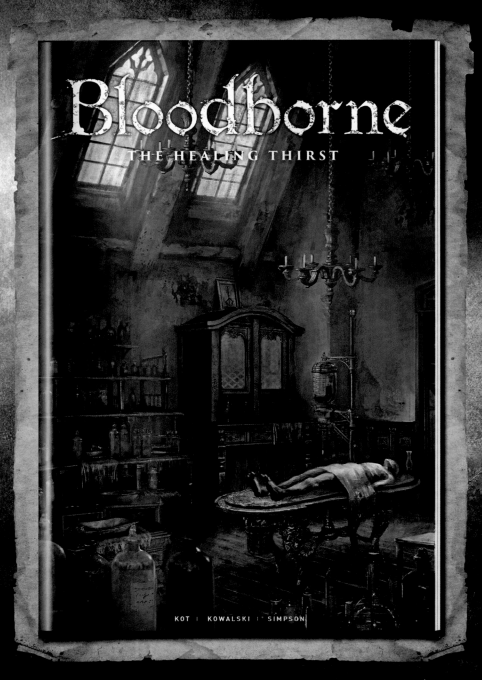